Barry,
Good reading

Stu

COUNTER-TERRORIST

COUNTER-

TERRORIST

by SAM HALL
with LARRY HUSSMAN
and FELICIA LEWIS

DIF

DONALD I. FINE, INC.
New York

DEDICATION

For my late father, my mother and two brothers, my children and former wife, Jan, as well as all those who have volunteered to wage war against terrorism.

ACKNOWLEDGMENTS

As the person who had the experiences, I am fully responsible for the information about people and incidents revealed in this book. I want to thank my writers, Larry Hussman and Felicia W. Lewis, for making my story so readable. And I appreciate the work of Evelyn Belcher, Eileen Sestito and Leanne Smith, who prepared the manuscript. Reviewing my past has been very painful at times. A few special people provided a haven of support throughout my earlier and during my more recent life. Therefore, special thanks go to my mother, Ann; my brothers Tony and Mike; my children Kelly, David and Samee; and my former wife, Jan. Also Pastor Ron Julian, Jimmie Bonbright, Don Wright, Ken Fletcher, Don Kemper, Bob Salerno, Steve Zax, Brenda Painter, Jack Walker, Ron Shaneyfelt, Jesse Phillips and Robert Klinemann. I want to recognize too the professionals, too numerous to mention here, who helped me gain the knowledge and skills I needed to fight terrorism. Remembered but nameless are individuals of the Special Forces, Navy Seals, Marines and 101st Airborne.

PREFACE

I n the spring of 1983 I was in Florida nursing a seeping hole in my side, my weight way down, the sight in my left eye gone, my resting pulse rate topping out at 116. While I slowly mended I started making notes that would throw some light on my life for my son and two daughters. We weren't seeing much of each other at that point since they were living in Ohio with my ex-wife. But it wasn't only the distance that kept us apart. Just over a year earlier I had quit my family business and taken a job with the United Nations peacekeeping mission in the Sinai. While I was working in the Middle East I had gotten myself trained by the Israelis as a commando. Once I had the skills I spent thousands on the black market for military equipment, frankly conned bureaucrats with fake names and papers, made lots of illegal border crossings, set up a counter-terrorist rescue team called Free Lancers, saw action in five different countries and got myself wounded fighting in Africa and spying on the rebels in El Salvador.

After expanding my notes into a rough account I started thinking maybe some other people would be interested in the story of a forty-five-year-old suburban businessman who decided to fight terrorists around the world because the thrills and the danger mated with service to an important cause proved to be the only way to fill his cup. Maybe these same people would be interested in the shadowy war going on at this very minute between terrorists and counter-terrorists. When a friend told me, "You've got a hell of a book there, Sam," I approached a couple of writers to help me present the tale that took me back over my earlier life as an Olympic medal winner, state legislator, reformed drug addict, and born-again Christian, showing how those early experiences set the stage for my counter-terrorist adventures—in Israel, Thailand, South Africa, Mozambique, Zimbabwe, El Salvador, Honduras, and Nicaragua. While the book was being organized I went back to Africa on several missions and then led the Miskito Indians in raids against the Sandinistas and received more wounds. On December 12, 1986, I was captured outside Managua, spying for the U.S. government. Forty-nine days later the Nicaraguans released me, for reasons I'll go into later.

In the process of telling my story I realized that, for security reasons, a few of the locales I visited and the identities and backgrounds of some of the people with whom I'd become involved would have to be disguised. Where I have not used the code names by which certain individuals were known, I have, in many cases, used pseudonyms to protect my sources. Major Shimer Weprin, Major Farouki, Arnold Koenigsburg, Lev Nadel, Oskar Mugange, Karl Martin, Micah Sharon, Tom Fenton, Richard Blake, Ron Dexter, Wassana, Sawang, Sawee, Harriet, Ida, Jacob, and Charlie are all pseudonyms. I also realized that not every conversation I'd had over the past five years could be relayed with one-hundred percent accuracy—that the best I could hope for in reconstructing the dialogue of a half-decade was close approximation. In many cases, to avoid any suggestion of recreation for its own sake, I have summarized dialogue representing as best I could what was said, but not the exact words. Despite these adjustments, I believe that the picture I've drawn here of the world of terrorism and my role in it as a counter-terrorist is a true and honest one. I hope my kids and the American public will understand what made me join the world-wide fight against terrorism.

—SAM HALL

INTO THE MIDDLE OF THINGS

THE CABLE that broke up my quiet hotel breakfast was from Brian in Pretoria, South Africa, and it read, "Peter, Raoul, Roger, Ernie captured STOP 15,000 *rand* ransom each STOP Advise soonest STOP." Brian had been acting as lawyer and go-between for the Free Lancers, the counter-terrorist rescue team I had assembled. In the past he had taken care of any sticky legal problems that cropped up. But this time his law books wouldn't help. There was nothing in them that covered what you did when almost half your rescue team needed rescuing themselves.

I was outside Pompano Beach, Florida, buying some equipment because we were supposed to be ready in a week to take a kidnapped priest out of Angola. But that would have to wait, along with the rest of my breakfast. Some quick hard cash was the order of the day if we wanted our four men back alive. That meant home to the midwest on the next plane out. While the Florida scenery visible out the cabin window got lost in the clouds I tried to read the airline magazine. But my mind kept rehashing the caper the captured Free Lancers had contracted for in Mozambique, a country on South Africa's northern border. It was an independent recon job mounted to gather intelligence for use against the Marxist Free Mozambique Organization (FMO). Peter was all for the mission because the chance to strike a blow against the FMO was too tempting to pass up. But he must have played down the enemy troops' numbers when we talked about the contract.

The fighting was supposed to be a few klicks (kilometers) from Mabote, so that was probably where the captured Free Lancers were being held, pending payment of ransom. How the men managed to get taken was tough to figure. They were too good. Espe-

13

cially Peter. He loved the military life as much as anybody could and was a born leader. We had met a few months before when I was in South Africa scouting for mercenaries to help in a Cambodian POW rescue attempt I was organizing. I now considered him my best friend. On the surface we didn't have much in common. He was Cambridge-bred upper crust and he spoke the King's English just like a real "His Majesty." Compared to him I was way undercouth with my new money and X-rated vocabulary. But despite our differences in manners and way of talking we were soulmates. Peter was a family black sheep just like me with more than forty years of far-from-perfect past. And both of us were trying to pay back a debt to the world as counter-terrorists.

Raoul was thirty-five and always second in command. He was almost as cool as Peter—if that were possible. And he was a world champion marksman to boot. He had once been an accountant in Cuba when there was something there to account for, but his family had the honor of being one of the first to be thrown out by Castro. Peter met him in Durban, South Africa, when Raoul was looking for some action there. They fought together after that in a coup attempt in the Seychelles islands. Roger, a South African, decided to be a mercenary right after high school. He was in his late twenties by the time I found him in Capetown and offered to put his talent to the best use for kidnap victims. Ernie came from Zaire. His native name was Kimbangula but Ernie had half the syllables. The shorter handle was a big plus if you wanted to stay in touch while your position was getting overrun. Peter had met Ernie on an African mission before Free Lancers was formed.

When my plane unloaded at the Detroit airport I hailed a cab and headed straight for a bank to get a fistful of Canadian quarters. The teller had a funny look on her face when she pushed thirteen pounds of the two-bit pieces over the counter. She probably thought she was dealing with an overaged video-game junkie. She had no way of knowing that she was just helping me make a discreet phone call from a location safe from F.B.I. phone taps.

I grabbed a hack outside the bank and told the cabbie, "Take me over to Canada through the tunnel." North of the border I had the cabbie stop at the first phone booth off the highway and dialed Pretoria. Brian's voice crackled through the static of a bad connection. "Peter and the others were snooping for the MRM when they were taken by a big FMO force near Mabote." MRM was the Mozambique Resistance Movement and the good guys—yes, I do believe there are good guys and bad guys—of the little war in question. I told Brian, "Start some talks with the FMO front man and say we'll buy back our people for six thousand *rand* each. Go to ten thousand if you have to. If the money doesn't work we'll have to go in after them." Brian asked, "By the by, what do we use for money?" I explained that my brothers were selling a hotel my family owned and my share would come to sixty-seven thousand dollars. Brian was happy to hear there would be about twenty thousand left over after the bills were paid.

We both knew twenty thousand wouldn't quite cut it, but Brian said, "I think we might be able to get a little more through Roger's and Raoul's families. I'll work on that and you get in touch with the rest of the team to put them on alert." After Brian hung up I headed on into Windsor, Ontario, and got the cables off to the other team members. Then the cab brought me back into the States and I flew out of Detroit to Dayton. As soon as I was home I went over to my ex-wife's place to pick up the three kids for a downtown restaurant dinner. I tried to do something with them whenever I got into town. That wasn't very often anymore. East time I saw the kids now they seemed to be a foot taller than I remembered. And each time I left them I hurt deep inside because it might be our last time together. After the waiter took our orders fifteen-year-old David asked the question that always came up at times like this.

"Why don't we get to see you more often, Dad? Mom doesn't tell us anything about what you're doing or where you're living."

"Oh, I'm doing some construction work in Florida, son."

That was the latest lie I'd told my ex. She probably didn't believe it, or maybe she just didn't care enough to let the kids know.

Now it was Samantha's turn to crowd me against the ropes. My twelve-year-old landed punch number two.

"Why can't you find a job around here? Mom says there are lots of construction companies in Dayton. She says she can't see why you have to live somewhere else."

"Well, things are pretty depressed in Ohio these days, Samee."

At this point "depressed" was a feeling I could strongly relate to. As always, the kids made me think about the way I let my duties as a dad slide. But there was no use covering that ground again. The feelings the Free Lancer missions gave me were too strong to think about stopping. Still, I just about hit the canvas when my seventeen-year-old beauty, Kelly, closed the discussion with her sarcastic slam.

"Oh, it doesn't matter where you live, Daddy. We'll just have to make an appointment when you're in town."

For the rest of the evening I forced back the supposedly unmanly tears and tried to lighten things up as much as I could. Our reunion only lasted a couple of hours. I had to get back to Florida to work on some rescue plans in case the talks in Africa broke down.

Weeks later a second message from Brian arrived in Fort Lauderdale, Florida, where I had a safe-address under a fake name. "Negotiations standstill STOP FMO prison map smuggled STOP Team waits plans STOP." I was expecting something like that. My cable back to Brian said, "Arrive Joburg next week STOP Make appointment me MRM rep STOP." Three days later in New York there was a seven-hour layover before the Johannesburg plane connection—just enough time to do the town with drinks upstairs at Sardi's and a great steak at Frankie and Johnnie's. There wouldn't be any cuisine like that where I was headed.

Two nights later in Pretoria the meeting with Brian and the MRM rep Oskar Mugange went well. They had the sketch of the POW compound that Ernie had somehow smuggled out. We could rely on the sketch because Ernie was the official Free Lancer mapmaker. His drawing of the camp fit well enough with the general plan I was mulling over. But the five free team members would need help. There might be quite a force of FMOs near the compound. Brian had my twenty thousand from the hotel sale and a few hundred from Roger's family, so we asked Mugange, "Can you rent us forty-five of your MRM fighters at $150 a day?" The MRMs were first-rate troops who spent their time harassing the communist rulers of their used-to-be homeland. Mugange was eager to help so long as we inflicted some damage on the terrorists along the way. We arranged for the Free Lancers team minus the four that needed rescuing to link with our "rent-an-army" 125 klicks northwest of the Limpopo River for the trek to the prison camp. When everything was lined up I went to my hotel room to wait for the other team members.

Within an hour the Bird—the first of the Free Lancers to arrive —was banging on the door and then perching on a chair arm asking about the situation. He still lived up to a nickname that derived from a semi-Schwarzenegger torso attached to two stick-thin legs. He looked like a Great Blue Heron with a bad thyroid. Knowing how gung-ho he was, I had a feeling he'd show up first. The Bird couldn't resist a good rescue mission, especially one in which his own friends were the hostages. We were lucky to have him on our team. When he joined the Free Lancers, he was a hero in South Africa and his fierce hatred of terrorists was legendary. Rumor had it that terrorists had killed a couple of his relatives, but I never spoke with the Bird about personal things because he preferred to keep to himself. He knew he couldn't stamp out terrorism by himself, though, so he was anxious to join a small team like mine that could contract for regular missions. Besides, we had the kind of unit that trained and fought with the fewest possible orders and picked its own causes. It wasn't the sort of regiment where you sat around waiting for a far-off general who worked for some bureaucratic machine to issue an order you didn't feel like following anyway. Our commando apartness was what we all liked about the Free Lancers. Especially the Bird, who would look for a different desert island to get marooned on if Friday ever found him. "When do we go?" he wanted to know, so I told him, "As soon as we can get briefed tomorrow on where the FMO units are and how many."

Gordon and Topper showed up next and the Bird said, "You two took your sweet time." It had only been fifteen minutes since he had swooped in himself. Topper explained, "Gordon and yours truly were 'skindiving' in the Capetown bars when we got the word." The two of them were always together. They were friends in Australia before they headed for Capetown looking for work as mercenaries. After they were briefed on the setup we all had a drink while we waited for Chippy. It turned out to be a short party. Thirty minutes later our star-tracker, who happened to be black, framed the doorway and needled us with "isn't this a fierce-looking tribe?" Topper yelled, "Fuck off, Black Beauty," and then after the handshakes we got down to business.

We went over the map and the mission a couple of times to make sure we had our roles straight. It didn't take long to polish the play, because we had been in Mozambique before to rescue some Canadian terrorists and knew the lay of the land. What we did need, though, was information about the up-to-the-minute political and military setup. That was always changing. To get brought up to speed we had a meeting scheduled the next day with Ron Dexter, a Vietnam vet who was the leader of a Zimbabwe-based anti-terrorist unit called the Selous Scouts. The Scouts were fighting in Mozambique too.

Early in the morning the five of us went to Brian's law offices to meet with Ron. He told us, "I've got a new unit organized that I've been taking into Mozambique myself. The situation there is as screwed up as ever." Different terrorist organizations including quite a few from Zimbabwe were fighting against South African sponsored troops and some terrorists were fighting among themselves. Ron said, "You can hardly tell the players without a scorecard. SADF is fighting SWAPO, and ZAPU is fighting ZANU, and ZANOA and ZRP are fighting ZIPRA." The mess was made worse, Dexter said, by Zimbabwe's Peking-schooled, controversial Robert Mugabe. His bands, helped by North Korean and Chinese regulars, were using Mozambique as a staging area for their deadly political actions. Mugabe seemed hell-bent to wipe out the last members of the Matabele tribe, which was fiercely independent but just about destroyed by years of persecution. The Free Lancers didn't like this Mugabe because Chippy, whose African name was Kamuzu, was a Matabele. He was also one of the most valuable members of the Free Lancers. None of our African missions could have worked without Chippy. I used to say that he could pick up the trail of an ant crossing a rain forest and track it for a hundred miles.

Anyway, we found out all about the fighting factions and the political situation in Mozambique. But there and just about everywhere else it was still relatively easy to tell the terrorists from the innocents by their actions rather than their words. Terrorism always meant violence or threats of it against bystanders who were just minding their own business. Those were the people Free Lancers was organized to help.

After Ron's briefing was finished we said our goodbyes to Brian and grabbed our waiting van loaded with arms and equipment. Six hours later we were in the Dakota flying over the drop site where our hired MRM troops were supposed to be waiting just ten klicks from the prison compound. When the pilot thrust up his thumb we knew we were just coming up over the prepicked spot. I stood up and fastened my T-clip to the static line wire while the pilot pantomimed, I like what I see. I grabbed the doorless jamb and stuck my head out to check for myself. The blast of hot African air hit me like a charging rhino and the noise from the prop engines crushed my ears. But I liked what I saw too, so I mouthed the order to the pilot, Take us up. Then I shouted to the men. "Stand up. Hook 'em up. Check 'em out." Everybody checked each other and confirmed everything was ready, so as soon as the engine throttled back each of my four teammates shuffled down the line with little Charlie Chaplin steps. First Chippy, then the Bird and Gordon and finally Topper gave me "thumbs up" and went out the door. My white knuckles choked the T-clip but there was no time to untense. An easy link-up with the others depended on walking out into the sky right now. When I did, I felt the prop wash, then the chute pop and the free floating till I hit the ground with a roll. When we were all free of our harnesses the others formed on me.

The bush at the drop site was very flat and treeless, with only a scrubby plant here and there. After we checked our coordinates the men lined up and I went over the mission one more time. "We're only two klicks from our join-up with the MRM force. After we meet them we've got an eight-klick march to the compound. We'll try to find some cover to check out the situation before we go for it." Then I made sure one more time all the details were taken care of. "Check each other for objects that might make noise as we move across country. Make sure you've blackened any metal surfaces that might reflect in this sun. Empty your pockets of anything valuable to the enemy and burn any letters or pictures or printed material." I didn't have to remind these pros what to do, but they expected the ritual. When it was done and everybody was painted with bug spray we moved out.

Half an hour later we joined up with the MRM force and started explaining our assault to them. We were about eight klicks from our target and we had to be careful because MRM intelligence reported a couple of North Korean units leaving the area on their way northeast to the town of Beira. For the last ten years North Korean civilian laborers protected by lots of their country's regulars were trying to help Mozambique build a rail line. Up to now the MRM was able to blow up sections of track so the little engine couldn't. We hoped the North Koreans were gone, because we just wanted our men and not a firefight. But thinking about the North Koreans kept us extra alert as we formed into three columns and headed southwest half a klick apart.

Thirty-five minutes later Gordon, on point in the now rocky country, drew fire. He dropped to all fours then prone with weapon at the ready so we all did the same. The fire was coming hot, but not too heavy, from a rise a hundred yards ahead, and Gordon yelled, "Looks like no more than a squad with AK–47s." With my whole body tingling and the fear sweat starting like it always did in combat, I yelled, "Let's take 'em out." Chippy translated the order to the MRM troops. Fifty separate bursts raked the rise for two minutes. Then some thinner fire answered ours and two of the MRMs in the middle column were hit. Both wounds were minor, so we concentrated on raking the hill again. This time we added half a dozen grenades to the greeting for good measure. As soon as the cordite cleared we listened hard and there was nothing but silence from the hill, so we took off on the run, dodging behind rocks on the way. When we reached the ambush hill three bodies in brand-new blood-soaked camis gave us their best death stares. Topper said, "Looks like the rest of them took off in a hurry." That was true, because ammo and food and even a couple of weapons were scattered around for the taking. I told Gordon, "Break those pieces against a rock and let's get out of here." That order broke some hearts, because there was a fifteen-hundred-*rand* bounty on the Russian weapons if they were turned in to the South African government. No time for them now. We couldn't be sure the troops who ran off wouldn't be back with half of North Korea for backups.

We had to move as fast as we could or we might blow the whole mission. So for the next two hours we made like Olympic sprinters and suddenly found ourselves peering at the terrorists' compound through some thick brush. The brush was supposed to hide the buildings but it made things easier for us too. Ernie's smuggled sketch was a masterpiece just as we knew it would be. There in the clearing between two kopjes (small hills) were the three small concrete buildings. Two looked to be divided into cells. The third, in between, had to be headquarters. Off to the right the radio shack tower stood about thirty-five feet high. A mud outhouse closer to us made up the rest of the skyline. Parked at scattered spots in the clearing were six sets of wheels, including what looked to be an out-of-commission fuel carrier.

We guessed that somewhere in the cells would be Peter and the others, in their second month of waiting for something to happen. Throughout the course of the ransom talks the FMO terrorists had assured Brian that the Free Lancer prisoners were in good shape. We didn't believe that. More likely they had been treated harshly and tortured for information. As we sat there in the brush we weren't expecting our freshly showered, after-shaved men to check out at the front desk with their bags packed once the fireworks started.

We couldn't be sure the North Koreans weren't still in the neighborhood either. Chippy and Topper moved out to run two-klick-wide semicircles around our position. If they could, they would get up close to the sides and rear of the compound to count enemy heads. In forty-five minutes Chippy was back with "No Asians sighted, but seventeen men guarding the prison and three women getting ready to cook a meal." The radio shack looked to be empty, and now we could all smell food on the fire. We knew this was a good time for an attack, so we were just waiting for Topper when he ran up holding my binoculars. He had news that changed the plan. He said, "A supply truck is headed our way with a driver and a woman on board. It'll take ten to twelve minutes to get here."

I decided to send Topper and three of the MRMs to intercept the truck before it got to our spying spot in the brush. That way we could throw an even better surprise party than we planned for the terrorists. Ten minutes later I was looking through the glasses and watching Topper and three MRMs jump out from behind some rocks with weapons drawn. They pulled the driver and his traveling companion out of the truck cab and one of the MRMs used his rifle to butt the male half of the twosome to the ground. While I watched the magnified scene through the glasses I was swearing under my breath at Topper, "Don't you hurt him, you bastard. Don't you hurt him. I need him."

The MRMs lifted the driver and herded him and the woman to the brush, while Topper wired the truck with explosives. Chippy translated my browbeating for the driver and his woman. They were already impressed with Topper because it was rare to see a white man in that part of Africa. But they turned pretty white themselves when I said to the driver, "I'll cut off your ears and stuff 'em down your woman's throat if you don't cooperate." That kind of forced feeding was a favorite practice among the local terrorists, but still I felt bad about scaring them with a threat like that. The driver was a pathetic-looking shirtless soul wearing ragged cami pants plus one black boot and one stringless brown. When he was sure he'd have to cooperate to keep his body parts from spoiling his lady friend's diet I told him, "Drive your rig alongside the radio shack and then jump out and run as fast as you can to the command center." After that he was supposed to warn the terrorists inside that they were surrounded by three helicopter-supported companies of trained commandos who weren't interested in killing anybody but did want the four Free Lancer POWs. Meanwhile my MRMs with FALs and AK-47s and RPG rocket launchers were set to hit the rusty fuel carrier but leave the five other vehicles alone for our own use later. The men all tensed and waited for my command.

We were all extremely nervous because it looked too easy, and Topper didn't help any when he asked me, "What if Peter and the others aren't in the compound after all? They could be on their way north with the Koreans." We'd talked about that possibility back in Pretoria. The answer now was the same as then. "That's a chance we have to take. We can't be sure it'll work out." But the driver was parking next to the tower already, so we couldn't turn back if we wanted to. We could see him running and hear him screaming my message on his way to the headquarters building. We didn't know what the result would be, but the driver was sure our bullshit story was the whole truth and nothing but. He was so scared he'd sound convincing if he told the terrorists Hannibal was bopping toward the camp dragging Dumbo by the trunk.

No more than a minute later the driver and someone else ran out of the hut just as the rigged truck blew up and parts filled the air. And dust. Mortar. Rocks. Wood. The tower collapsed in a heap. At the command "Go" my assigned marksmen opened up on the old fuel tanker with the rockets, but one missed the truck and hit the bottom of the outhouse and the air was filled with unlovely detritus. We all fired one short burst from our automatics but didn't need a second because two minutes later a white rag attached to a broom handle waved from a window of the command building. We moved into the compound, alert for any tricks, and took eighteen men and the three women prisoners. The truckless driver and his luckless lady got put back together again. Meanwhile the Bird and Chippy questioned the prisoners. Gordon and Topper searched the cells for our men. Three minutes later all four of them plus four strangers, including a couple of women, joined us in the center of the compound. There were a lot of mixed tears and smiles as we hugged each other. Then Peter laughed and said, "You took your bloody good time getting here, Yank." I told him I was busy cleaning out my sock drawer and asked, "How have you been?" Peter said, "I'm none the worse for wear, but you'll have to ask the others. We were separated the entire time." Raoul and Ernie said they were okay too, but Roger was pretty weak, so he sat in the middle of the group. "I've had diarrhea for I don't remember how long and I haven't been able to eat much." Topper said, "One of those big steaks back in Joburg will straighten you out." But Roger didn't look up to a steak right then.

The other three were all in good spirits and, surprisingly, seemed to be okay physically, except for a couple of just-healed scars from flesh wounds. I congratulated Ernie on his sketch of the compound and asked him, "How did you smuggle it out?" He said, "I made what I believe you call a 'pass' at one of the women every time she brought food to the cell. She decided to help." I told him it was a good thing the FMOs didn't have male jailers, but he just smiled and said, "I am such a beautiful one. Even they would be unable to resist me."

Once the backslapping was over we found out who the strangers from the cellblock were. They turned out to be two villagers and their wives held for ransom. The price in cases like that was usually food and whatever weapons the rest of the villagers could get their hands on. This kind of hostage was only held a day or two, so it was plain these were brand new victims. We gave them the pleasure of helping to tie the terrorists' hands behind their backs with radio wires from the command post while Ernie and Chippy destroyed the weapons and checked out the wheels. Only four out of the five trucks had fuel and we couldn't find any extra gas, so we decided to leave the one sitting on empty and booby trap it. When we were satisfied with our work the back-together Free Lancer team, plus the locals, boarded the four vehicles and headed south while the MRM force marched north with their twenty-one prisoners. We dropped off the villagers just outside the clump of huts they called home and felt lucky it was on our way. The last homebound leg to the Limpopo was so smooth I had time to think back to Israel and beyond. Back to all the crazy twists and turns in my life that had brought me, finally, to the satisfaction of missions like this.

ONE

EVEN BEFORE I made my entrance into the world I was already kicking to a different drummer. My mother told me later how hell-bent I was to end the womb-wait. Her doctor even linked my thrashing to the blood clot that left her blind in one eye.

Once I made my debut, my restless streak was up-front for my father too, and all the relatives unlucky enough to be held captive while he showed me off. I banged my head against the crib walls for hours at a time. Then after my escape to the living room floor I did mini-marathons on my hands and knees while my parents tried to figure out what made Sammy crawl. For my first birthday my Dad rigged up a contraption that was a kind of scaled-down rub-berized parachute harness that clamped onto a convenient door jamb. Within three minutes I learned how to fly by bouncing off the floor as hard as possible. My mother was afraid I was going to do my head-banging act on the ceiling instead of the crib walls. After my graduation from potty paratroop training I went on to free falls off the living room couch and the kitchen counter, till my dad found me a set of toys that kept me grounded for at least part of the day. I split the regiment of lead soldiers into warring companies that fought for weeks and months over every inch of carpet in the house.

One day when I was six my career as a serious diver got under way. My parents took me to a neighborhood pool. While they were busy kibitzing with some friends a bigger kid teased me with a dare no good sport could pass up. He said, "I'll betcha a dime you can't jump off that diving board at the deep end." That sounded like an easy dare to me, since I'd been flying off an upper bunk bed higher than that board for a couple of years. The only problem was learning how to swim on the way down. "Let me see that dime." Sure enough, there was the shiny coin in his unclenched right hand. Less than a minute later I was bouncing on the board. With my palms pressed together like a praying plaster saint I dove head first for the water. Just before I hit it I remembered to hold my nose so the first few seconds in the drink weren't too bad. But then it came to me where this was all happening, and I started thrashing around and yelling for help.

About that time the life guard got distracted from leering at the local bathing beauties or whatever he was up to. He dove in after me and dragged my soaked but satisfied self on to the cement. My father and mother came running up to the spot where a knot of adults was already standing around me. Mom was speechless and Dad was white as a sheet. Finally he said, "What in the name of God possessed you to do that?" I didn't think I'd better tell him about the dare. Anyway I never did get the dime because the bigger kid was nowhere to be found. But at least my dad made up for it when he said, "You're going to get your first swimming lesson this afternoon."

I was a hyperactive ten year old when we kids played a game called "capture the flag" at summer camp in Wisconsin. Teams of boys would plant their colors at either end of the lake to see which could take the other one's fort first without getting tagged. We would swim the lake and hide behind boats and logs on the way or run through the woods as quiet as we could on pint-sized missions. We played day after day, rain or shine and on into the night. That game was the highlight of my best summer as a kid. It brought out all the competitive spirit my dad had nurtured through constant dares and double dares to do whatever the other kids were afraid to try because it was dangerous. I soon found out the really thrilling things always meant risks. That was a lesson not everybody learned or at least accepted. So many people shunned risks and then led "if only" lives. I never wanted to have to say, "If only I'd done this" and "If only I'd done that." By then I knew the biggest "if only" I had to smash when I was old enough was military service. I already had a dream of fighting for my country and having enough medals pinned on my chest to bow my back like Quasimodo's.

The year after the Wisconsin war games my dad enrolled me at a special summer camp in Indiana. That's where I began to build the love for my country that's been getting bigger ever since. The military officers who served as counselors there were always stressing America's greatness and its gift of freedom. Their impromptu late-night history lessons about Bunker Hill and the Alamo and Iwo Jima riveted me to my seat. That didn't happen very often in school. I also got to wear a uniform every day and stand at attention outside while I recited the pledge of allegiance. Not to a flag hanging limp in a classroom, but to one flapping in the morning breeze. The pride made my socks creep up my ankles when I marched around the parade ground to the beat of the band. I won more medals than any camper. They weren't military medals. There were athletic awards in boxing and track and swimming.

During those years I really got hooked on diving. Dad took the family every winter for vacations at a Florida hotel where all the world-class swimmers and divers used to stay for year-round training. I watched them for hours at a time, especially the divers with their tip-toed poise and long leaps off the high board. I loved the way they hugged themselves into balls and seemed suspended in the air for a long second before they stretched out and started down to make nearly splashless entries into the blue water. I wanted to be the best diver ever, so I started copying the form I saw at the hotel pool. By the time I was fourteen and back in school in Dayton I was getting really good, thanks to practicing three or four hours every day.

Since Dad had made a lot of money in real estate development, he was able to hire the famous diving coach Bob Maxwell to work with me. I found out later that Dad insisted on my getting the strongest kind of discipline from my coach. He told Bob, "Be tough on him. I want you to drive him way past his limits. Curse him till he cries. If he's got the talent you say he has I want him to use every ounce of it." That was about the time my practicing at the local YMCA pool jumped to five or six hours a day. In fact I was spending so many hours on the board, the time to drop out of high-school football was near. But my brothers were both doing great with the pigskin and the pads, so I was afraid Dad would be disappointed if I quit. He got the word one day after school.

"I've got to ask you something, Dad."

"If it's about quitting diving you can forget it."

"Oh, I'd never stop diving. It's football. If I give it up would you think I was yellow?"

Dad let me quit, but only after he gave me a lecture about putting all the leftover effort into my diving and maybe some track and field events. To make sure I got the message he added a PS that sealed the bargain. "Next month some workmen are coming over to start digging an Olympic-sized pool in the backyard."

Pretty soon my diving improved to the point where Yale wanted to recruit me for their team. Dad took the high school counselor's advice and had me transferred to Williston Academy in Massachusetts for some high-powered math and English classes. Prep school was great, but not all that studying in the cramped library. And I was afraid there might be four years more of the same at Yale, so I talked Dad into bringing me back to Dayton to finish high school. There was no military training at the Dayton school, but there was athletics. My discipline won me three state diving championships and a national YMCA title, and I set a couple of local pole-vault records.

By now I knew Ohio State was the school for me. It had the reputation of excelling in sports. When I got there I added nine Big Ten and NCAA and AAU diving titles plus Army ROTC training to my record while I prepped for the 1960 Olympics in Rome. Thanks also to my diving there were trips to Europe and the Far East, with Dad going along to cheer me on. My best dive before Ohio State was always off the one-meter board, but that wasn't an Olympic event so I concentrated on the three-meter with a practice and conditioning program that took nearly every waking hour. I pushed and pushed myself, and if my willpower began to wilt Dad drove me with his demands. The payoff came in the NCAA three-meter championship just before the Olympic trials. The competition was really rough and I was in fourth place after the qualifying rounds. Just before the last round Dad took me aside and gave me one of his tougher talks.

"Why don't you get off your ass and show me some effort?"

"I've given it everything I've got. These guys are good."

"No you haven't given it all you've got. And those other divers haven't got half the talent you have."

"But . . ."

"Don't 'but' me. I paid good money for Maxwell to make you the best. And what the hell did I build you that pool for? So you could piss and moan about the competition? Haven't you got the message yet? You can be the best at anything in the world if you've got the basic talent and the drive. No son of mine is going to quit on me. Get out there and show me some guts."

Somehow that day the lecture worked better than it ever had before. I wanted to please the man so much. His will was so strong that it became the stimulus for everything I accomplished. When the final round was over I was teary-eyed on the top block clutching the championship medal.

Four months later my 170.38 in the Olympic trials in Detroit made me the favorite to take the Gold Medal. But I had to settle for a silver in Rome when my feet brushed the board on my last dive and Gary Tobian from USC beat me with a great performance. What a crushing blow, after all that hard work for all those years. Especially after *Sports Illustrated* and other magazines rated me the best diver in the world. And all because my father was my personal Vince Lombardi. God knows he wanted me to give him that gold medal and that would have been the best thing that ever happened to me, but now I was second best. I didn't know how he'd take it or what he'd say when he made his way poolside. But he clamped me in a bear hug and whispered, "I'm so proud of you," and then hugged Gary Tobian too with the tears flowing all around. That's when I knew that the whole Olympic episode would glow brighter in my memory than any mere bronze or silver or gold. When I stood on the block with the stars and stripes above my head I felt ten feet tall and the national anthem sent those shivers down my spine like it always has. But especially that day. Ever since then I haven't been able to watch any Olympic ceremony on TV without the tears starting. The 1960 games hooked me way past unhooking on challenges and excitement. Going head to head with athletes from all over the world and making friends from Europe and South America and Asia and Africa—those things were burned in my memory. I wanted the rest of my life to be that intense and to me the only way was military service.

After the Olympics I enlisted. The Air Force seemed to be the best bet for me to express my love for my country that had already given me such great opportunities. I had grown up close to Wright-Patterson, which was one of the biggest bases in the world and served as headquarters for a SAC operation that made me excited every time I drove by. As a high school brat I would even take girlfriends up to a hill that overlooked the base and between gropes watch the B–52s take off and land.

Shortly after joining the Air Force, I was asked by Special Services to dive for them, but running track sounded better. I was pretty good on the cinders and I needed to master something besides diving. Staying in the Air Force for twenty years was my goal and I even passed the OCS exam. But I ruined my right leg getting ready to compete in the World Wide Air Force Track Meet. While attempting a vault, I failed to notice a two-by-four hidden in the sawdust around the pit. It caught my spikes and twisted my leg so bad I looked like I was running north and south at the same time.

After a series of operations and a complete rebuild of my leg the Air Force decided their doctors were too busy to spend so much time on a lost cause. They gave me a medical discharge, not realizing they were getting rid of one of the most gung-ho flag wavers in the service. I knew I'd missed my calling and would probably feel frustrated the rest of my life. As it turned out, though, even I underestimated the sense of loss, because after the discharge I felt empty with an ache that stayed with me long after the grief a death or a divorce or a lover's loss would have. In fact it was impossible to shake that sadness and it tinged every joy that came later.

Once the Air Force cut me loose I didn't know what to do. One night in a bar one of my friends got me thinking about a new career. He was a Republican, and when he started slamming Jack Kennedy he got my dander up.

"If he hadn't been killed he'd have ruined the country by now."

"Kiss off. Jack Kennedy will go down as one of the greatest presidents we've ever had. He said a lot of things that I really believe in. Like 'America has got to be the watchdog of the free world.' "

"Well, if you believe so much in what he had to say, why don't you run for office yourself? "

Now that was a thought. I did have some political connections from my days of working as a college intern for Governor Di Salle's office, not to mention my Olympic name recognition. But what to run for? When my brother Tony found out there might be a chance of me trying for office, he mentioned the State Legislature. He always had an interest in politics and some political ambition of his own, so his advice sounded good. Winning the nomination as a Democrat wasn't too tough, and when the election was over I found myself facing a two-year term in Columbus. I really wanted to do a good job to show that other Halls besides Dad could make their mark, whether it was in business or athletics or politics. But it didn't take long to get disillusioned. Within a couple of months I was offered bribes two different times by lobbyists. Right in the middle of the damn House chambers no less. Those guys really turned me sour on politics. Especially since I knew that some of the other representatives changed their votes on the same issues after huddling with them. That convinced me to get out after my term was up in 1966. I guess I wasn't much of a political mover and shaker anyway. I just didn't go for all those smoke-filled rooms and the slow-motion results. But I did get behind a couple of bills that I hope did some good. One made it law that gravel-pit operators had to fence their property. So many kids around that time were drowning in those dangerous pits because the owners didn't give a hoot about them. My other bill was aimed at saving kids' lives too. It made it illegal for newsboys and girls to deliver their papers without wearing clothes with patches that glowed in the dark. Not earthshaking, I grant you.

When I left the legislature my brother Tony ran for my house seat and won. Later he turned out to be a U.S. Congressman with a name for helping the little guy, including the starving poor of the world. I was always proud of Tony's political career. He was one of the few in the game who was honest through and through. Most of the rest you couldn't trust any farther than you could throw a truck. But over the years my views about America's military role in the world got a lot more conservative than Tony's and we found ourselves arguing about politics. I still respect him, though, and hope he feels the same about me.

In the middle of my term in the Ohio House I got married for the third time. My first wife had been an Ohio State May queen I met in my junior year. All our friends thought the match between the campus beauty and the dashing diver was made in heaven, but the marriage turned out to be fourteen months in a much warmer climate. Thank God there weren't any children, because we didn't really have much in common. We were both at fault. Then three years later I married a woman with money in her background and she was quite a beauty too, but we didn't have a whole lot to talk about either except new and ingenious ways to spend the bucks. We were always arguing, so we broke up and that marriage only lasted half as long as the first. But in 1965 I married Janice. We were really in love and she gave me three very special children. When Janice came into my life I settled down as much as was possible for me. After the last year in the legislature I took over my father's real estate development firm so he could take a break and think about other things he might want to do. I built the business and played the role of husband and father the best I could. Janice and I might have been lifers if all the things that finally pulled us apart hadn't happened. Those things started when my restless streak drove me to volunteer for the Israeli Army.

Not that my life was boring up to that point. After the Olympics I took up all the things the family money made possible, including big game hunting and fishing, sky and skin diving, jet-set hobnobbing, and non-stop woman chasing. I suspect I had bought more adventure by my early twenties than most men do in a lifetime. I killed gazelles over in Africa. Mountain goat in Hawaii. Wild boar down in Tennessee. Bear up in Michigan. Antelope out in Wyoming. Caught marlin in the Bahamas. Skin-dived in all the oceans and most of the seas. Sky-dived with the latest equipment, in faraway places. Romanced more women than I could count. Travelled to fifty-two different countries. Met and shook hands with royalty and Presidents Kennedy and Johnson and Nixon. Even after I married Janice I got away on trips as much as I could. And I barhopped every chance I got to make sure I didn't get too "settled down." I always wanted more, even though I sensed back then that none of it touched my real need. After leading a life most pampered playboys could envy I still wanted more. Excitement was like a drug to me and it gave me a high I couldn't get from anything else. But it too let me down when it was over.

When I was growing up my dad taught me that competition was the most important thing in life. I learned the lesson so well I couldn't do anything unless it measured me against somebody or something else. And in all those years I just knew that putting my life on the line by pitting myself against an enemy in war was the one and only form of competition that could fill the bill. That was shut off from me, though. I was a disabled veteran even though my disability didn't have a damn thing to do with combat. If I could have passed the physical I would have headed for Vietnam in a minute. Even if it meant leaving my new wife and baby. That's why, when the Middle East began to heat up again, I started dreaming about joining the Israeli military. Not only did it offer the competition I wanted, but it was a way of showing my respect for the country I had heard praised all the time I was growing up.

My love for the Israelis went way back to talks with friends of my dad. We weren't Jews, but a lot of his business sidekicks and my best buddies were. I loved them for the way they lived their lives with *chutzpah* and for the way they could make me laugh. When I was still in kneepants I went to their *bar mitzvahs* and weddings and I was always getting invited to share their bagels and lox and kosher turkey.

All the while I was growing up my spiritual godfather was Arthur Beerman, who made a big local reputation as a business genius and good-doer. He started a tradition by giving huge Thanksgiving dinners for all the poor people in the community. And he gave me advice about everything from money and girlfriends to sex and athletics. He was my father's best friend and business partner. They topped their success in retailing and services with smart real estate investments that made them both millionaires. I think they're probably up in heaven now running the harp concession with title to six of the pearly gates and options to buy the other six.

Over the years my Jewish friends told me about the Israelis' struggle to survive free and I got caught up in those stories as much as I did in the American history classes at school. My Jewish buddies taught me to admire the Israeli military power and the Israeli soldier's reputation for cold skill and total discipline. All of that was probably in the back of my mind as I got more and more restless during the Sixties. My itch wasn't like most Americans' in those days. It didn't have anything to do with peace marches or hippie communes. My problem was that I couldn't get into the Vietnam war that so many would soon be trying to duck by heading to Canada.

Then one crisp fall day in 1967 I came backpacking out of the Idaho mountains after an elk hunt with four friends. When we made civilization the radio news was all about the Israeli-Egyptian war. That's when it hit me that the Israelis might not be as snooty as the American army about a gimpy leg or a thirty-year-old body.

I hired a bush pilot to fly me to Montana, where I caught a jet to O'Hare and another one to Dayton. As soon as I got to the house I remembered I'd have to tell Janice what I was up to. The easiest way out was a cock-and-bull story.

"I'm sorry, honey. I've got to go to New York on business. I'll be back in a couple of weeks."

"A couple of weeks? What are you talking about? You just got back from a week of hunting. And what business in New York could take two weeks?"

"Oh, I'm trying to sell that land out by the new university to a New York investor. It means a lot of money if I can swing the deal."

"I just don't understand you. You've got a wife and a year-old baby and you're willing to leave us for three weeks for an elk and a New York huckster."

I didn't know what I'd do to explain a longer time away if the Israelis really wanted me. But I went straight from the house to the Jewish Community Center and told the director and his assistant I was eager to fight for Israel. Within half an hour I was talking with a local leader who was willing to be my sponsor.

"I've got a condo in Tel Aviv, Sam. And connections. If you're really serious, I can have an Uzi waiting for you. You'd ship out with the American group tomorrow."

"Where do I board the plane?"

The next thing I knew I was crouching with forty-two other volunteers in the belly of a C–160 on a not-much-used runway at O'Hare, waiting to slip the surly bonds. The only problem was that rumors about a quick peace were already flying before the plane could. After a three-hour takeoff hold a man came on board and yelled, "The party's over. A treaty's been signed." When we climbed off that plane we were all frustrated, especially me. I had been sure this was my one chance to see some action at last. But the war in the Middle East was so short, the only way for me to get in on the action would have been to spray the Sinai from Idaho with my elk rifle.

That same year of the Six-Day War my father gave up his seat on the city commission and ran for mayor of Dayton. The family couldn't have been more proud when he won. We all supported him with our love, but the happiness didn't last long. In a matter of months Dad was hit by a string of cruel diseases that would make him an invalid and slowly kill him. He had to have four operations, and the worry took its toll on everybody in the family—maybe most of all on me. I was already into liquor and a few uppers to dull the pain of my growing list of regrets. The worst of those letdowns was my forced role as a suburban businessman who really wanted to be a soldier. When Dad got sick I increased my intake of booze and drugs and began the long slide into my own private hell.

One day in 1970, while my dad's health was getting worse along with my addiction, he told me the blackest news of my life. He took me aside and said, "I'm sorry to have to tell you this, Sam. Your mother and I are getting a divorce." The shock was terrific. Who could have any idea something like that was about to happen? My parents had their fights like all married couples, but could they split after thirty-eight years together? Impossible. But it was true. My brothers were stunned too. We all tried to talk Mom and Dad out of their decision, but they wouldn't listen. And what was worse, they wouldn't tell us why they wanted to split. We knew Dad was tough on Mom because he was so sick and there was no pleasing him, but we thought she would cope and come through stronger. We couldn't believe she'd go for a divorce, but she did. Within a week Dad was living in a penthouse apartment and my life was a lot more unbearable than before. I was trying to hold down the family business and felt forced now more than ever to be with my dad and help him with his physical problems.

By the next year he needed a wheelchair to get around. It was apparent he couldn't keep his political career going, so he didn't run for reelection. While all his problems were mounting I managed to keep up a pretty good front, so my friends thought everything was on an even keel. They even got me elected president of the Women's Olympic Diving Committee and head of the Dayton

Draft Board. Then a national group put me on a Multiple Sclerosis Board with Joe Garagiola, Mamie Eisenhower and Ara Parseghian.

Since my intake of steroids had been steady, my strength was still good enough, in spite of all the other drugs, to make a try at the unofficial American bench press record for my weight class. Some of my buddies brought the world champion, Larry Pacifico, to Dayton for a check of my attempt. We all assembled at a Holiday Health Spa in town and a crowd of friends cheered my series of lifts. But at a body weight of 158 pounds, I missed the 370-pound record by six pounds.

That near miss didn't give me the big self-image boost that would snap me back from my drug daze. It only made me ripe for the dare my friends hit me with the next week. We were sitting at a motel restaurant having lunch when one of them tried to bait me into doing something crazy to prove I was the same old Sam.

"When are you going to pull your next stunt, Sam?"

"What do you mean, stunt? You know I'm just a conservative businessman."

"Sure you are. I'll buy you dinner tonight and pay your cleaning bill if you jump off that diving board out there with all your clothes on."

"You're on, sucker."

While my friends gathered around the pool I put my off-the-wall plan into action.

"Excuse me. I'll be back in a minute."

As soon as I was out of sight I grabbed the lobby elevator and rode up to the eighth-floor roof. From the edge I yelled down to my buddies, "Here I come." Then I made a perfect leap off the roof into the pool. My buddies were flabbergasted, but the stunt didn't do me all that much good. I was only trying to tap a well of nerve that was drying up with each successive drug injection.

In the summer of 1972 something happened that shocked me back to my senses for a while. It converted me into an instant student of terrorism. I had been watching TV a lot because the Munich Olympics were in the news. When the report flashed on the screen I couldn't believe it. A Black September group had gunned down eleven Israeli athletes in cold blood. I was too full of rage to do anything for a couple of days. I just sat around the house with my anger getting more and more out of hand. Not only had the terrorists killed citizens of a country I deeply admired, but they had gone so far as to invade the Olympic Village—the place where I'd met the greatest bunch of people in my life. I had total respect for everything that had to do with the Olympics. You don't go through all that training and the competition and friend-making and those goose-flesh ceremonies and come away without a deep and lasting feeling.

In Dayton, the week of the massacre, the city's biggest synagogue held a memorial service. Since I was an ex-Olympic athlete I was asked to say something consoling. When I got up to the microphone I was too shook up to say much more than a few words and that sure wasn't like me. But I did manage to give my Olympic silver to the synagogue in memory of the dead Israelis. I put it around the neck of the Jewish leader in charge and somebody snapped a picture which was later featured on the cover of a national magazine.

From that time on, in my book terrorists were the lowest of the low. To get back at them any possible way was always in the front of my mind. I started reading and collecting everything I could get my hands on about terrorist acts around the world. My new album was full of magazine and newspaper clippings that detailed all kinds of political crimes, from a death-squad machine-gunning of hundreds of innocent Central American villagers to the poison-tipped umbrella murder of a European diplomat. The collection also bulged with clippings detailing the Israelis' responses to the terrorism directed against them. They were leading the fight that the world would have to join some day soon. My loyalty to Israel derived to a large extent from the fact that it was so much like America in its will to be free. More than ever the perfect place for me seemed to be by the Israelis' sides, helping them fight for their beliefs and heritage. Especially since my own country wouldn't let me put my life on the line to show my thanks. Feeling helpless again when something like this Olympic massacre happened the next time would be too hard to take. I didn't want to be one of those people who could make a difference but sit on the sidelines watching. And still the damn drug doses that were slowly turning my brain into cauliflower kept getting bigger.

Probably my slipping self-esteem made me do crazier things than ever to try to regain self-confidence. At a business lunch a few weeks after the Olympics a friend named Charlie kidded me about being washed up. The sports pages had recently carried stories about my diving mark being broken. Between 1960 and 1972 I had held the record for total points, but now I was reminded that I wasn't the champ any more. When Charlie laughed and said I was a "has-been" I told him, "I can still break a diving record even if I can't get back in the Olympics. I'll just beat the unofficial world high dive record." When Charlie said, "I dare you," I knew I couldn't resist.

The unofficial record at the time was 153 feet, but there weren't any 154-foot platforms around. Charlie wouldn't let that spoil his fun. He checked out some statistics about the heights of nearby bridges. The best bet was a 206-foot span over Lake Cumberland in Kentucky. My sky diving days told me the difference between 154 feet and 206 feet was no big deal. Either way your body reached its top speed before you hit the water. The next weekend found me perched on the catwalk with a goading Charlie at my elbow and eight other friends stationed in a boat below. They looked like specks floating down there and for a minute the idea of backing out on the bet seemed like the only sane thing to do. No chance. To test the depth of the water I decided to take a preliminary jump off the bridge, but halfway down it occurred to me there was no bubble machine in the lake to cushion the shock like there was in a high dive pool. Just before splashdown a gust of wind caught me and blew me into a sitting position. The 120-mile-per-hour force broke my back, and after a hospital stay I had to wear a brace for six months. All the time my back was mending I thought of how stupid the jump had been since it could have killed me and left my dad worse off than he was. On the other hand, it proved I could still beat a dare, so there was still some of the old nerve left.

The next year a lot of jumps at the local sky diving clubs kept my real hopes hidden. And just to prove that Mrs. Hall didn't raise any dummies after all, my pack included a parachute. The year 1973 was also the year when yacht racing first appealed to me. I was just getting into it and dreaming about maybe training for the Americas Cup crew when the doctors told me about my lung cancer. That was quite a jolt to an athletic type who never smoked. The bigger jolt came when, the very same week the operation was scheduled, the Yom Kippur war broke out. By the time the surgeons took one-third of my right lung and laid me up the war was history. The Israelis cleaned the Arabs' clocks in just seventeen days.

Missing the action again depressed me more than the cancer, but I would go into much deeper depression months later when my drug-clouded brain told me to do something that proved a major embarrassment to my family. The problem came about because I'd begun to make it a practice to carry a gun, thinking—naively maybe—that someone might try to steal the receipts I sometimes collected for the family business. One day, while alone in an elevator, I pulled the stunt of attempting a quick draw and ended up shooting myself in the thigh. What hurt most was the realization of how stupid I'd been. But then I compounded the problem by making up a story about being attacked. At that point my self-esteem was so low I couldn't face the pain of more humiliation.

After the truth came out about what had really happened, I made a pact with myself at least always to own up to my failures. Though the drug problems would still haunt me, some inner voice told me that part of my problem was the need to live up to an unrealistic standard that couldn't be met.

When I was recovered physically I went back to work taking care of my father. Within two years he was in such bad shape that the doctors told me to get him ready to die. How do you let your father die? Especially one like mine, who was the main motivator behind all I did. Sometimes his pressure made me hate him and cry a lot alone. But thinking about it long enough convinced me he was only trying to show his deep love. My mother never approved of Dad's methods and they were a source of dissension between the two of them. But Mom was a persuader in her own gentle way just as much as Dad, and her support for her boys was like a rock. She was a churchgoer who never cursed and didn't look too kindly on those who did. When we were with her after being with Dad we had to change gears fast. She was so set on raising her sons to be gentlemen that there were times when we had to wear sport coats to the dinner table.

But it was my father who was the real power behind me. He was the one who shaped my character for better or worse. He could have spoiled his three boys since we lived pretty much in luxury with servants and fancy cars and the best prep schools and tutors and traveling companions. But Dad leaned on us all the time to beat the other guy. He pushed me and pushed me and made his goals for me my goals till it wasn't possible to resist him. Even though most of it didn't take, he never seemed to be disappointed in me because I was willing to try anything twice. My mother was very disappointed later with my drug dependence and the depression and the screwed-up business career. But over the years His Honor the Mayor and I got closer than most fathers and sons get, and sometimes it was almost like sharing one mind.

Dad was suffering from too many diseases by 1975. They took away too much of his great store of energy. That's why his doctors told me to do what was necessary to help him get ready to die. They gave me the sad duty because Dad was so close to me, and my brothers' commitments kept them away from Dayton. But I didn't have any intention of letting my father die. I was going to dare him back to health, or at least see to it that he wouldn't go out an invalid. In the six months before the doctors told me it was about over he had major surgery, so he needed round-the-clock care. A lot of my time was being spent trying to run the family business, but every spare minute was devoted to my dad while I averaged about three hours sleep a night. There were no bar-hopping escapades or pleasures of any kind. Except for the damn dope. Every morning it was Dad's house before work, then back for lunch with him, then supper.

Even though he couldn't roll over in bed I bundled him up in a wheelchair and took him on visits to friends and political cronies. That seemed to revive his spirits a little. He always loved New York, so I started driving him there and pushing him around Manhattan in his wheelchair. Then later I started taking him to a Dayton hospital for physical therapy. The therapists taught me everything I needed to know to help him myself, and they even gave me the run of the place when there was no one around. I began going to the hospital every day at the noon lunch break. He didn't know what my goal for him was or he might not have gone along. If there was any chance at all, he was going to walk again.

At first he couldn't stand. Then after a lot of therapy that was supposed to make standing bearable, he just wouldn't. That's when I started to batter him with the kind of name-calling he used on me in the old days. The emotional pain was probably as awful for me as the physical pain was for him.

"Stand up, you chicken son-of-a-bitch."

"How can you talk to your father like that?"

"I said stand up, you helpless old bag of bones."

"I can't."

"Yes you can. No-guts Hall. That's who you are. Just a worthless old ass. You're not worth the time of day, you old coward."

About that time he would cry in hopes I would let up, but I just piled on more abuse.

"Where's all that nerve you made me show all those years?"

"To hell with you. I can't take this anymore."

"Yes you can. And you will, you goddamn yellow bastard.

Stand up." By now he wouldn't be able to control the crying, and he'd have to get a few minutes to himself in the exercise room. In the meantime I'd hide in the bathroom with tears in my eyes. Crying myself to sleep got to be a way of life in those days. But if the pressure wasn't kept up Dad would die on me and there was no accepting that.

Every day he was pushed to do more and the progress came glacier slow.

"Okay, Dad, you walked two steps yesterday. Let's see you do three today."

"Fuck you."

"Fuck you, too, you chicken shit son-of-a-bitch."

After a month of his physical and my mental agony, my treatment showed the first sign of really working. One day his exercise effort didn't please me and he heard about it.

"You're a lazy quitter. I don't know why I waste my time on you. You're a wornout useless old motherfucker."

He looked at me with the glint in his eye I hadn't seen for so long and said, "Not any more, remember. Not since the divorce."

The tension broke with that comeback and after that he started to laugh at my language and the tone of my voice, and he would try to do more than the day before, until he was making real progress. Each night at home I'd study the words of some great leader, like Douglas MacArthur or George Patton, to quote them to my father the next day. We began going places that meant something in his youth and seeing people who could motivate him. A couple of times friends managed to get famous athletes like the Reverend Bob Richards and Jesse Owens to come by for visits. Sports heroes always inspired him and Richards and Owens were a great help with their competitive drive. But what was even more impressive was their feeling for an old man in trouble.

During all that time of pressuring and goading my dad into keeping up his therapy I was neglecting my wife and kids. But there was no other way, because without my pushing we would lose him. The strain on me was terrific and the depression bought me a couple of forced bed rests in the same hospital where Dad was getting his therapy. But the reward came six months later when Dad walked out of the hospital on his own. That made all my efforts worthwhile and took care of some of the guilt about my wife and kids. Dad's words to the doctor were, "My son and I want to thank you, and I won't be back because I can walk again and we won some time." He didn't have to explain to me or the doctor who he meant by "we." He was a severe diabetic taking two insulin shots a day. He had heart and lung disease that couldn't be treated because of his weakness. And he suffered from seventeen different complications. But he was able to walk with two canes and relight the spark of his spirit for a while.

When he died two years later I knew the extra time he'd been given was at least in part because of my challenges and that part of my debt to him was now repaid. But I was still devastated with an emptiness that no other person would ever be able to fill. And there was a balance due him because toward the end of the long trial of his last months he was stronger than I was. And he would never have accepted my surrender to the pill and the needle. My drug use was getting more and more serious, partly because I couldn't bear seeing him dying before my eyes in spite of his own and my best efforts. Those days taught me that a person like me, who could thrill to incredible highs beyond most people's dreams, was prone to the deepest valleys of despair too. I was so caught up in trying to beat the odds against my father that I needed a steady diet of downers after my earlier binge of uppers. Now I was mixing fixes in more combinations than Dr. Jekyll could think up. The more ashamed I was of my weakness, the further I slipped into addiction. When Dad died we sold some of the family properties and I took a job with a local construction operation. I managed to keep my mind on business during the day most of the time but the nights were unbearable. Janice and Mom couldn't talk to me about Dad and how depressing it was to see him fall apart. By now the uppers took the place of the downers again. One night, sitting in a warm bath I got a strong urge to end it all. My razor was on the sink, so I stood up and took out the blade. Afterwards I couldn't even remember slashing my wrists. Good thing I hadn't locked the bathroom door. When Janice heard me thrashing around in the tub she came in and found me soaking in blood and called an ambulance.

After that dumb-assed incident I went to a counselor "for Janice and the kids," but faked getting help. The counselor just wasn't getting through to me. Every night it would be: slip out into the garage and shoot more and more drugs to deaden the pain. But self-hate was always the side-effect. I was going from really bad to a lot worse. When the construction company went belly up it gave me the excuse to become a full-time addict.

About this time too I started looking again for that one woman who would make the pain in my life go away. Even though I loved Janice (and by now we had three wonderful kids) the feeling dogged me that she wasn't really the love of my life. The idea grew without my really being aware and it sent me out hitting the local bars again. Before I tried making myself into the good husband and father for Janice I had to have as many women in my life as possible. That way the perfect one would find me if she ever came my way. Life couldn't be its most intense otherwise. A weakness for the ladies was always one of my biggest downfalls, but that wouldn't win me any prize for male originality. I loved women not just for sex, but because they could be so soft and tender and strong and stubborn all at once. And most of them could love you and forgive you way past reason. Not only that, but each one was so different from the last one you had and the next one you wanted that you really got wrapped up for a while and you almost had enough because everything was so strong. At the same time that made life pretty frustrating, because days and nights were only long enough for so many women. Not to mention all the friendships with men I craved and my need to be alone a lot of the time. Sometimes I think God goofed when He made us with such a nagging need for opposite things and then squeezed our time on earth so we couldn't possibly try all we wanted.

Anyway, I was never able to resist a gathering spot full of people, whether it was a sports arena or a theater lobby or a barroom. Places like that were electric with excitement because you never knew who you might meet or what they might be like. Who was the guy on the next barstool and what did he do for a living and what were his hobbies and did he have a family and what kind of car did he drive and did he know any good jokes? Who was that one over there and why did he look so down? Could I say something or do something to make him feel better? Did he just go through a divorce or a death in the family? I always wanted to know the answers to questions like those, so I always tried to get them when I was in a bar. And that was quite often.

But the sharpest single tingle in a bar always came from the "Ezio Pinza time." That was when you made eye contact on "some enchanted evening" with a pair of female blues or browns "across a crowded room." Nothing could match the turn-on of those first minutes of a new relationship with a good-looking woman. There was always the slightly awkward conversation and the come-hither smile and the light playing in her hair and what more could a man ask? That was the kind of set-up that helped make life worth living, even though sometimes you couldn't make it go much further. If you found out she was a terrific person on the same wavelength and you wanted to really know her, she usually got crowded out anyway by the others you had to have. Or maybe it was all sex appeal and then just bed and bored. But my problem was usually the opposite. Sex made me fall in love so often a doctor might have prescribed something for genital heart disease.

Anyway, late in 1979 Barbara turned up at a local bar and turned out to be my lifeline for a while. She was so full of faith in my could-be future that she sparked some of my old zest and made me think about going cold turkey from the drugs. But I put that off even though Barbara tried hard to bring me back to life. After a while she gave up trying, so the affair was already going downhill when we were followed to a motel. The next day at home Janice gave me the news.

She told me that she wanted a divorce and that I should leave that night. When I told her that I still loved her, she said she realized that but that she'd known for a long time that I had to be free. I suggested more counseling but Janice had made up her mind. It was over.

We stayed separated until the divorce a couple of years later. The shock of the family break-up was enough to push me into a new round of drugs and booze. I tried suicide again. This time it was an overdose, but I couldn't get that right either. Maybe a small voice was telling me that whatever it was I was really looking for might turn up if I could just pull myself out of my funk. In a few weeks at least another job did turn up. This time with a real estate development firm. But within two months I was so strung out that a leave of absence was the only way to save face. That's when my old friend Don came to the rescue.

Don was a high school buddy whose life was also pretty wild— up until we ran into each other in 1980, that is. Now Don was born again and very much changed. He was in his forties too and suddenly satisfied for the first time in his life. When Don started telling me all about the good news for sinners in the Bible and the tears filled his eyes, the inner peace he talked about seemed real to me. He wasn't smoking or drinking or running around, and I really envied him. My Presbyterian past never had much effect on me, even though I'd always believed in God. The trouble was, I thought, He never seemed much interested in my problems. I felt I needed a God who could be the best possible personal friend, not a way-off father figure. Don talked about Jesus as if he was his best friend, and the kind of spiritual high he was on seemed a lot better than those phony drug rushes.

When Don suggested I go see the pastor of his church, I balked a bit. I told him that I wasn't much for religion. But Don kept pointing out how much alike we were, and how what worked for him might work for me, and I finally decided to give it a try.

Right after that talk I looked up Don's fundamentalist pastor and accepted Christ as my savior. The pastor assigned a man in his congregation to give me one-on-one teaching, and once a week for six months we would have breakfast together. We talked about the Bible and he would answer all my questions. Then for an hour or two every week the pastor himself would counsel me. For the first time in my life I felt some peace.

But the drug problem wouldn't go away. The pastor tried to talk me out of it, but, naturally, he didn't succeed. It would take more than words to cure me. Then Don came to the rescue again, or maybe it was God acting through Don. I had all the willpower of a roll of wallpaper till that night when he said, "Sam, you're a mess. You've got to get back to the discipline you used to have or you'll be dead in six weeks." Dying wouldn't have sounded all that bad except that lately I'd been praying a lot for the guts to change. But feeling that Jesus loves you doesn't buy the groceries. Don was telling me that my full cure was going to take more work than I'd invested so far. And that little voice in my head said again, Maybe someday if you stay alive you'll find what you're looking for. So I locked myself in my apartment with enough food to last six weeks and went cold turkey from the liquor and drugs. But I underguessed the recovery time by about a hundred percent. Two and a half months later my apartment was still my prison and I wasn't able to do much of anything except hallucinate. But at least I was off drugs and maybe on the way to winning.

The struggle to kick the drugs almost killed me and afterward my doctor gave me hell for trying it alone. He said the shock to my body could have bought me the farm. He was surprised it didn't, because my weight went from 165 to 128 pounds. There had been no sleep the first week because every part of me jerked out of control with no letup. I lost control of bodily functions. When sleep finally came the second week it only lasted an hour because of the exhaustion. By the third week I couldn't even raise myself out of my chair for four days. Drapes closed. Lights out. Sweat soaked.

I told myself more than once to die those first three-and-a-half weeks. But I kept pushing myself to keep at it, because if this thing could be licked anything was possible. After four weeks I managed to drag myself out for a walk at night, only to get completely lost a block away from the apartment. All through my fight I tried to keep my mind on what could be done with my life if my habit could be controlled. It took a lot of stupidity to get myself into this situation and it would take a lot of work and prayer and luck to get myself out. Even after all those cold-turkey weeks, sometimes my body would jerk so much that my arm would shoot out and smash into anything close by. My forearms and wrists were swollen twice their normal size from hitting tables and walls and the headboard of the bed.

During all that time Janice was calling every day, even though we were separated. But answering the phone took too much of my strength. She worried herself sick. After a couple more weeks I managed to go out for a walk one night without hallucinating the whole time or getting myself lost. So I called Janice. She was crying, but she was relieved to hear my voice. The next day she came over and took me to my daughter Samantha's soccer match. It was my first time away from the apartment or the streets around it in almost two months. I didn't even remember how to talk to people, but at half-time Samantha came up into the stands and knelt by my right side to hold my hand. The sun was over her right shoulder and it cast her shadow in front of me. I looked at it the whole time instead of looking right at her because the shame of being an addict was so sharp. I was modeling weakness and stupid-ity for my own adolescent daughter—the girl I loved so much, despite having pissed away most of the time that could have been used to get to know her.

I felt terrible for Janice too. But at least she was old enough to try to understand the pressures that brought me to this point in my life, and she did try. During the rest of the soccer match Samantha was on the field, but her shadow was still next to me. And it was by my side for the next month. All my other hallucinations got weaker as that dark copy of my daughter's shape got stronger. Always on my right. Bending with me to pick up a dropped scrap of food. Staggering with me to the bathroom. Walking alongside to help me get my bearings on night walks in the fresh air. That shadow served me all through the fight to free myself from the drug devil for good. Then after a month it faded as my body healed and my mind centered more and more on the real.

At the end of nearly two months my weight was still at 128, but I felt a little better and slept two or three hours a night. That gave me enough strength to hug Janice and the kids goodbye and drive out to Colorado to put the finishing touches on my new self with the help of some mountain air. From my rented apartment each morning's drive brought me up to a height of about 8500 feet for some physical training. At first, walking a hundred yards in the thin air brought on a fagged-out collapse. But each day it got a little better and easier and very slowly my strength came back. Eight weeks later, running and climbing three and a half miles a day in heavy boots was no problem, even with my back bent under a knapsack stuffed with full water bottles to weigh me down. In another six weeks my form was almost as good as it had been for the Olympics. Aside from my reconstructed leg. And I felt great at 162 pounds of muscle. Off drugs I could lick the world, and with Jesus' help I meant to stay off them.

In the early spring of 1982, with my faith recharged and my health revived, I grabbed an opportunity to go at last to the land of the Bible, as a man of peace instead of the fighter I longed to be for so many years. My résumé got me an interview for the job featured in a New York *Times* held-wanted ad. The interview was in Dallas. My family business background helped out, but the job was so appealing, I think I could have talked my way to an offer even if I only had a third grade education. My one-year contract made me a personnel specialist for a support element of the United Nations

Multinational Forces and Observers. This MFO outfit was part of the Camp David Accord drawn up by the law firm of Carter, Begin and Sadat to oversee the transfer of the Sinai from Israel to Egypt and to protect the peace afterwards. At last I was going to see Israel firsthand and at the same time contribute something to a historic peace process. I've often wondered since if I didn't know deep down even then I would end up fighting for the Israelis.

My first chance to mug for the camera. Age—one week.

The Hall boys. From left to right: myself, age five, future Olympian; Tony, age nine months, future All-American tailback and U.S. Congressman; and Mike, age four, future nationally known educator, lecturer and writer.

My first year at Culver Military Academy's summer camp, 1948. I'm in the front row, second from left, next to my brother, Mike, who is wearing glasses.

The Hall family, 1949. Standing, from left to right, are myself; my father, Dave, who would later become Mayor of Dayton, Ohio; Tony; and Mike. Seated is my mother, Ann.

Graduating from Ohio State in 1960. My father, Dave, proudly stands alongside.

Taking first place in 1959 Pan American Trials.

OFFICE OF THE VICE PRESIDENT

WASHINGTON

October 22, 1960

Dear Mr. Hall:

This is the first opportunity I have had to offer my congratulations to you for your outstanding achievement at the 1960 Olympics by winning a silver medal in the Springboard Diving event.

You may be justly proud of your well deserved award and very sure that the people of our country join in commending you for the exceptional manner in which you represented the United States.

With every good wish,

Sincerely,

Richard Nixon

Mr. Sam N. Hall
351 Faunwood Road
Dayton, Ohio

Letter of congratulation from then V.P. Richard Nixon.

Olympic medal presentation, Rome, 1960. Gary Tobian, center, gold medal winner; myself, right, silver medal winner; Juan Botella, left, bronze medal winner.

Jumping off a 206-foot bridge that spans Lake Cumberland in Kentucky. After jumping to test for depth, I'd planned to *dive* off, thereby breaking the world record that existed at the time (1972) for the highest dive. But I broke my back and had to wear a metal brace for six months.

TWO

By the third of February in 1982 I was looking down on Tel Aviv's Ben Gurion International Airport. It was the fulfillment of a dream that had spanned fifteen years. Now my future was waiting for me down on the runway. When the plane landed, I didn't. Instead of walking to the terminal building I soared. If there'd been dung piles on the tarmac I'd have stopped looping the loops just long enough to dive into each pile and say to myself, Isn't this great! Israeli camelshit!

Once I came down to earth everything about my new temporary homeland interested me. The airport policing seemed pretty lax. The last leg of my flight began in West Germany and at Frankfurt all the travelers put up with a full search, not only of bags but of clothing and body. Tanks were parked on the runways and machine guns could be spotted everywhere. But at Tel Aviv there was no search of my bags and no heavy armament in sight. I only spotted one Israeli soldier carrying an Uzi. No other security forces. Even the New York and Miami airports looked stricter. A little later I found out how wrong I was. If there were 500 people in Ben Gurion terminal building at any one time, over twenty percent would be plainclothes guards. All of them carried weapons under their civvies, and after you were in Israel a while you could spot the teams working the airports in pairs, with automatic pistols or Uzis strapped under their ski jackets. When something suspicious happened the security man or woman walking behind a partner would just reach under the partner's coat and pop out the automatic or the Uzi.

If somebody spotted a box or a bundle that looked as if it had been planted by a terrorist, the security forces swung into action

63

and within seconds a loudspeaker was giving the order to "clear the terminal, clear the terminal!" The loudspeaker was mounted on a van manned by security guards. One of them opened the rear doors and out on little tank tracks rolled a mechanized human-looking midget robot with a gun for an arm. It fired twelve-gauge .00 shot. I called the first one I saw at the airport "Irving." While I was admiring him he went into action. He shuffled up to a suitcase and blew it apart while his human partner stood behind a column. Irving's computerized cousins also patrolled the streets of Tel Aviv.

On the way to my new apartment the bright seashore-sand-blasted buildings on the bustling tree-lined streets dazzled my eyes. And so did the physical beauty of the Israelis. During the drive from the airport their individual appearances really struck me. I fell for them at first sight, especially their dark shiny hair and high cheekbones and the way both the men and the women carried themselves with such pride. Not to mention the different styles and colors of their clothes. They looked to be in great physical shape too. In my letters to friends in the States that first week I said not one Israeli was overweight. They all looked as if they could do a sub-three-hour Boston Marathon. Maybe being one of "God's chosen people" took care of your waistline along with your soul. I was anxious to ask these Israelis all about their lives, but I only spoke a few words of Hebrew. I knew I'd be frustrated till I learned enough of the language to carry on a decent conversation. Once the language barrier was broken we'd surely have a lot in common. All of the American products were on display in the stores. The array of items—everything from Wheaties to Levis—gave the impression that the country was a smaller version of the States.

My first day on the job taught me plenty about the organization I was working for and what the work was like. The MFO was made up of military units from twelve different countries, with offices on the twentieth and twenty-first floors of the Ramada. My apartment was on the seventh floor. The MFO answered to a council called the Joint Commission, housed in a bomb shelter deep under the downtown library across the street from the IBM building where some of the Israeli defense command was dug in. The Joint Commission was made up of the Egyptian and Israeli military brass. All security matters were cleared through them. The Camp David Accords stipulated that the Commission had to keep track of everybody connected with the MFO. My personnel specialist job ran me from the Ramada to the library and then over to the IBM building and back to the Ramada.

E–Systems had hired me for the MFO job. The company was a private outfit with headquarters in Texas. It was subcontracted by the U.S. government to support the UN soldiers with logistics, and I'd heard all the top executives were retired military brass or ex-CIA. E–Systems did ninety-nine percent of its business with the military and had contracts to service all the communications gear of important planes, including "Air Force One." They dealt a lot in high-tech equipment like advanced spy planes and twenty-first-century communications networks. One of their most interesting gadgets was a miniature radar device that looked like a jungle plant. It had been dropped from planes flying over Vietnam. It could pick up how many people walked by it, not to mention their weight within fifteen pounds. And it looked real enough to defoliate.

E–Systems also put devices like that all over the Sinai where they had a field mission set up in 1978. The mission amounted to the first peacekeeping force in the northwest section of the Sinai. But E–Systems' job in the Middle East now was to take two Israeli bases in the desert—a northern base of about two hundred acres at Eitam and a much smaller southern base at Sharm el Sheikh—and turn them into liveable cities for the Egyptians. In 1967, which was before the Israelis took it, Eitam was a big Egyptian military base with an important landing strip. About seventy-five percent of the people working toward the Sinai turnover lived there and the rest were stationed at Sharm el Sheikh. The cost of the work to build the new cities was to be split, with America putting up sixty percent plus Israel's and Egypt's twenty percent each. The whole complicated project needed to be "go" by the time the Israelis handed the Sinai back to the Egyptians on April 24th. Some advance paper-shuffling was done in Washington to clear the way for the turnover, but all the hands-on work was still ahead. As personnel specialist I had to do "whatever needed to be done." That meant getting things organized for the twelve countries' military that were coming in every day. Plus fixing clearances for cooks and laundry workers and mechanics and drivers. Then buying food and setting up offices and housing in warehouses and hotels. A great staff had been already hired to serve under me, but it was clear right away that it really wasn't big enough.

I was in charge of transportation for the MFO too. That made me a kind of go-between, meeting the new military and workers at the airport and holding their hands till they were settled. The job demanded twelve to sixteen hours a day with only the Saturday Sabbath off. Or as the Israelis call it, *Sha-bott*. There were plenty of snafus to straighten out. The screw-ups you always found in military detachments were even screwier in the MFO, because this was a brand new outfit. But the fast pace didn't bother me, and I liked being on the front burner. I knew what a big deal the Camp David agreement was for Israel. When the Egyptians had controlled the Sinai before the 1967 war, they hadn't done a damn thing with it. After the Israelis got it they built highways and power stations and piped water in from the Jordan river in the north and turned desert into farm land in the south. The pipes carrying the Jordan water were so big you could drive a jeep through them. Still, with all their investment the Israelis agreed at Camp David to give up all these projects plus about two billion dollars a year in Sinai oil reserves.

Once the job routine got squared away, I started to check out the night life in Tel Aviv. Sleep was something I had never needed much of. I could top off a twelve-hour work day with a high time and still need Sominex after the last partier was long since dead to the world. The Ramada Lounge drew big crowds of military brass and international jet setters to listen to Sammy Villa. He was Israel's number one pop singer. He had a thin body full of muscle

that worked like a magnet on women. The night I met him he
needed a stick to beat them off the stage so he could finish his act.
When we were introduced I stuck out my hand and said, "I'm
Sammy." He took it and said, "You must be Sammy One because
I'm Sammy Too." We hit it off right away when I told him about
my feelings for Israel.

"I've been itching to get to this country for years. I love the
people already. I only wish I could talk to more of them."

"We'll have to get you some Hebrew lessons, Sam. I'm having a
party at my place Friday night. That's the best way to learn. Come
on over and let some nice-looking woman use her native tongue on
you."

There was a balcony above the Ramada Lounge where I usually
stopped on the way from my room to check out the social scene
down below. Sammy would always spot me up above and pound
out "Here She Comes, Miss America" on the piano. The fanfare
got to be so popular with the lounge lizards that Sammy put it into
his act. I reminded him once that the Miss America contest was for
women. He just said, "What a shame, since you and I are so beautiful."

At Sammy's condo that first Friday night I met all his friends. It
was his wife's birthday and an excuse for one of his famous posh
wild parties that he always video-taped with himself as star of the
footage. All night long he was clowning for the camera or doing a
dance with a gorgeous guest or attacking the lens with mock karate
chops and kicks that you could splice into a Bruce Lee flick.

About midnight Sammy stopped clowning long enough to intro-
duce me to a big-league-looking Israeli officer named Major
Shimer Weprin. Sammy said, "Major Weprin works over at the
Joint Commission office. I'm surprised you two haven't run into
each other yet." The major sat down next to me while Sammy went
back to his other guests. By the time the party ended Major Weprin
was on his way to being a good friend and had pledged to be my
future tennis partner. Sammy had told him before about my reputa-

tion around town as the crazy American who loved Israel. I couldn't resist telling my new friend about my old dream of fighting for Israel.

"The American military wouldn't take me for Vietnam because of my bad leg," I said.

"Well, that doesn't matter now that you're here on a peace mission. If you ever decide you want some action, though, you ought to check out the volunteer squads being trained around the country. They're run by ex-Israeli officers with medical discharges like your own. Some of the volunteers are going across the Lebanese border to interdict the PLO."

After the first few pulse thumps I got all the information Major Weprin had on the squads and filed it away for future reference. The thought crossed my mind that maybe the squads might be my ticket to a little action someday, but I didn't want to think about it too much because my peace-keeping job would keep me so busy. But I could dream.

Those first few nights in the Ramada lounge, a lot of Israel's most attractive women were on display too. Being born again, I was naturally trying to reform. But stopping the skirt-chase altogether was too much. If you were addicted to women, it was tough not to fall once in a while. And at the Tel Aviv Ramada that first month Ida and Harriet had what it took to make me question my self-inflicted promise never to get serious about marriage again. Ida was in her late twenties and she had wild red hair like King David had in the Bible descriptions. We danced one night past closing time and I was already in love by the second set. But Ida turned out to be married to a man thirty years older. He had given her and her mother a home after the Yom Kippur war and took care of them, so Ida said thanks by marrying him. But she wasn't happy now.

Within two nights we were really intense. Her sense of humor and turned-up personality were fatal for me. She could talk about anything, from Moses to modern music. I loved listening to her stories about growing up in Israel and what impressed her on her one visit to the States and what her ambitions were. She wanted to be a doctor, but the breaks had been against her so far and she was worried that time was passing her by. I gave her advice about getting along better with her husband, but she told me through her tears the third week, "I may want to leave him—maybe even for you." I held her for a long time and tried to explain. "I can't make a commitment till I know for sure what to do with my own life after the MFO. My stay here is only scheduled to last until the Sinai cities are humming and from then on who can tell?" All the time I was trying to cushion the "no" that came from my head, my heart was calling me seventeen kinds of jackass for not grabbing the happiness Ida could give. But when she left the next morning I knew "no" was the only right answer, because not even Ida could cure my thirst for that "more" that always seemed to call me.

Ida still wanted to see me and I sure wanted to see her. But the spell needed to be broken or it would get us both into more trouble than we could get out of. Two weeks later the spell-breaker showed up in the Ramada Lounge. Her name was Harriet, and she was a little blonde all of twenty-two whose mother and father had brought her as a child to Israel from South Africa. She was a college grad who spoke five languages and typed four as a secretary for an International House. She loved to dance too, and when she asked, "Will you teach me the new American steps?" I tried to show my strong interest in her, but at the same time I wanted to look blasé in case Ida walked in. I couldn't resist Harriet because fun was her middle name and at the same time she was as bright as anybody I ever met, and that's a considerable combination to go up against. She knew all about the military history of the Middle East and the political setup too. She gave me a crash course in the subject that was already my favorite. There was definitely chemistry between us, and within two more weeks she had me really thinking long-term contract. She said, "I believe in open relationships and I don't mind you keeping all your women friends." But that kind of attitude couldn't last, and besides, I'd just be wanting complete freedom at the same time I'd be jealous of any other man whose roving eye landed on Harriet. So the best thing for both of us was to move on.

My first Sunday in town had been all work, but by the second weekend there was some free time for a little exploring. Netanya was a resort on the Mediterranean a short drive north of Tel Aviv. It was a pretty town at sea level, flanked on one side by high bluffs and on the other by a Daytona-like beach. The sand-colored buildings and houses really contrasted with the dark blue harbor clogged with white boats. North of town luxury apartments and condos climbed a steep hill overlooking the sea. People went to Netanya for the great skindiving in the coral-filled inlets, so I rented some equipment and checked the Med for coral, fish and, I confess, mermaids. The rest of the day I spent window-shopping the local ladies and the tourists in the public park. That trip to Netanya turned out to be the first link in a chain that finally got me hooked up with the Israel forces. Back in Tel Aviv I got so carried away describing my trip that Sammy Villa suggested our group move the next weekend's party to there. A caravan of "Ramada rats" headed for the resort the following Friday night.

That Saturday we all swam and boated and fished with a native net, and made such a smash out of the whole trip that Sammy said all of us should get together next at the Lido Kenneret in Tiberius. The resort hotel there was owned by a friend I'd made at the Tel Aviv Ramada. His name was Anthon, and he did me some favors early on, because being in charge of transportation for the MFO, I got asked a lot where to go for R & R. Recommending the Lido Kenneret was easy for me, because my friend was supposed to be a terrific host and his hotel offered a spectacular view on the Sea of Galilee.

When Sammy and his troop arrived the next weekend in Tiberius, the site of the great biblical dramas truly moved me. I spent the first couple of hours walking the shoreline and imagining parts for myself in the wondrous story of Jesus, even to throwing the net and rowing the boat for the Apostles on make-believe fishing trips.

But for me the most appealing fantasy role was fighting the Roman persecutors of the Christians.

The next week the tension buildup that led to the June 6th war was everywhere in Tel Aviv. There was a hurriedness to the good times my friends were having, and a lot of them talked about being called to active duty soon. But nobody who knew Israeli history was too surprised by the sudden shift. Actually, from my first day in the country reminders of war had been everywhere, even at the Ramada which was like a prefab fortress. The first floor front was at ground level, but a couple of stair-flights at the back of the building led to the beach about sixty feet below. The lounge was in back too and the windows gave a sweeping view of the sea. One night Sammy Villa pointed to them and said, "Those windows were designed to be removed in a minute so two eight-inch guns can be set up and trained on any hostile warships."

By now uniformed Israeli soldiers were everywhere and street attacks against the troops were getting more common. Car bombs were going off right and left, and in the middle of one week the stepped-up city violence got close enough to smell. I remember walking from the Ramada to the "BBC," a favorite restaurant for Americans in Israel, and hearing a loud explosion. I asked an old man next to me, "What was that?" but he just mumbled, "When will it stop?" A couple of blocks further on a small crowd was already watching the clean-up operation. A woman standing there with her two children told me, "Someone was just blown up" and a teenager said, "I was walking right behind them. It was two soldiers and a woman. Somebody on a Vespa threw them some flowers and one of the soldiers caught them and they exploded." The flowers must have been arranged with a stick of plastique about the size of a cigarette pack. Plastique was a favorite weapon of PLO terrorists. It looked like a harmless piece of putty, but it was really more potent than dynamite. This time the windows were blown out of buildings for two or three blocks. The soldier who caught the flowers probably thought they were a sign of friendship, but now the only way the police could tell anything about him or his buddy and the woman with them was by the epaulets that by-standers picked up off the sidewalk. The acrid smell of the explosive was still strong, and the grim firemen were washing down the walls of six or seven building to clean off the splattered remains. Incidents like these and newspaper reports that terrorists were lobbing shells at Israeli border positions from their hideouts in Lebanon made it pretty clear that the "winds of war" were blowing up a major storm.

My regular working trips to the Sinai kept me reminded of Israel's history of trouble—the rusty relics of the Six-Day War still littered the desert. There were battered jeep bones and half-track corpses and tank remnants. I also learned that about ten million land mines had been laid in the Sinai but that only about thirty percent were ever removed. The ones still there needed a lot of respect from the MFO personnel. We could never be sure where they were going to turn up next. They were blown around the desert in sand masses called "waddies" that created a whole new breed of animal called the three-legged camel.

At about the time the soldiers were blown up on the sidewalk I went to the airport on business. A big stone wheel just inside the terminal caught my eye that day. In the previous visits to Ben Gurion I'd noticed it from a distance but hadn't given it much thought. This time I found out the wheel was a memorial to twenty-six Israeli civilians gunned down in a terrorist attack at the airport in 1976. Somebody had hired a Red Brigade suicide squad to do his dirty work. I remember speculating at the time that the mastermind was probably Carlos, the world's number one terrorist. All his hired murderers had been killed in the airport attack. But by their sick standards the mission had been a big success. Up close, the memorial brought back a flood of memories. I remembered the terrorism scrapbook I had kept and my thoughts about getting back at bastards like Carlos. Checking out the wheel memorial started me fantasizing again about joining a commando team and striking back at terrorists.

It now seemed that would be the best role for a military man. Terrorists' tactics made me burn to join in a small group-action against them or even go one-on-one. A terrorist seemed like an enemy you could relate to. Not like rows of tin soldiers mowed down a mile away or bombed to kingdom-come from the sky along with half the civilian population. There was a time when any kind of combat role was attractive to me, but no more. I longed for something more personal.

The Sunday after reflecting on the wheel memorial at the airport, I headed with Sammy Villa's group to Tiberius. This time the trip got me closer than ever to the war that was coming. Tiberius was almost next to the Golan Heights, which was where the Israeli troop movements relit the fire in my belly to fight. My hotel-owner friend, Anthon, knew about my interest in the army, so we spent the afternoon talking till he said, "You know, Sam, there is going to be a new war for sure. There are too many signs. This evening I'll drive you up to Golan and show you the maneuvers."

When we got there we couldn't get close to the bunkers or the training centers because of all the barbed wire and road blocks, and there were patrols everywhere. We saw a lot of tank maneuvers plus caravans of soldiers and heavy artillery being moved around. There were some sightseers, but I blocked them out because I wanted to focus on the military. The tingle was real, but so was the trouble I had understanding what was happening to me. Here I was on a peacekeeping mission and the sight of the Jews getting ready for war made me hungry again to join them. That Christian faith I'd developed was supposed to preclude such feelings. It didn't. Some violence in me couldn't be erased, and that worried me. A Christian shouldn't want to fight. So the trip to the Golan Heights had me confused. Maybe somewhere in the back of my brain my big reason for coming to Israel was that I was really hoping for war. Driving back to Tel Aviv I prayed a lot and it seemed to me that God might be answering that I was needed in this fight. Or maybe my wish was father to the desired answer.

* * *

Back in my office on Monday I started to put a new plan into action. My Hebrew was still too weak for me to be accepted by the right branch of the Israeli Defense Forces, and I'd also heard that they enforced an iron-clad three-year enlistment. A year would be plenty for me. That was long enough without seeing my kids in the States. So becoming a legal full-fledged member of the Israeli army wasn't the likely solution. The more I thought about it the more the answer seemed to be the "civilian" commando squads that Major Weprin told me were being trained at different sites in Israel. I thought I could probably sign up with them for weekend duty and still keep my job with the MFO till the Sinai cities were finished.

That afternoon when we met for tennis, the major supplied some more facts about the special forces and how to join them. At first he acted surprised by my relit fire.

"I thought you were here to keep the peace."

"I was until yesterday. Anthon took me up to the Golan. Tell me again what those squads are like."

"The units are being trained in commando tactics and current weapons by ex-IDF officers. Most of them weren't able to stay in the military for medical reasons. They set up training sites to add to their civilian incomes and stay in touch, and their students are mercenaries from everywhere and a lot of volunteers. Are you serious about joining?"

"Very serious."

"Then I'll call an ex-officer friend of mine. His name is Arnold Koenigsburg. He helps train a volunteer unit over at Nahariyya."

That was in the northwestern part of the country, on the Med near the Lebanese border.

No question, by the time this Koenigsburg called the ants in my pants had St. Vitus' dance. I was primed and ready.

"Major Weprin vouches for your loyalty to Israel and he says you've had some prior military training. You sound like the kind of person we're looking for. My unit is working out of Nahariyya. Can you make it up here next weekend?"

"Of course I can."

Then came the problem of sitting on my feelings for a week that seemed longer than ever. When Friday night finally came, I borrowed a car and headed for Nahariyya. The training area was a big farm belted by barbed wire. My identification got me past the gate and the Uzi-toting guard dressed in IDF fatigues. He waved me through and pointed to a two-story farm house about a mile up the path. Koenigsburg and thirty other men were sitting around a huge fireplace in the main room when I knocked on the door. The group was introduced to me and then Koenigsburg, who was a thirty-year-old ramrod, took me into the kitchen and poured a couple of shots of cognac. They were designed to oil our talk about the training site and the kinds of military teaching the volunteers would be getting, in addition to the role that was planned for me.

I was told the abandoned farm was as good a spot as any IDF camp for training. There was so much unused land around that nobody from the nearby kibutzes ever bothered the people here. He said, "There are five ex-officers working with me at the moment, and we have twenty-five volunteers. About half of them are American Jews working to qualify for the IDF. The other half are mercenaries from around the world. They sign up because we've got a reputation for tough training. We'll teach you to think like a terrorist. That's the only way to counter them." I was wondering at about this time why Koenigsburg took me, since I was at least twenty to twenty-five years older than the other volunteers. The IDF didn't interest me. Neither did a career as a mercenary. I didn't need the money and on principle I would never take any for helping Israel. Why I was accepted was a mystery, but thank God for Major Weprin and the fact that he knew Koenigsburg.

The ramrod told me, "The IDF knows all about the civilian commando training centers like this one. There are two others in the country. The army and the government are careful not to officially sanction them but they don't do anything to stop them either. They're grateful that there are volunteer squads that will do some jobs without being told to. Jobs that need doing but that can't be done by the regular army because of political situations. For instance, we can go across the border to stop PLO units before they get down here to do their dirty work."

I was anxious to find out what kind of training was in store for me, and Koenigsburg said there was no secret about it. "You'll get plenty of calisthenics and you'll be shown all the techniques of commando operations. You'll have to learn all there is to know about small-team weapons and you'll get lectures on counter-terrorism. You'll have to study in your spare time in Tel Aviv. And you won't have as much spare time as you think, because there will be assignments in observation and concentration we'll be giving you." That all sounded great to me, but the best part was Koenigsburg's next line. "If you're good enough you might see some action soon."

That first weekend at the center was basic weapons work and commando demonstrations from experts. I was kept very busy crawling through obstacle courses, jumping in and out of pillboxes, countering mock-terrorist attacks, joining in small team work, and practicing hand-to-hand combat. Twenty-six years earlier in Ohio State's ROTC program I had qualified with the old M–1 rifle; I did it again in 1961 with the Air Force. Then after the service there was big-game hunting with different weapons. I even built a gun collection insured for $36,000. But those guns were for hunting animals, not terrorists. At the center we were trained with the M–16 and the Uzi and the Czech AK–47, not to mention Israeli and Soviet grenades.

The commando lessons in the classroom and the field stressed behind-the-lines tactics and night missions. In college I wasn't what you'd call a student. But now at the center I put all the Rhodes scholars to shame, eating up manuals that were printed in English and French and Hebrew and Arabic and Russian. There were lessons to be learned in handling grenades, such as how many seconds you could hold on to Brand-X with a pulled pin before it turned you instead of your target into chopped liver. And how to electric-tape the tension on a triggering spoon. With a few of those taped babies you could go looking for military vehicles. When you came across one you could pull the pin and drop the grenade into the gas tank. In four or five hours the gas ate through the tape, and vehicle parts got blown across the countryside.

When I was back at work the next week the training manuals took the place of my *Time* magazine. No more living it up in the Ramada Lounge after dinner either. Lunch had to be skipped too because Koenigsburg gave me a week's worth of mock missions for that hour. He told me to keep in touch with a Lev Nadel in Tel Aviv. He was to be my case officer and military mentor and he would be giving me assignments. I called him my first morning back on the job and he said, "I want you to go to the lobby of the Sheraton and sit during your lunch hour. Observe everything you see taking place there. Remember everything. Don't take any notes until you go back to the office. And by the way, on the way back to the office, memorize three license plate numbers. I'll call you this afternoon to get your report." The assignment was the first of such training missions in different parts of the world in the months ahead.

At the Sheraton I found an overstuffed lobby chair and started taking mental notes. I didn't really go for this caper because it seemed boring and what it had to do with being a commando wasn't clear. But I kept checking the lobby and the happenings because I wanted to do whatever was needed to pass this mental obstacle course and get my chance at a real mission.

About ten minutes into my watch a young Israeli sat down in a chair across from me, and it was obvious after a while that he was a trainee too, making observations of the same lobby scenes. I knew enough not to make any sign to him and he didn't act as if he noticed me. Just before the end of my lunch hour a scuffle broke out at one end of the lobby. Two men started arguing over a satchel, and at one point they were playing tug of war with it. One of the men finally cursed and left the hotel. The other one gave the satchel to the concierge and got on the elevator. About that time my lunch-break was up, so I went back to the office and scribbled a few notes.

About three o'clock my phone rang and Lev Nadel started the questioning. "What color was the chair you were sitting on?" I answered, "Green." I thought, "This isn't so tough." But Lev was just warming up. "Did the man who gave the satchel to the concierge wear a belt? Did he have a limp? Was the clasp on the satchel gold or silver? Were the glasses on the man who went out in the street the kind that change colors with the light or not? What floor did the man who got on the elevator go to?" By the time Lev was finished with the grilling I knew I had a way to go before I mastered this part of commando training.

The next morning before work Lev called again with some kind words. "You did well, Sam. You scored better than most recruits the first time out. You're being trained in scanning. You may think it unimportant now but you'll realize later how wrong you are. To scan means to use your eyes like a radar sweep. You sweep the environment at frequent intervals and never let your whole concentration fix on any one thing for any length of time. I'm talking seconds only."

Lev knew about my next afternoon off and told me to take a bus to Ashdod and check out everything and at the same time lose two tails that would be shadowing me. "I want you to practice using any available reflecting surface—mirrors, store windows, car doors, whatever will give you an image of the tails. And when you get back I want five license plate numbers." That afternoon I gaped at car bumpers and led the two volunteer tails on a merry chase through the city. Ducking in the front door of a yard-goods store and then out a back window was my way of saying goodbye to the tails.

The next few weeks set up a pattern of mornings and afternoons on the MFO job with lunch-break games styled by Lev and weekends at the training camp. One afternoon I was set to go to Haifa to check on a shipment of MFO goods from the States. Lev called about the time I was ready to leave, with an assignment for me. He wanted me to go to the west window of Room 834 in the Hilton from 3:00 to 3:15 and diagram the traffic pattern in a six-square block area. And memorize *ten* license-plate numbers. These things had to be done in my head and not on paper. All the time I was listening to Lev I kept wondering when he'd quit upping the ante and what any of this shit had to do with stopping terrorists. But I wasn't allowed to question any of his "requests." Doing that was a sure way to be cut from the program. So I did my duty and tracked the cars and bicycles and motorcycles until the flow was pretty well memorized.

The next night in Tel Aviv my regular contact with Lev on the street cleared up the Haifa traffic-pattern assignment. "I want you to put together a simulated attack by a nine-man squad on Room 834 at the Hilton. The attack has got to be completed in a quarter of an hour in the afternoon. Use the back stairs and the six-block area you studied as your escape route."

The next weekend, back at the training site, there were more one-on-one and team maneuvers. In late March I got a week off from work and spent the whole time at the farm. The highlight of the training for me was the day we were taught the rudiments of hand-to-hand combat. Years earlier I had received some training in the martial arts. When I was a kid my dad rented space in one of his buildings to a karate school, so I got some free instruction. Over the years I thought there might come a point when I'd be glad for the karate. Say in a street fight or a bar brawl. But in Israel the hand-to-hand exercises were intended to be used, and the notion of applying my skill in combat made my adrenalin flow. That day in Israel I would never have guessed that almost three years later I'd be using the lesson of the day against the Sandinistas in a Nicaraguan free-fire zone. I just wanted to show the Israeli instructor what the brash karate kid from the States could do. And as it turned out, I was his first volunteer.

I thought he'd be impressed with my talent. Very funny. His opening move exploded before I realized I was supposed to be ready. It sent me flying to a one-point landing right on my nose. I bloodied up about half of the Israeli countryside while the instructor just planted his foot on my back and told the class, "This schmuck should have been alert at all times."

One day just after lunch one of the instructors used a little psychology to start the afternoon session. We were sitting in a group under a shady tree finishing our food when the teacher walked over and, calm as a kumquat, took a grenade out of his pouch. Then he pulled the pin and tossed it on the ground where we were sitting. Everybody dove in opposite directions for cover, but he just stood under the tree and yelled, "Now that I've got your attention let's get to work." Naturally the grenade was a dud, but the afternoon lesson about surprise sunk in deeper than we expected.

For the first month the training at the center covered the most important work of the unit, such as scouting and gathering intelligence and patrolling and tracking. The ex-officers taught about knives and bayonets. How to use demolitions and how to read maps and aerial photographs too. They spent a lot of time psyching out the typical PLO terrorist and studying his ways. Arnold Koenigsburg was the best on that subject. He was a walking dictionary of terrorist tricks, and he taught us how a terrorist fighting in the city would save his ammunition. For instance, "If he isn't sure there are any potential casualties inside a building or a room he'll throw a grenade through a window or door without pulling the pin and then yell 'grenade' as loud as he can. Anybody inside comes running out. Then he greets them with a burst from his AK–47. Or if nobody comes out, he goes in to retrieve his unused grenade."

A training day at the center usually began with physical exercise at six in the morning. Then breakfast from seven to seven-thirty. Two forty-five-minute classroom talks on military theory and tactics. An obstacle-course run just before lunch. After lunch an hour of weapons training usually began the afternoon classes. Each volunteer got to choose his favorite weapon to work with. Then came an hour of hand-to-hand combat exercises and some demolition work and grenade games. But the class that was always worth waiting for came just before dinner. It dealt with the latest intelligence information about PLO strength and a talk-through of an actual mission behind enemy lines in Lebanon planned for the next night. Needless to say, becoming good enough to go along on one soon was my top priority.

After the commando training started it was tough to concentrate on the MFO work. That wouldn't do, though, because I had to hire and clear 362 Thai workers. They were supposed to be stationed in the Sinai by the time the Egyptians took control on April 24th. I had full say-so for getting the Thais put in vital support jobs. They were really needed because things were beginning to fall apart at the bases in the Sinai. A lot of the American civilian workers were quitting because the heavy workload and a few lousy leaders were getting them down. Naturally my combat training had to stay secret, because if the MFO found out it would be "Goodbye Sam." But most of my spare time went to thinking about the coming war with the PLO and planning my part in it.

In the middle of one week in early April I took time out from work to take a good friend up on an offer. Amir was the owner of a fleet of rental buses that ferried MFO personnel. He ran a business that gave tours of the Holy Land. We always talked about the Bible and especially Jesus. Amir called him "a good Jew." We rented up to thirty-five of his buses a day sometimes, so he said, "Sam, I'll give you a free tour of the Holy Land to show my thanks." Now we were tooling through that bleak countryside in his Mercedes— "on location," where all the great biblical stories happened. In fact I had to pinch myself to be sure it was all for real. I kept checking each sandy hill, half expecting to see Anne Baxter and Charlton Heston on the next one, delivering dialogue while Cecil B. rolled the cameras for *The Ten Commandments*. But of course this was much better, this was for real and it was awesome.

About three hours from Jerusalem Amir said, "This is the Valley of Armageddon." We got out of the car and Amir pointed to the sun-baked places where the real Biblical prophecy was supposed to be played out. Standing on the spot where the last great battles on earth were going to be fought really excited me. Amir started quoting: "The people of the North will be defeated by Israel and in a second war there will be so many deaths that blood will be running from twenty-seven miles one way to two hundred and fifty miles the other, and it will deepen to the height of a horse's bridle." He was getting so revved up himself telling the story of Jewish heroes that he ended by crushing me in a bear hug. Just at that moment an Israeli jet broke the sound barrier right above our heads. It was like the plane was putting the finishing touches on the story I just heard. Chills literally ran up and down my spine and I had to fight back some tears. Anybody who has stood where I stood for the first time knows the feeling.

The following Friday at the training center I got the word I would be part of a counter-terrorist mission into Lebanon the next week.

ALL MY life I had been chasing challenges and the Israeli counter-terrorist missions promised the biggest payoff of all. The week of waiting for the night of the mission was almost too much to bear. Focusing on my work was just about impossible. My boss thought his personnel director was losing it. My daydreams about firefights kept fogging up our talks. And I nearly got myself killed in Tel Aviv traffic running three red lights on one short jeep trip. But Friday and the time to head for the training center finally came. I could hardly control my nerves on the drive that seemed twice as long as usual. At the farmhouse Koenigsburg was already prepping the six other members of my team for the mission. He backed up and briefed me too as one of the other volunteers blackened my face and handed me the uniform of the day—black pants and black boat-neck sweater, along with brown Israeli hightop gym shoes. After David described our duties he issued us Uzis and automatics. We got grenades and three knives each. Commandos always needed knives at the ready, but concealed in different places so as to get at them lying or crouching.

You couldn't ask for a more hated enemy than the one my team was looking for on this mission. The principal aim was to take out members of the fanatic PLO unit called the "Djibril Division." The Djibril was the most hated and feared of all the PLO outfits in those days. For years before the Lebanese war broke out they had tried hundreds of times, with some success, to cross over from Lebanon into the Israeli town of Nahariyya just to kill everybody in sight. One time they invaded the house of a woman doctor in Nahariyya and killed her, along with her husband and two children. Another time they took over a whole apartment building and mas-

sacred all thirty of the tenants. They even tried to shell the mater-
nity ward at the Nahariyya Hospital. The Djibril were the kind of
murderers you could never change or bring to the peace table because they hated with such a white heat. They always seemed to
find the easiest, most vulnerable targets. But the Israeli teams had
their own intelligence network now, so the teams crossed the
Lebanese border to take out the terrorists before they could do
more of their dirty work. Sometimes they ran into PLO squads
going in the opposite direction, toward their assignments in Israel,
and they cut them off at the pass.

Our job was to jog just five klicks over the border to check on a
PLO squad our reports told us might be moving toward Nahariyya
to shoot up the streets. It was the same squad that had killed six
Israeli teenagers the week before. Another part of our mission was
to report on any armament we might see, so we'd know where the
enemy had moved from the night before. The moon made things
twenty-twenty clear. We needed that, because the ground was
rocky and hilly and a broken leg was easy to come by. My adrenalin was pumping so strong I felt like I could have made Syria in
record time on the palms of my hands. All the natural sights, like
rocks and trees, looked to have sharper edges that night, and the
insects sounded like the Mormon Tabernacle Choir. After crossing
the enemy's land-mined area with the aid of our mine-sweep detec-
tors, my nerves told me this had to be my line of work. But I tried
to center on the goal of the mission and let the feeling fill in the
gaps. The lives of my comrades were at stake—*not* just mine.

We were under strict orders not to bother any PLO units headed
deeper into Lebanon, but we were authorized to take out any terrorists running towards Israel. We had to be sure to finish anything we
started. If any of us got taken prisoner we'd probably buy a bad
press in some of the world's newspapers. And that would jeopar-
dize other such operations.

About halfway through our run, the team leader, a mechanic in
civilian life, signalled us to take cover, so we all hit the dirt and
crawled for the nearest rock. A group of about eight PLO were

moving from our left toward our right. They didn't see us, so it looked like an ambush was possible. But just as we were about to surprise them the column of terrorists made a hard left and disappeared deeper into their sanctuary. When they were long gone Itzhak, a one-time grease monkey, gave the signal to resume our run. When I stood up I felt an abrupt chill. My shirt was soaked with sweat even though the night was very cool. And my cami pants were soaked. My first brush with a near firefight showed me how right it was all those years, for me, to link combat with exhilaration. I felt more alive than ever before. The downer came when we didn't see any more terrorists the rest of the night. Back at the camp I enjoyed the review of the mission. It would be tough to get through the next week at work.

On Sunday morning, at the office, I remembered I had to hire and transport those 362 Thai workers as soon as possible. The April 24th deadline was bearing down on me. That was the day the Sinai would turn Egyptian, so the border would be closed. We needed laundry attendants and cooks, not to mention mechanics' helpers and drivers and groundskeepers and janitors for the Sinai. There wasn't a lot of time to hire and get clearances for each man. The clearances meant dealing with Thailand's Central Intelligence Division (CID) along with Israeli and Egyptian intelligence. Once the workers were cleared, an airplane had to be hired to get them to the Sinai on time because after the 24th all the checkpoints would be closed.

As soon as the order came from Washington during the first week in April, I started looking for a Thai employment agency to line up the workers. That part was easy. A lot of Thais were working in the Negev for the Israelis. The military had a feel for which employment agencies were the best, so based on the track records, I chose one and flew to Bangkok to meet two agents named Wassana Koochai and Sawang Malatip. Wassana was a tiny man in his mid-forties who was married to a Chinese woman, and they had four young kids. Sawang was in his late thirties and a bachelor. We started kidding Sawang right away about him being Bangkok's swingingest single. The three of us hit it off and after the first couple of days together we were well on our way to being close friends. Wassana and Sawang had gotten together in the early seventies to set up one of the most profitable employment agencies in the Far East. They really enjoyed the work, particularly the chance to meet people from all over the world. When they found out what the MFO needed, they introduced me to about ten would-be camp bosses. I chose two of them, but the clearances were up to Wassana and Sawang because they were used to dealing with Thai red tape and knew how to cut it.

The applications came flooding in because the Thais could make five times as much working overseas as they could at home. The contract with E-Systems called for free daily food and living quarters, with transportation and medical care and other fringes too, besides a good salary. The Thais could send ninety percent of their money to their families and keep the rest for pins. The long lines waiting for interviews told us there were twenty times more applicants than jobs. I felt very sad walking along the lines introducing myself. The men wanted the jobs so much they bowed to me from the shoulders with their heads down and their fingers to their mouths like beggars. I wished we could meet in a more equal way, because knowing each one of them as a friend would be a gift. They all seemed to be so proud, even though they were hard up. Over the next couple of months I would be able to get close to some of them.

One night, while we were doing the hiring in Bangkok, my two new friends, Wassana and Sawang, took me out for a night on the town. They picked me up at my hotel and drove me first to dinner at a restaurant that should have been next to a fire station. The local food was so hot you needed two or three pumpers to put out the blaze in your belly. But the really spicy time came later. After dinner we pulled into a courtyard in front of a new-looking building in downtown Bangkok. The only identification on it was a small neon "coffee house" sign. Sawang said, "Now we show you how Thai have good time." When I walked into the lobby I got the surprise of my life. The room was humongous. It was divided for a hundred feet by a glass partition twenty feet high and on the far side was a ten-tiered platform with a bright red carpet. All around the room three hundred gorgeous women and girls stood dressed in silk Thai get-ups or western dresses, and all of them had big numbers pasted on them.

Bangkok had a big name as a flesh market, but I wasn't ready for anything like this. The whorehouses in the States were pretty sleazy operations on back streets, or they were masked as health clubs or massage parlors. This coffee house looked more like the Bangkok branch of Bloomingdale's, except that every department featured women's underwear. It had been years since I had availed myself of store-bought love in the States. My Dad had warned us when we were in our teens never to bed a woman we weren't ready to marry unless it was one who made her living loving, because that kind of woman wasn't looking for respect. I stopped making the rounds of the houses in my hometown after a few visits, though. I couldn't help asking the girls all kinds of questions about where they were from and how they got started and why they kept at it till eventually they got ticked and told me to shut up.

Anyway Wassana and Sawang introduced me to the head pimp, called "The King," and when he saw he had an American customer he said, "I have just itchy bon tok son girl for you. You like this one. She good one. She only start today. She still virgin. And smart too." I wanted to tell the little Thai I was in the Far East in the fifties and just might be his old man. But he pointed out the object of his sales job across the room and she did look like the best catch. The pimp called over the P.A. system, "Number fifty-six, please," and the woman answered to the number. Without much fanfare she was introduced as Sawee and we went upstairs.

The pimp turned out to be right on at least two out of three counts, because Sawee was bright and gorgeous. We had a terrific talk about everything from world events to Thai cooking. Not to mention the back rub and massage. We found out right away how much we really liked each other, and the next day we did more of the same. Three days later we had our first real date. That was the day she surprised me with her résumé.

"I Thai CID. you know this, yes."

"You're kidding. You mean I was set up?"

"Yes. King is agent too. I pay to service Americans. You want know this."

"Thanks for telling me. But why did you tip your hand?"

"I like you lot."

I couldn't care less if Sawee was head of the CID, since I didn't have any juicy secrets anyway. Between the Israeli commando school and Sawee, life was beginning to feel like an Ian Fleming novel and I confess I loved every page of it. Especially with my own beautiful spy for a friend. All that was missing was Ms. Moneypenny and a couple of ugly villains to complete the cast. Sawee turned out to be a real find, though, and not just a fantasy sidekick. She would help me a year later with some false passports and black-market arms.

By now time was getting short to arrange all the details for my 362 Sinai-bound Thais. The plan called for renting a jumbo jet from Holland Air Leasing, which was the cousin company to Dutch KLM Airlines. That cost the UN $278,000. Two pilots had to fly me from Amsterdam to Bangkok to pick up the Thais and bring them all back in the plane to Ben Gurion. But that was when a problem surfaced. KLM flew cargo for most of the Arab states that were boycotting Israel. The Dutch pilots wouldn't land in Tel Aviv or even cross into Israeli air space. So after we left Bangkok we had to fly to Athens and get hold of an Israeli travel agent. For an extra $48,000 two El Al 707s flew to Athens to pick us up and take us to Tel Aviv. The logistics just about wore me out, but the Thais made it across the border into the Sinai with one day to spare before the deadline.

While all this finagling over the Thais was going on, I was still spending my Friday nights, plus Saturday afternoons and nights, training and going out on counter-terrorist missions. We went across the Lebanese border three more times. The fourth time occurred on a Friday night after working later than usual in Tiberius on my Thai problem. It was so late in fact that I was afraid there wouldn't be time to make it to the training center. When I punched out there were only three hours to get myself and my gear to Nahariyya, and to make things more complicated, the curfew was in effect. Outside my hotel there was no traffic going north. I was in my civvies, carrying a suspicious-looking ditty bag full of night gear, and trying to spot a car heading in the right direction. The curfew meant anybody on the streets after dark whose looks or actions caused doubts would be shot and, if he lived, questioned. This wasn't just Israeli skittishness. Terrorist bombings were common.

The action at the training center was about to happen without me, so I had to think fast. The motor pool where all the UN vehicles were parked was next to my hotel. As a teenager I had made a career out of sneaking into neighbors' unlocked cars and coasting down their driveways backward into the street. Now came the chance to use that talent gained long ago. But my prey this time wasn't a suburban station wagon. Any vehicle flying a UN flag could go anywhere, so I practiced my commando shtick and slipped into the motor pool without being seen. Inside, I jumped behind the wheel of a likely looking jeep and started it. Lucky for me the guard at the gate saluted when I tooled past him.

I drove straight for the training center, and made it just in time to dress up like a GI Joshua and join the night patrol looking for some Djibril who had murdered a group of senior citizens on a bus near Nahariyya the week before. About eleven-thirty our unit jogged five klicks into Lebanon and stopped behind some big rocks while Itzhak checked the map for our bearings. We were all wheezing from the run. In about three minutes Itzhak had us pinpointed and ready to take off again when all of a sudden we heard what sounded like a delayed echo of our wheezing from a minute before. The others realized before me that it was Djibril wheezing coming from behind a rock not more than thirty yards away. One of their squads was resting there in the middle of a run, probably into

Israel. We listened to their wheezing for a few minutes more that seemed like an eternity. We knew they'd probably run right past us, so Itzhak signalled the order to unholster our sidearms. My gun hand was shaking, but I managed to pull out my .45. Within seconds the rested terrorists broke from behind their rock, on the run. When they reached our rock the firing started and seven terrorists went straight to Allah. Three others took off so fast they were probably in Beirut by midnight. When it was over I couldn't tell whether my fire made any contact with terrorist flesh or not. I was going to have to control my nerves if my squad was ever going to get any good out of me.

All the next week at work was spent rerunning those first combat sensations. Except for my lack of cool it was no disappointment. I'd never forget the sound of those terrorists wheezing—the fear and exhilaration. The only other thing I could compare them to was my first bear hunt twenty-five years earlier in Michigan. At one point in that hunt I was working part of a fourteen-square-mile swamp alone, and my jitters peaked when the dogs started barking closer and closer to me. They had to be chasing a bear my way. I wasn't in the best shape to meet him, because the night before the hunters had drunk straight shots of Jack Daniels into the wee hours while we tried to outdo each other with wild bear-hunting stories. The stories were still in my mind the next morning as my own bear bore down on me and the Jack Daniels worked its way down from my brain to my bowels. I didn't want to be caught with my pants down by a pissed-off bear. To add to my misery a freezing rain began to pelt down. But what brought my bowels to the brink was the sound of heavy wheezing from an oncoming bear chased by a couple of dogs in hot pursuit.

I had to pull down my pants and relieve myself, so there I was hanging on to a tree limb with one hand and gripping my rifle with the other one. While I was squatting that asthmatic bear got closer and closer, till all of a sudden he broke through the brush right in front of me and literally scared me shitless. I let go of the branch and tried to get off a late shot at the bear's fast-retreating behind, but I slipped and sat in my own "Jack" shit and that was the first time I ever wished I'd fallen between two stools. By the time my pants got pulled back up Yogi was long gone, but he left me with the memory of that wheezing ever after. On that mission in Lebanon, the wheezing PLO patrol gave me an even stronger rush, because this was for a real cause. Up in Michigan the bears never formed into killer divisions bent on terror.

Working was harder than ever back in Tel Aviv the Sunday after my first combat experience. Resigning was a possibility, but the peace between Israel and Egypt was still worth contributing to. Besides, my dad had taught me never to leave a job undone. There were new headaches, though, like the strike that was ready to break out because about fifty MFO hands were bitching about their working conditions. There was a big turnover rate and you couldn't really blame the men for thinking about a walkout. The management was pretty shaky and the workplace wasn't very pretty, surrounded as it was by wire and cyclone fences. Things were especially bad for the Thais. In the beginning they were housed in dingy garages. The E–Systems management finally answered my pleas and got them some trailers, which cost E–Systems about a million bucks. But the men still couldn't leave the base. Eighty percent of the time there wasn't enough water to shower or do personal laundry, since the PLO, disguised as Bedouins, kept blowing up the water lines.

Living in the Sinai was always a war against the sand too, because it kept us feeling grimy and it wrecked our equipment. Sinai sand was superfine; like graphite, but a lot dirtier. Even though all our offices were inside rooms with no windows, still our people were kept hopping, cleaning the typewriters and copiers once a day. Besides the annoyance of having to do their jobs in a huge sandbox, the men didn't have any place to get together. Not even so much as an open spit of ground between trailers. But there was a kind of courtyard-like area close by that had promise. It could be made into a patio where the workers would be able to socialize. After a few "midnight requisitions" of crushed stone and slabs, plus a case-of-beer bribe for a British truck driver, we had the makings of a patio that would be the showplace of the Sinai.

Too bad the big E–Systems boss from the States arrived on the scene just after Thais had finished the patio. He was pissed off because so much time and so many materials had been "wasted."

"What the hell is this cement parking lot for?"

"It's a patio for the men, sir."

"What do you mean a 'patio?' Who do you think you are? We're not paying you to waste our money on 'patios.' "

"Well, it will be good for morale, sir."

"Screw morale, Hall. You're on notice. One more deal like this and you're out on your ass."

I felt like shoving one of my taped spoon-grenades where his sun didn't shine. I didn't tell the men about it, though. They were sure to quit if they knew the visiting honcho was threatening to cut off Hall's balls for trying to make their working conditions better.

The night the boss left for the States a group of Thais and Aussies invited me over to our new patio for a drink. After a hard day at the office and about ten beers I was feeling less pain than the mayor of Luckenbach. The talk turned to the Israeli forces and their commando skills. That's when my bragging started.

"I'd make a pretty good commando myself. Those Israelis wouldn't have anything on me."

"Can you prove that, mate? It's easy to say, don't you know?"

"You good, Mr. Sam. You show. They know."

Resisting that kind of fun was always tough.

"I tell you what," I said. "I'll get past the guards at the gate with this beer can and park it on top of pumper number three. Then I'll get back in without the guards seeing me. You clowns can check the beer can tomorrow when you inspect the pumper."

"You're on, mate."

My mission would take me over the part of the desert used by the Bedouin wanderers. They were mostly peace-loving souls, but their bands were occasionally infiltrated by the PLO, not to mention drug dealers. A camel is great camouflage. When you saw a group camped you couldn't be certain they weren't really a bunch of terrorists. If they were they would just as soon cut your throat as eat their dates. The fake Bedouins had blown up water mains and some of the MFO's houses in the Sinai and they had tried to destroy the airstrips a couple of times. Our units were stationed to protect water pipes during the day that the terrorists blew up at night. The next morning there would be a little lake with a sandy shoreline. Before the Sinai turnover the terrorists came through fences at night to put egg-shaped mines with fins on the airstrip. They could be set off by the wheels of our planes if we didn't watch out. Our security forces had to put sandbags around them and dynamite them. *If* they were lucky enough to find them.

Anyway, while my disbelieving buddies razzed me on I got started on Operation Beer Can by crawling under the wire past our guards. Which was easy enough, since the two Colombians on duty were checking the desert for arrivals not departures. Once past the gate I hung to the left and crawled a couple of hundred yards out of the guards' line of sight. Then I got up and set sail for the pumping station. The night was cloudy, but in the desert there wasn't any need to worry about running into rocks as you might on moonless nights in Lebanon. So I was tooling nicely along in overdrive when I nearly fell over a damn camel. He was either sleeping with one of his buddies or humping his wife, but he got up and brayed at me with murder on his mind. My near somersault must have looked like part of an Olga Korbut floor exercise, but I kept on running to put the aluminum evidence of my visit at the agreed upon spot—which I did ten minutes later. On the return trip a Bedouin fire told me to veer right and avoid the Sinai social scene. By the time I got back to the base the sun was up. I didn't want to crawl under the wire and risk a round in the rump, so the best thing to do was walk up to the fence and tell the guards, "I was drunk last night. I must have wandered outside to pass out." They bought the story and I walked back to greet my patio comrades. They weren't really impressed until the water-pumping station inspection crew came back later in the day with my beer can in tow.

Forays like the beer can caper kept me sane during the wait for the commando weekends, especially since the MFO work setup was getting more and more annoying. There were always petty problems connected with the job. Even the Israelis caused a few, such as the time during Passover when they refused to let anybody eat any of the eggs that were delivered because they were stamped with ink that wasn't kosher. Since not a soul Jewish or otherwise could crack any eggs during the holy season, fifteen thousand a day ripened in the Sinai sun. When the Egyptians took over, the problems just changed nationalities.

One Egyptian problem was a major named Farouki. We didn't particularly take to each other when we met but I decided to work with him if it could be done. He was one of the head men in the Sinai and we needed his customs stamp to approve the men that were hired. Since I had something to say about transportation I figured maybe the major could be handled. His daily rounds took him from his home near the north base at Eitam to the south base at Sharm el Sheikh. In our business dealings he tried bullying me and at one point he demanded the men's passports. I could just imagine asking, say, a U.S. citizen thousands of miles away from home to give up his passport to a complete stranger, especially for a full week. Besides, to be frank, the Americans with the MFO were often ready to quit, so they needed their passports with them at all times. The major just wanted to do his work at home that week in El Arish.

"I must have those passports, Mr. Hall. Please get them to me before I leave today."

"Listen, major, I'm in charge of these men and you're not getting their passports for a week or even a day."

"We'll see about that, Mr. Hall. Your superior may tell you something quite different."

"I don't give a jackal's ass if you go see Ronald Reagan. Every dick that's my responsibility is going to keep his passport."

For a couple of days we fought to a standstill. But the trump card was up my sleeve, because the wheels and the wings that

Major Farouki needed to get home to El Arish by five o'clock quitting time needed my approval. My strategy to win him over was to begin my work day earlier so he could finish earlier too. Then I plied him with transportation. The only way from the north base to the south base and back was a bumpy ten-hour jeep ride that was guaranteed to give you hemorrhoids on hemorrhoids. Or you could ride an Aussie C–140 airplane in comfort. After a few days testing the difference between the two kinds of travel, the major saw that we, indeed, needed each other. "I think we two can become friends," said he, and pretty soon we were on a first-name basis.

One afternoon Major Farouki was flying with me over the Mediterranean to the south base when we spotted the skindiving paradise called the Red Devil. The month before, I made a couple of trips there to enjoy diving that was the best in the world. The water was clear deeper than anywhere else, and you could spot the evil eye of a baracuda fifty to sixty feet away instead of the normal twenty-five-foot range. Major Farouki was surprised by my skindiving, which gave us a shared sport. He started describing other parts of the Med that were choice spots to enjoy the diving. By the time we got back to work we were talking about our families. When we parted company for the last time we shook hands and then in the old European way hugged each other. The two of us had wasted our early days together being pissed off. The chance to make a friend like Major Farouki was what made life a kick, and I was especially happy to get to know an Egyptian well, since my weekends were spent fighting terrorists who could warp my view of all Arabs. In fact most of the Arabs I dealt with on a day-to-day basis were quite likeable. And I really respected Anwar Sadat for being willing to work with the Israelis to bring peace in the Middle East. What a gift to the world that peace would be.

In late April a new disaster hit that would lead me to quit my job. There was a rumor flying that the Egyptians would welch on their promise to hire my Thai workers for a full year because they wanted their own people to have the jobs the Thais were contracted to do. Getting the Thais to the Sinai before the deadline was such a bitch the rumors had to be bunk. Besides, Wassana and Sawang were my good friends by now. The whole group they helped me find through their employment agency had to be protected. If the Egyptians got rid of them it would be curtains for the Thais because most of their farms were sublet back home. They'd have to go back to Thailand with no way to support themselves. About their only helper in the Sinai was Sam Hall. I was ready to go to court for them if the rumor was true and if something couldn't be worked out. But Wassana and Sawang back in Bangkok were a worry too because employment agents there were killed for less than setting up a broken contract.

For three or four days I read all the telex messages coming into the Ramada in Tel Aviv to check out the rumor about the Thais. When I learned for sure they would be fired on June 25th I met with the Thai camp bosses and called Wassana and Sawang with the news. There was a seven-hour difference in time between Israel and Thailand, so it was about ten at night in Israel and three in the afternoon in Bangkok when I finally got through to the two agents. After twenty minutes on the phone Wassana said, "We stay, we die. Revenge. No give mail two three day. Wassana Sawang go country hide." They had a money-making business that had just cleared $98,000 on the MFO contract, but at this point their lives were worthless and there wasn't anything to be done about it. The more I thought about the Egyptian welchers, the more my blood boiled.

It would be up to me to help my workers cope because I had a better relationship with the Thais than anybody else in the MFO. When they came to the Sinai I'd tried to make sure they were treated well, even though it was a losing battle. They only got to live in my trailers for about two weeks before the news broke that they would have to go back to Thailand. Sanitary conditions weren't the best either, and every night they had to battle to do their laundry in what water they could get from one of the fire hydrants. Before they moved to the trailers there weren't any fans to cool off the galvanized garages on those 120-degree days. I bought them some fans and twice I gave them a hundred dollars to throw a party for themselves and got repaid a thousand times with smiles and invites to join them.

The worst problem was they weren't understood or liked by some of the American workers. One day a foreman named Kevin, who was in charge of the only bar on the base, pulled a really cruel stunt. Like some of the other Americans he was pissed off by the fact that most of the Thais didn't speak much English, so his bright idea was to crack them on the head when he couldn't understand them. Touching a Thai's head was a definite no-no because they thought it caused some of their soul to disappear. The evening of the head-hitting incident the workers told me their gripes while we all squatted like they did out of custom. My gimpy recontructed leg gave me a fit, but my pain was only physical. Kevin's smart-assed stunt had crushed the Thais and they expressed it by writing with their fingers in the sand over and over his English words, "God-damn" and "Fuck" and "Slant Eyes." The next morning I chewed his ass to shreds and sent him shuffling off to see the base manager, who took a dim view of race-baiting.

Once I was sure the Thais would be forced out I wrote and asked for an extension at least until August 31st. I reminded the powers-that-were that they had to give thirty-days notice or pay extra. I told the Thais to threaten a lawsuit against the MFO and the United States too, and thanks to the pressure they got two months more salary for a total of four months' pay out of the contracted twelve, plus one-third of the bonus they were supposed to get when they completed their work. The base manager collected a little money from the other workers to give to the Thais before they left for home. It was beginning to look easier to deal with terrorists than political hacks. I remembered why my term in the state legislature back in Ohio was such a crock. That job had given me my first inside look at the ways the special interests of the big guy were protected while the little guy suffered with little or no chance.

Since the Thais would be lost, I went back to Tel Aviv in disgust and typed my resignation. My peacekeeping job was unravelling anyway, and there wasn't much to gain staying with the MFO. Besides, my commando team could use me full time. I went right to the north base to turn in my resignation, and when that was done went back to the Sinai and packed my bags. As the bus taking me to Tel Aviv was boarding, all of a sudden the area was filled with Thai workers taking pictures and shaking my hand. Their camp boss handed me a letter they all had signed, and when the bus pulled out and the waving hands disappeared I read the letter and damn near cried about leaving the Thais. But they had their lives to lead too.

Back in Tel Aviv I made arrangements to join the anti-Djibril squad full time. The next week at the training site we saw enough action to remind me I was alive again after all the political pussy-footing trying to help the Thais. At the end of the week our squad was sent to a different part of Israel to take out some terrorists and their vehicles that were turning up in big numbers across the Lebanese border. The war was just a couple of weeks away by this time and we were headed for the 144-square-mile area called Fatahland that was occupied by Al Fatah—the terrorist group that had killed 7500 to 8000 people in northern Israel between 1965 and 1982. We knew there were about 1500 Karame Brigade killers moving into the vicinity of Haskaya a few klicks from Metulla in Israel. When we got to Metulla we got a briefing from the leader of the squad stationed near there, then moved out fifteen klicks deep behind enemy lines, checking the whereabouts of moving artillery and looking for vehicles bunched together so we could do damage dropping taped grenades into gas tanks.

After half an hour's search we found a terrorist outpost, but there was only one truck there and no one guarding it. We passed it up and looked for bigger game. Another klick-and-a-half of searching brought us some Arab singing up ahead. At the top of a rise we trained our night glasses in the direction of the music and the dim lights of a tiny village. This time there were four or five vehicles and a couple of small buildings with two sentries on guard with AK–47s. There was only one road into town and one road out. The sentries and the vehicles made my pulse race, but we didn't have time to exploit the moment because we had to concentrate on a quick plan to take the trucks out and then get out of the area.

When one of the sentries went inside a building, that reduced our problem about fifty percent. But we still needed to take out his partner. We all volunteered for the job, but our "number one" knew I was itching for more action so he chose me, with an Israeli named Jacob for my backup. We waited, crouching on top of the rise for five minutes that seemed like fifty. When the time was right we both ran up behind the sentry without making a sound. He was singing along with the small radio he carried. When we got to him he was standing still instead of walking like he was supposed to, so I grabbed him from behind by the throat and hit him hard in the back of the neck with the heavy handle of my knife.

I was almost sick when his neck cracked. Even with the action of the last few months this was the first real moment of truth for me and it affected me in my gut. But there was no time to throw up or even think about what just happened since we didn't know for sure if the sentry was dead. Jacob helped me drag him forty or fifty yards over a knoll to a tree. He wasn't a big man, but he was dead weight and the two of us were worried about the noise. We had a little trouble dragging him away without tipping off the other terrorists. But our adrenaline was pumping hard, so we didn't mind the effort. When we got to the other side of the knoll Jacob started unrolling the duck-tape that was wound around my waist and said, "We'll tape his arms and feet to this tree." Then he slammed the terrorist's head against the tree to make sure he didn't wake up. After the neck blow it was doubtful he would, but if he did he might scream and rouse his partners. As soon as we were certain our job was done, we signaled the squad to go to work on the trucks. Within ten minutes we had a tiger in each tank, then started for home and ran the fifteen klicks with just three short breaks.

Back at the training center I had a chance to think about the night's work. Doing everything as I was supposed to during the attack made me proud. For example, watching the sentry's hands when my arm was around his neck to make sure he couldn't surprise me in some way or get off a few rounds to wake the other terrorists asleep in the buildings. Hemingway was right when he said a soldier's best feeling is getting his job right. The only thing that would have made it better would have been staying to see the trucks explode one by one. The one problem I had was making peace with myself, because the sentry was probably dead. If he was, I had killed for the first time in my life. My mind kept replaying the scene over and over again in Cinemascope and technicolor, and the sentry's neck bones cracked another forty or fifty times in Dolby stereo before the sensation began to fade.

When I had time to think without the breaking bone sounds I felt grief for the sentry and wondered how much his mother and father and wife and children would suffer and how the news he was dead would reach them and if they could carry on. Those thoughts tortured me for weeks, but at the same time what helped me was Itzhak's description of the terrorist attack on Metulla the week before our mission, when twenty innocent townspeople were shot and left for dead on the main street. I still wondered whether my sentry and I would have liked each other if our fates had brought us together in a different way. Which wasn't too likely, because most terrorists were fanatics whose hate wasn't reasoned and you couldn't talk with them or change their minds with all the good intentions in the world. It was better to break their necks before they broke a few million guiltless ones on the way to making a new world where your own mother and father and wife and children were at risk.

Still, how did my new line of work square with my born-again Christian religion of love? Who could know what God thought of the killing that was so common down here on earth? What did He make of songs like "The Battle Hymn of the Republic" or "Praise the Lord and Pass the Ammunition?" I knew that the Old Testament God, the God of Moses, could be vindictive. But then Jesus came along, turning his other cheek. Maybe it didn't matter that nobody could figure it out, certainly not Sam Hall. The people who would rather make love than war made a lot of sense, but if somebody didn't wage war against the terrorists there wouldn't be any lovers left, at least not in the Middle East. And I sure wasn't going to quit this work, not when I was finally on the edge of achieving what I'd been reaching for all my life.

Just after the mission in Fatahland some bad news put an end to such action for me. All outsiders were told to leave Israel by June 2nd, since war in Lebanon was right around the corner. America especially didn't want its citizens involved. That made me bitter. Now that war was about to be *officially* declared, nobody wanted me in it. I tried everything I could, but Major Weprin's words had to be accepted. "I'm sorry, Sam. I've looked into every possibility. There isn't any way for you to stay in the country and fight for us." Not, that is, without officially joining the Israeli Defense Forces and risking loss of citizenship.

Going home by way of the Greek Islands and France might be better than a nonstop flight to New York. A short vacation would clear my mind before I spent some time with my kids. On June 2nd I got a flight to Athens and the next day took the island cruise. When I got back to Athens the Lebanon war had already exploded. On June 4th five hundred mortar rounds hit Israeli positions in the Golan Heights, and on the sixth the Israelis began the offensive that would push the PLO back to Beirut in three weeks. In Paris my mind was still on war. After a night there I went out to Normandy Beach where the great battle took place almost exactly thirty-eight years to the day before my visit. I stood on the beach and tried to imagine the fighting, my mind filled with images of World War II documentary film footage I'd seen as a kid. The soldiers landing and the bullets hitting the surf and the sand. Would there be a decisive battle to end World War III—the war against terrorism? It wasn't too likely and it sure wouldn't have the look of Normandy, with waves of rifle-toting GIs storming fixed positions.

This World War III would probably end, if it ended at all, on some airport tarmac or restaurant roof or hotel lobby somewhere. Most people were already worried about the nuclear holocaust, but that would be World War IV; and if we lost number III to the terrorists, well, it wouldn't matter so much if the world blew up anyway...

When I got back to Paris, I was missing my kids so much I flew straight back to the States for the first time in six months.

David and Samantha and Kelly all seemed so changed. We spent the next few weeks getting reacquainted while I was calling Tel Aviv once a day trying to get the clearance to go back. But how to explain another sudden departure to the kids and my ex-wife?

Finally in August, after more fibs to my family, I was cleared to go back to Israel. By this time the PLO had been pushed back to Beirut. Major Weprin was headed by convoy for Beirut when I caught up with him and he offered to take me along.

During three days in Lebanon we got a look at the setup for the American mercenaries. Most of them were serving under General Saad Hadaad. They were out-of-work Vietnam vets looking for action and the 125-pounds-per-week pay. But their money had to rent their own living quarters, plus buy food and equipment. They were a sad lot because the only action was guard duty on the roads leading in and out of Beirut. One boy wanted to go home, but couldn't because he didn't have enough money. I told him to go to the American Embassy in Tel Aviv and ask for a friend of mine who would pay for his return as long as he was willing to use his passport to secure the loan.

One of Major Hadaad's aides offered me 200 pounds a week, paid by Israel, to stay and work as a merc for him. He said, "Major Weprin tells me you did good work at Nahariyya." Fighting for pay still didn't interest me, and there wasn't much to do anyway. Outside of a few small incidents, the war was halted and the multi-national peacekeeping forces, including the ill-fated American marines, were already arriving. My future was in fighting terrorists. Just where wasn't clear yet, since the Djibril was on the run.

But there was another kind of mission I'd thought about for years that could actually be put into action now. It would take more training, but paying somebody for that was always a possibility. I decided to find out what could be done the next week. Then I would see about the chances of rescuing American POWs and MIAs in Cambodia.

M Y FATHER was sitting with me in his living room the night in 1972 when Nixon announced he was bringing our troops back home from Vietnam. Together, my father and I had followed the "progress" of the fighting, feeling an anger that kept growing and a sadness that got deeper over the years. Our leaders, it seemed, didn't seem to want to win that war. Still, we sent our men and boys and, yes, even women over to be killed and maimed and mentally broken. That's why my dad's first remarks when the President told the country that our forces were leaving Nam hit me so hard. "Sam," he said, "I wish it was over, but it isn't. Not till all the POWs and MIAs are home or at least accounted for." A little later he was dead, so he didn't see his Vietnam wish come true. Maybe none of us will live to see that wish come true, but the next time Dad and I meet I'll at least be able to look him in the eye and tell him I gave it a good shot.

The idea of a POW-MIA mission appealed to my head as much as to my heart. My new combat skills, plus my logistics work with the MFO, equipped me to carry out such an attempt. And I had reason to believe that I could get the reliable intelligence I'd need.

But a weekend soldier needed extra training to get ready for that kind of mission. My first move was to call an El Al Airlines security guard who was a friend of Sammy Villa's. He knew of places around the world where a mercenary or volunteer could get himself properly trained.

"I suggest a warfare school I know about in England, Sam. There are some real pros running it. But you'll need a letter or two from military brass with some connections."

"Sounds good to me. I think I can get a couple of letters."

After we hung up I called Major Weprin and asked him to recommend me to the school.

"That will be no problem, Sam. And I think Saad Hadaad will
write for you also."

"I didn't think of that. His word should cut some ice."

A couple of weeks later I got a yes and grabbed a flight for
London.

The English school lasted six days. It was a classified operation
taught by officers from special services and one-time intelligence
agents. Our number-one teacher was named Phillip. He had a British accent so he might have been with the SAS at one time, but
nobody wore insignia and we couldn't be sure. We all got plastic
cards and were told they listed the rules for the next six days and
nights. The cards read: "No cameras are authorized. There will be
no discussion of politics or personal questions of fellow students.
No souvenirs such as class notes or spent shell casings or defused
grenades are to be taken from the class or from the training site."
On the flip-side the card read: "For security reasons everything
here is on a 'need to know' basis."

Phillip turned out to be a forty-year-old more-or-less Roger
Moore type, though hardly as handsome. He had been in on the
planning of a commando rescue caper at an embassy in London
that had been taken over by Iranian terrorists in 1980. When he
talked about that mission his eyes lit up. I was just sorry there was
no way we could talk one to one and maybe get to be friends. But
the fifteen other men from different countries needed his time too.
They all seemed to be in their twenties and that suited me fine.
Someday every branch of the U.S. government that turned me
down because of my age in the past might get a surprise. With
sheepskins from this school and maybe a couple of other war col-
leges I could prove that a man in his mid-forties wasn't necessarily
ready for the boneyard.

My classmates' home countries weren't clear, so getting a fix on
why each student was there wasn't easy. I tried to fix their looks in
my mind because I was thinking about hiring eight men for my

POW-MIA mission. Who better could you want than gung-ho young fighters like these?

We worked mostly in groups of two and three, and the instructors were up-to-date about tactics and weapons. They taught every kind of trick; for example, how to tighten your body while you were being tied up so when you relaxed you had more room to maneuver, a la Houdini. We all got demolition training with a lot of different homemade explosives, such as the "Wild Turkey Bomb," which was mostly alcohol. It turned out you could kill somebody besides yourself with booze. And all you needed were a few recipes from the school of counter-terrorist cookery to pull off an explosion that could incinerate a building full of terrorists. You didn't need any help from Oppenheimer or Teller.

The grand finale of the six days was Phillip's replay of the rescue try at the embassy in London in 1980. With the students starring in the counter-terrorist roles, Phillip showed us how to rappel down the side of a building and then swing out on the rope to crash in through locked windows. Once we'd made it inside the building we had an inkling of what it must be like to carry out such a mission.

The last exam was a mini-mission alone at night. We had to run and walk thirty klicks from Point A to Point B in twelve hours or less. Along the route three different way stations were set up, and at each way station a plastic-covered clipboard was hung on a tree. Each volunteer was supposed to put his John Hancock on the clipboards as he passed them. We were sent off at ten-minute gaps. It wasn't until nine o'clock that I started out. All night there were noises in front of and behind me as I ran through the woods or rested on a log or rock. I didn't have any trouble, except for stepping on a slimy snake about midnight and brushing past an angry farmer just after sunup.

When we got back to the camp we were checked out and given the okay to leave. On the way out of the main hut I asked the Irishman in charge what the bill was for the training. He said everything was free. That didn't figure. Somebody must have been paying for me, but there was no telling who. Maybe whoever it was would spring for another semester. "Are there other places where I can get more training?" The Irishman said right away, "There's a school in Germany that could give you the kind of instruction you're looking for. Go back to the States and you'll get a call." My record must have been clean, because he seemed to know everything about every one of the sixteen students. He could help you or hurt you. If you got too nosy he'd clam up. He sure wouldn't refer you to other schools if he thought you might be a risk. I didn't know what the tie between the two schools was. And the Irishman didn't offer any clues.

By noon I was on my way home to see my kids. I worked at keeping in shape in Dayton while the wait for the call to go to Germany stretched over a month. I pulled on my combat boots and sweats every day and ran six miles in the hills around the city. The joggers in their warmups and Nikes probably thought some bumble-brained Gomer Pyle was out of step with the National Guard unit out of sight over the next rise. Some work every day at the nearby firing ranges kept my eye sharp too.

After two weeks I was restless, so a quick visit to Hilton Head sounded good. It was always one of my favorite R and R spots and now it could help get my mind off training for a while. Maybe some new people talking about their humdrum problems could freshen me up and help me sharpen the rescue-mission plan.

The first night I headed for my favorite lounge in the middle of town and spotted a couple of white dresses stuffed with sun-tanned blondes who looked to be local. When I introduced myself their drawls told me I was right. We danced for an hour and then grabbed a table with four chairs that had just emptied. We were in the middle of one of those laid-back South Carolina palavers about the heat wave when a fortyish tourist from Indiana joined us. He was interested in the smaller blonde named Laura, so I homed in on Jennifer while I kept one ear cocked to catch the Hoosier's line. I always tried to collect good lines. The Hoosier's was so white-label-black-lettering generic you could use it to turn off a smart woman on the singles scene from Seattle to Key West. Naturally he started asking Laura if she came here often and what her sign was. Since there weren't any right answers he didn't even listen for them. Instead he moved right to the third question which was what did she do. Laura told him she was a student. Naturally he wanted to know where. When she named a community college our hero praised higher education and asked what she was studying. That's when I almost choked on my drink, because Laura answered, "typing," and the Hoosier shot back, "Wow, heavy!" But the crazy thing was it must have worked. When Jennifer said goodnight at closing time, Laura and the Midwest Don Juan were headed for his car. That proved that no amount of corny dialogue could keep two people apart if the acid and alkali were mixing right. So maybe Doris and Indiana Jones would find some of the significant otherhood that was always just out of my reach.

When I got back home to Dayton I tried to pick the pins and needles out of my butt while I waited for the call from overseas. In a couple of weeks it finally came. The training camp in Germany lasted four days and five nights. Three of my classmates from the warfare school in England were students at this school too. None of us asked questions because we were all worried about the ban on loose lips and we kept pretty much to ourselves. There were twenty-six students and their IDs were as much a puzzle to me as mine was to them. All, though, were in great shape. The instructors were special forces commandos from different countries who went up against the very same terrorist outfits they talked about, including the Red Brigades and Black September and the IRA and the Baader-Meinhof gang. One instructor, who had to be an Israeli, was said to have been in on the Entebbe raid.

There were more classes on homemade bombs to get rid of a bridge or a building. One day some of us were standing around on a break before the start of a class in explosives. All of a sudden an instructor took a Zippo lighter out of his flak jacket and without so much as an "oh, by the way" tossed it into a pile of leaves. There was a loud explosion that scared the hell out of all of us. The instructor showed us how he did it with the unit from another Zippo plus a nail file and a little plastique. By the end of the day all the volunteers were able to pull off explosions from cigarette lighters. But I was the only one who blew up his bunk mate's laundry bag.

There were lessons about Claymore mines that I felt would help on the POW-MIA mission. A Claymore expert was a must for Cambodia. The scenario in my head called for an "escape and evasion" route ringed with the mines. But even if somebody expert volunteered for the party, I wanted to know everything about the Claymores myself as a backup.

The German school featured mortar lessons too. I remember thinking that a few of them might come in handy in Southeast Asia. We got to where we could break down and put back the fourteen pieces of the 60 mm. mortar trigger housing in less than two minutes. In a couple of days we knew all about NTH/Naphtha explosive and peroxicle bombs and potassium/sulphur bombs and soap-dish charges and cigaretter-lighter grenades. A smart counter-terrorist could make acid from aspirin and blasts from sawdust. He knew what to look for in letter bombs, although we were told they hardly ever worked. We got pretty good with C–4 plastique, even to the point where we could tear off a piece and fire it up to boil coffee.

Now if anybody asked, we could tell them how to switch detonating fuses between three kinds of hand grenades, including American and French and the Russian F–1. There was more training in hand-to-hand combat too. We focused on alertness and vulnerable points and falls and takedowns. We learned how to take a weapon from an enemy and how to attack with knives and pistols. The instructors were trained to kill with rifles and scopes and spent a lot of time showing us greenhorns how to shoot at long distances. We all qualified with a 26X scope at one thousand yards.

The big deal at the German school was military psychology. A lot of sessions were spent on ways to make a captured terrorist talk. Dishing out pain wasn't the best way, we were told. Your subject might just pass out while he was giving you the six o'clock news and then you'd have to wait for "details at eleven." That wouldn't do when time was short, as it almost always was when you were fighting terrorists. The shortest way to get what you wanted was to make your prisoner fear you. There were lots of ways to do that, such as pouring gasoline over him and then threatening to flick your Bic. Or if you had a group of prisoners, you could take them up in a helicopter about 600 feet off the ground and tie their hands and feet. Once you put them next to the door and slapped them, you screamed at them in their language, if you knew it. If their seats next to the helicopter door didn't make them talkative you'd keep shouting, "not good enough." Then if you threw one out the door in plain view of the rest you could point out that the unfortunate guy didn't have a parachute. That would get everybody's attention. It was a technique used in Nam as well, and frowned on by some. But we were talking about terrorists who majored in murdering the unarmed and innocent. I make no apologies for it in that context.

Another way to get information was to tie the hands and feet of three terrorists laid on their backs side-by-side. Three of you held the legs down and two forced the others to watch. Then you questioned the third while you sat on his chest. You asked for the facts you wanted. Politely. No answers? If the terrorist you'd selected had a strong rib cage you got up and kicked him. If that didn't work you put a pistol in his mouth and asked again. If no secrets were forthcoming you loosened his teeth with the pistol. If you still didn't get any answers you pulled the trigger. Even hardened, fanatical terrorists tended to become talkative under such circumstances.

Such interrogation methods were the only kind terrorists understood. And we had to learn how to hold up under the same abuse, and worse. We got one of the hardest lessons in mental toughness the last day. We were each put into a fifty-five-gallon drum for three hours in near total darkness. There was a lid on the drum and holes in the bottom. The drum was cocked at an angle so the person in it had his head below his feet. The instructors then spent three hours pounding on the drum and dripping water on us and screaming insults while we suffered inside. When my time came to get in the drum I told myself I could take that kind of torture, but those were probably my worst three hours ever. We weren't supposed to tell our names to the instructors banging on the drum, but they kept asking, "Who are you?" and "Don't you want a drink?" My legs were so cramped I could hardly stand it but I managed to keep yelling "Fuck off" to the instructors. That just brought more yelling and dripping water and pounding. I was scared and mad as hell, but got through it by telling myself the time in the drum would be over soon.

Midway through the German training the head man told me about another school that could give me the last bit of instruction I'd need to prepare for the Cambodian mission. I'd done a lot of skydiving during the sixties. Now I had to update my jumping with the new hardware military jumpers were using. The German administrator said he'd try to get me enrolled in a warfare school that gave paratroop training. And he said my way was paid up-front by somebody he wouldn't name. By the time the German school was over I was scheduled to start jumping in Holland in October.

I had just over a month before the jump school was supposed to start, so I went back to Dayton for a little more R and R. That's when I met Donna, a tall Hitchcockian blonde lady who seemed more mature than other women I'd been involved with in the past. Right away Donna had me reading about the life of Beethoven and listening to Mozart. That shows you how much I loved her, because I was never too much on high-class music or art or literature. In fact, before I met Donna I thought *Moby Dick* was the last stage of herpes—well, almost. Donna was divorced and in her early forties. Beautiful women of that age with real class can't be resisted, at least by me, although they often seem not to know it themselves. Maybe I only knew it now because *I* was in my mid-forties. When I was younger I couldn't figure falling for a woman in her forties, but I guess your point of view changes with age. I guess that would explain why Masters and Johnson found a lot more going on in those nursing homes than shuffleboard. And I knew that even though I'd probably never lose my yen for young women, my range someday would run from puberty to Medicare. Anyway, by forty a woman knew a lot about the joy and the heartbreak life brought, so her beauty was connected to character. Donna's fine features and her young ideas made the fact that she had a teenage daughter hard to believe. On the night we met she was wearing a tan skirt and a high-necked long-sleeved white silk top that set off her good looks and said more than words could about her role as a mother and her strong religious beliefs. She was sexier in that outfit than all of Hugh Hefner's fantasy mates put together. But what really had me convinced was her Christian commitment and the love she expressed for her daughters.

Donna was the kind of woman you could relate to in every way, not just in bed. You could share your feelings with her and be sure you'd get understanding back. I wanted to tell her how much I loved my own kids, even though my behavior didn't prove it, and how hard it was to tell them what was in my heart. I could tell Donna things like that. In two months I bought her a wedding ring, but she never got it. The night I planned to give it to her I realized that marriage to each other wouldn't be fair to either one of us. I didn't want Donna to have to worry each time I went away. And I couldn't risk holding back in combat because of her. So the next day I put the ring in a safety-deposit box and kept it there for those times when I needed to feel that life was better than it ever was.

In early October I got to Holland ready to become a paratrooper. There were twenty-four of us signed up this time, including the same three who trained with me in England and Germany. Those three would make good recruits for the Cambodian mission. But they couldn't be asked, because it was clear enough from their small talk that they were Americans. And if they were connected in some way to the military they might turn me in for planning my off-the-books rescue mission. At least part of that planning was going on in the States, which might be interpreted by some as a violation of the Neutrality Act.

Jump school lasted five days. We ran everywhere we went—to meals and to the airplane and even to the john in the name of physical fitness. There were more classes here on terrorism and counter-terrorism to sharpen our skills. We talked about the political fallout of covert activity. A lot of the training was in demolition—everything from the recipe for TNT car bombs to ways to use civilian fireworks in combat. We even blew up a bunch of mock buildings each about the size of an outhouse. I got used to the command, "Sam, you're on the shithouse." Which meant to blow the sucker up with the chosen explosive of the day. If I made some mistake strewing timber fragments around the countryside, the officers bawled me out in proper fashion: "Mister, you shouldn't detonate that charge until everybody is at a guaranteed safe distance. Are you trying to deplete the population of this unit?" Anybody who's been in the military can recognize that as an ass-chewing with respect. We were always treated like people, not lowly grunts.

But, as I said, what I really went to Holland for was the paratrooper training. My first jump ever had taken place at a sky-diving school in a suburban airport in the late fifties. That was still near the start of my search for the so-called big thrill, when I thought jumping out of an airplane might be it. Floating free over the curved earth and hitting a paper or painted bullseye thousands of feet down satisfied me, for a while. I logged 248 jumps before I quit, but never loaded down with weapons and full military gear. In Holland the weapons were strapped to your side and the full gear turned out to mean heavy packs stuffed with everything from food to clothing and military materiel. The packs could weigh up to ninety pounds, and with your chute on you carried them between your legs. If you ever meet a paratrooper who brags about being well hung you should make sure he isn't talking about his jump pack. The packs were attached to long ropes and they hit the ground first to keep wind gusts from blowing you into the next time zone.

You only needed five jumps to qualify, but you had to do your jumping from different classes of planes, at different altitudes, using different methods. You sat on the floor of the plane waiting for the order to "stand up and hook 'em up." Getting up with all that equipment was like pushing a boulder up Mount Everest. Once you accomplished that task, you attached a hook to the steel line because you didn't want to trip on the way to the door. Three seconds after you jumped the chute opened whether you wanted it to or not. This was called static line-jumping and it didn't call for any action on your part except for getting out the door of the plane with your head down. But you could get creative in "hop and pop" jumping. There you weren't connected to a line of any kind, so you could exit sideways like Ronald Reagan's son, the ballet dancer. Or backwards the way Jacques Cousteau left the *Calypso*'s dinghy to look for Neptune. The third method was the free-fall, which gave you the option of pulling the ripcord and opening the chute at any point going down.

No question, for me every jump was a thrill. You needed to be a little scared of each one because it was when you weren't that you were in the most trouble. The jumping in Holland was different because the hardware was new to me, especially the bulk. When the fifth day came and it was time to pack up and leave, I felt a real letdown. But when my bags were half-stuffed one of the instructors brought me a mystery telegram from the States. It said to contact a man named Snyder back home about more training. Though my instructors in Holland acted as if they'd anticipated something like this, I was very surprised.

Snyder gave me an even bigger surprise. "Sam, we want you to have some more training before you go after those POWs." He wouldn't tell me who he meant by "we." Then he knocked my socks off by telling me to board the next plane out to a town just outside one of the biggest army bases in the country. At the base I received more jump-training and learned new rappelling techniques. I was also given additional instructions in hand-to-hand combat, weapons, demolition, world politics, spying and counter-spying. After a month of that I was sent by Snyder to a marine base for another two weeks of hard work. By the time it was over Snyder was still a mystery. But he had me ready for Southeast Asia.

As soon as I was settled back home most of my time was devoted to gathering information about the Cambodia setup, including long hours watching films in different Ohio POW-MIA offices. The films told me what to expect about the countryside, as well as the kinds of torture a captured American might look forward to. Surprises were something I didn't want.

After every angle had been covered, my top priority became recruiting a rescue team. Since the best mercenaries could often be found in South Africa, I decided to make that country my first stop. To get leads about mercs you needed to deal with the American consulate. That was easy for me. My time in Israel made me something of an expert in contriving IDs and other papers. I even knew how to avoid the long job of making them myself by buying them on the black market in any country, including America.

If you want to apply for an American passport through regular channels but under an alias you just head for a small town with a lot of people out of work. There you find a hard-up citizen to play your uncle and the two of you go to the local post office. Once there you tell the clerk that you are the nephew who lives thirty miles away with a maiden aunt because your parents are long since dead. Nine times out of ten the clerk will give you a sheet of paper to sign. After you've signed it, he has it notarized and you have a legal-looking ID. Now you can apply for a passport. Odds are you'll get it, because the federal worker who sends it through doesn't give a damn if you live with a maiden aunt or a cape buffalo. He couldn't care less if your parents are dead or alive and working in the politbureau.

If you want to forge your own papers you have to work at it a while. Interpol catches a lot of people who try to cross borders. The easiest papers to forge are the ones in plastic, because when the ID is sealed the weight and feel of the paper or card stock isn't so easy to spot. You can use different kinds of material. A professional photographer comes in handy to clone the details of an official picture if there's a standard pattern. The photo you use should match how you intend to look undercover, with your hair dyed and your face bearded or disguised. After you've got your picture and a couple of official seals, you run a thin strip of pink plastic from the bottom lefthand corner of the soon-to-be pass to the upper right-hand corner. Then you laminate it. Hardly anybody except the ones in the inner circle know about the pink plastic strip. A good forgery won't be questioned. The coded cards are changed all the time, though, so the forger has to keep the ID up to date.

If you need a real-looking intro letter you head for the nearest print shop, because the printer can reproduce any sample of letter-head by taking a picture of it and having a "fourth grade professional artist" or negative stripper retouch it. Then you print duplicates that can't be detected as artificial.

Now you're ready to put the next phase of your operation into motion, and the next phase for me was to find my soldiers of fortune. I left in mid-January for Johannesburg with the ID of a correspondent. At the American consulate the officer in charge was a big help.

"I want to do a story on the life of a mercenary. Could you point me in the right direction?"

"You might get some help over at the American Information Office. It's in the African Life Building."

There I was whisked to the desk of a low-level intelligence officer. After an hour of rag-chewing, I said, "I'd like to do a feature story about mercenaries. Could you give me some tips about where to find some." He said he'd heard about a couple of places where they hung out. "Try the 'Waterfront' in Capetown or the 'Rhino' in Durban. Or the 'Top of the Morning' here in town. And there's a skindiving equipment place called 'Gino's' in Capetown."

The next day the "Top of the Morning" didn't produce anything. So the next step was to take the famous Blue Train to Capetown and a place called the "Zebra Lounge." A Vietnam vet friend in the States told me it was a hangout for mercs. My contact was supposed to be one who answered to the code name "Candle," but the Zebra Lounge turned out to be closed down. The other Capetown bars such as "Andy's Boat" and the "Sailfish" and Steve's "Waterfront" didn't produce any contacts either. The skin-diving shop was deserted, so I went back to the hotel and laid around the pool. Late in the afternoon an attractive cocktail waitress named Ingrid came out for a swim and we spent some time together that night doing the discos and bar-hopping. She was indeed an eyeful, but I kept the other eye out for potential recruits, looking for any clues that might indicate a likely prospect. My moving version of "What's My Line?" was a miserable failure.

The next day I flew to Durban, and my first night in town turned out to be lucky. Sitting in the "Rhino," trying to watch the sun set beyond the beach, I had my view blocked by a young officer in the South African army sprawled on the next stool. He was a few sheets to the wind and we started talking about the military.

"Do you know any mercs?"

"This country is crawling with them."

"I'm doing a story on their lifestyles. I haven't been able to find any."

"You must be looking in the wrong places, chap. If you want to meet one here and now look for Karl Martin. He's a security guard here at the hotel." Immediately I wrote said Martin a long note about an American who was looking for some action and, if he could get me some, to come to room 209. I left the note at the desk with my MFO badge.

It turned out Martin didn't get off work till noon the next day. In the morning my nerves were on edge from waiting for his answer. I decided that three or four hours skin-diving in the Indian Ocean might help me relax. The certification card that would enable me to use the full hardware was back home, so snorkle gear would have to do. I started by checking out a strange school of fish. All of a sudden a shark the size of a baby *Nautilus* showed up about twenty yards to my left. Sam Hall, intrepid counter-terrorist, shot out of the water like a Trident rocket. A burly fellow hauled me onto the deck of the nearest launch and a lady sipping a martini on board told me her husband had taken a picture she was sure would show me on friendly terms with "Jaws." While he pulled off the picture she mixed me a martini. When the big skipper showed me my shark caught by the camera, I downed the drink in one swig and ordered another one. Olympic coaches would do a lot better if they trained their swimmers with a greedy great white in the lane five seconds behind each would-be Mark Spitz. So long steroids.

Badly shaken, I went back to the hotel to wait for the merc, and found my room had been searched while I was out. My friend had to be there ahead of me, so I went down to the lobby and spotted him right away from the description my go-between had given me the night before. Martin would make my brush with the shark seem like a tender moment with Marie Osmond. A colder person would be hard to imagine. He told me he'd see me later in the lounge. When he did he said, "Let's go outside but leave your jacket here." He was probably afraid I was a setup who would tape our talk to get him in some kind of trouble with the South African government. He was from Durban and thirtyish with a typical merc's big neck and biceps and narrow hips. I reminded him I wanted some action and he said, "I might have something, there's a squad going into Zimbabwe next week to look for some Canadian tourists kidnapped a couple of weeks ago."

Ever since the warfare school in England, when Phillip replayed his Iranian Embassy rescue, I had been itching for a chance to participate in a mission like the one Martin was describing. And this one promised to be in a particularly good cause. Further, it was a perfect way for me to meet mercs who might be interested in a Cambodian try. Martin seemed satisfied I was for real, because he made a quick phone call and then came back saying, "You're on."

The next morning he drove me in his dusty Toyota to a ranch northeast of Durban, where we were greeted at the gate by an armed guard who waved us through. In a field near the ranchhouse about fifteen men were doing calisthenics. Martin pulled up to them and yelled, "Peter, here's your ninth man for next week's mission." It was this same Peter who would mean so much to me in the months ahead. He seemed to accept me right away and said, "Come over and join the misery," so I melted into the group doing situps. The rest of the afternoon was spent in tough training, at the end of which we all dragged into the ranch house for a big dinner. At the table I was introduced to Gordon and Chippy and Ernie and Topper and a lot of other men. While we destroyed some big South African steaks we talked about the upcoming mission and the soldier's life in general. Then I asked, "Why did you take this rescue job?" Right away Gordon answered, "We've been on a lot of missions together and we always make sure we're on the good guys' side before we say yes." That didn't satisfy me. "How do you decide which side that is?" Topper said, "Sometimes it's easy, like tomorrow, but if it gets complicated we let Peter decide. He keeps up with what's going on in the big world and we trust his judgment. Tomorrow's job is sponsored by a Canadian interest."

I liked these men already. I could ask them almost anything and get straight answers. "Do most mercenaries care who or what they're fighting for?" I asked. Peter said, "Just about all of the ones I've met are good men. They do want to know who and what they're fighting for. Mercenaries have gotten an unfair press for a long while. Most of them are more honorable than the men I've met in many other professions. Of course, there are times when we have to work with someone who will do just about anything for money or even somebody who's a bit off the wall. We call those types "rikkies." You'll meet one tomorrow. His name is Werner and he's from Austria. He'll be going with us because no one else is available. But the Bird is coming in tomorrow too and he'll keep Werner on target."

My ears pricked up at the Bird's name. His reputation was pretty wild too. Steve at the American consulate said there were all kinds of stories going around about a merc called the Bird who was a kind of South African Audie Murphy taking out terrorists by the dozens. You can bet the idea of meeting the famous Bird made my day and occupied my night.

I figured the time was ripe about midnight to pop the question. "Would any of you be interested in a POW-MIA rescue? I've got the money to arm and train a unit to go into Cambodia and I think I can get the info I need from contacts in Thailand." Gordon said, "I've read a lot about your Vietnam War and about the men that are probably still prisoners there. I'd have to know a lot more about your plans, but I think I'd be interested." Peter added, "Let's talk about your idea when we've come back from Zimbabwe."

After dinner we headed for the big front room of the ranchhouse and Topper broke out the booze. We talked for a couple of hours more while the men dropped out one by one to head for the sack, till I was left alone with Peter and his bottle of Beefeaters. We knew we were on the same wavelength the minute we had shaken hands earlier out on the training ground. We'd been looking for the chance at a one-on-one talk and covered the waterfront by the time the sun came up. Peter was forty-one and divorced from a woman he still thought about a lot because she was the only one who could almost understand him. But she couldn't live with his drinking and the need to fight, something he couldn't explain. She was back in England with their three kids.

When Peter filled in his background and talked about his life I was knocked out by how we'd come to the same point from such different starts. He said, "I like to call myself the 'bastard barrister,' because I was groomed at Cambridge to wear a powdered wig on behalf of lords and ladies in trouble with the law. My family received their first disappointment when I announced after Cambridge that I wanted to play professional soccer. But I didn't go through with that ambition, even though I was offered a contract. I married Jillian instead and within four years we had three children without thinking what we were doing. In the meanwhile I was commissioned in the SAS and the training was satisfying, but there was no war to apply it to. I was getting more depressed by the month because I knew for certain I couldn't sustain the role of a husband and father. I wanted some excitement. I *needed* it."

That was when Peter fell in love with the bottle, and while he was rising to the rank of captain in the SAS he was sinking in his life at home. Finally, just at the point where he was about to make a mark at the Judge Advocate Bureau the army had to give him a quiet discharge. I could tell that, like me, he still felt a lot of guilt when he talked about the sad ending of his marriage. "Things went from worse to worst, until Jillian left one day with the children and I haven't seen her since. I drifted to London and drank myself right into the gutter. All the time I kept asking myself what I was doing and what I wanted from life. The only thing that was certain was my need to *fight* someone. I thought I could prove my worth to myself in that way. One day, long after I'd given up on myself, a family friend found me and talked me into coming to South Africa to dry out. I know Jillian must have sent him and I'm grateful to her for that."

Peter told me how he'd met Gordon and Topper at a bar in Pretoria when they were loosening up before a mission. When they found out he was an ex-SAS they talked him into joining them. "That was the beginning of my life, Sam. I loved everything about that first mission and especially the way it made me feel alive for the first time in my life. That was seven years ago. I've joined over a hundred missions since and I have never been disappointed. They've not all been successful in serving their purpose, but the raw edge of fear and tension are always there. What more could I ask?" Peter didn't have to tell me. I knew he was my new best friend who could understand maybe too much about me.

Just before we finally broke up the talk—a short hour before the Bird and Werner were supposed to show up—I asked Peter about the Zimbabwe mission. He said, "We'll be assigned to C-team and we'll split from A off the coast of Mozambique. B-Team will move overland all the way from the south." I wondered how the Canadian tourists were kidnapped, and Peter told me, "They were in Kruger National Park when they became separated from their party. Ottawa thinks some of Mugabe's killers got them, and if that's so I pity them. Their chances of surviving this long aren't good. But at the worst we need to verify their deaths."

I was too keyed-up to sleep. I paced my room till two hours later, when I was at the training site with Gordon and Topper. The Bird drove up with the rikki sitting next to him in the front seat. The Bird asked Gordon, "Who is this?" and Gordon said, "He's OK. A new mate who's going out with us." That seemed to satisfy the Bird, but Werner looked through me with the weirdest eyes since "Dawn of the Living Dead." He didn't say a word all through breakfast or on the way to the coast to meet the boat, but then he couldn't get too much in anyway because I was asking Peter about every step of the mission. Right up to the point when we boarded the boat that would take us north to my first action in Africa.

Here I talk with some of the Thai camp bosses I'd hired as part of the support element of a U.N. peacekeeping mission in the Sinai.

Talking with members of the Israeli Defense Forces in 1982. I carried an M-16 but was ordered to carry my magazine *out* of the weapon unless fired upon.

At my communications station in the Negev Desert, Israel, 1984. One week later a terrorist bombing at the Beirut Airport would kill 248 U.S. Marines.

Any U.S. Marine would recognize this obstacle course as being on an island in the Carolinas.

On an aircraft carrier somewhere in the Atlantic.

In a submarine somewhere in the Atlantic.

THE PRIVATE launch headed north out of the harbor at Durban. Peter and seven of the mercs from the ranch stood surrounding me on the starboard deck. A few feet away stood the nine men from A-team, their faces filled with the same tension. Off our port side a series of long ropes trailed back to four inflated rafts that looked like sucker fish attached to the side of a shark. The launch hugged the coastline to keep away from patrol boats. At dusk we spotted a sleek cabin cruiser that looked like a police watch out from Swaziland. Our captain headed northeast full speed in the direction of the island of Madagascar to keep us clear of any questions we didn't want to answer.

After dark the moon stayed tucked in behind the clouds, so the launch could be pointed due north, then west to our landing sites. About an hour and a half before daybreak we got to the coast of Mozambique. A-team left the launch in two of the rafts at a point three klicks south of the port city of Beria. Five klicks north of Beria my C-team partners and I swung over the side and dropped into the two other rubber rafts. Though it took only twenty-five minutes to get to the beach, it seemed like a couple of lifetimes. We slit the rafts and buried them in the sand.

The first leg of our trip was now over. But we still had to get through Mozambique into Zimbabwe by walking and running or grabbing any wheels we might meet. We were to link up with A- and B-teams six days later at a spot about fifteen klicks southeast of Salisbury. A few hours before A- and C-teams had boarded the launch, B-team had left Durban by truck, headed northeast to the Limpopo River. That was a quicker and safer route to Zimbabwe than through Mozambique. But part of A- and C-teams' mission

135

was to train for an amphibious strike set for later in the year against the dictator of another African country. Once the three teams joined up we were supposed to raid a terrorist camp in an attempt to rescue the six Canadian tourists. They might still be alive, but intelligence reports said two of the eight who'd been kidnapped had been already killed for not keeping up with their fast-moving captors.

When we hit the beach we were wearing cami pants and olive tops made to look as much as possible like Mozambique army uniforms. We also carried an extra set of duds that was a dead ringer for the khaki uniform worn by Robert Mugabe's terrorists. We knew we might run across units of both forces, since the communist state of Mozambique was crawling with Mugabe's private army. For extra insurance the whites among us blackened their faces with grease paint, which prompted a lot of ribbing from Chippy and Ernie. "Up close and personal" we looked like clones of Al Jolson loving his "dear old Mammy," but we felt the disguises would be effective from a distance. Our firepower wasn't any match for the Russian tanks or bands of assorted badasses that roamed the area we were about to pass through, so it was important we not be spotted. It we were spotted, we could not make any radio transmissions.

Early in the first day's trek one of the mercs named Glen let out a soul-piercing scream. He had gotten entangled in some razor wire just before dawn. Half the bush seemed to be bloodied from the squirting wound. When we cut him loose he was able to walk, but his lower left leg gave him a lot of pain. We couldn't tell how long he'd be able to keep up. He sure couldn't run. But he was a gamer and he moved out with the rest of us as soon as his leg was patched up by Topper.

In the middle of the morning our disguises were tested on a couple of herdsmen with what seemed like good results. They only looked away from their cattle once. If they recognized us as mostly whites in black face they must have decided we were just another one of those crazy camera crews from *National Geographic*. By afternoon we were relaxed enough to begin enjoying the scenery. After the swamps and sand dunes near the coast the landscape stretched out in broad plains that climbed to plateaus and then mountains. Walking through the heat and dampness was easier on my forty-five-year-old body than I'd expected. We were moving close to Kruger National Park, so we were flushing animals along the way. In fact the only scarce species seemed to be the one I was itching to endanger. That was the two-legged terrorist. At dusk we made camp and congratulated ourselves on so far so good.

Just before daybreak the next morning we skirted a tiny, sleeping village and stumbled onto an inviting old Dodge truck. Gordon had it hot-wired in no time and C-team was suddenly riding in style toward Zimbabwe. We made another forty klicks by mid-morning before the truck's bad case of bronchial asthma told us we had a dry gas tank.

On foot in the early afternoon, we walked into our first firefight. We had been moving along due west at a fast clip and had just reached the top of a rise when we suddenly found ourselves staring into about twenty surprised faces a hundred yards below. We knew right away we were the uninvited guest of an enemy patrol because we recognized some North Korean regulars plus one officer with lighter skin who looked to be Cuban. We knew too that we had the advantage over our new friends because we were above them and they were off their horses. Not more than a couple of seconds passed between the startled looks of recognition and the shooting. Every C-team member had his weapon on semi-automatic to save ammo. About half the terrorists were dead after our first burst. The others, including most of the North Koreans and the Cuban, took cover and were returning our fire when Peter gave us the order to stop shooting. After a few minutes the terrorists figured out that we would let them leave. We knew they might tell their buddies about us, but that would be better than making us spend all our fire power on them.

We watched them mount their horses and ride past us from our right to our left toward the sun. All of a sudden Peter ordered

Raoul to put a round into a rider who had a radio strapped to his back. Raoul raised his rifle and lined up the target. He held him for a couple of seconds in his open sight and led him a little so he'd ride into the squeezed-off round. When the bullet hit, the man was lifted sideways off his horse like a puppet jerked by a string. His face-first landing sent the dust flying and then he sprawled still. The radio on his back looked for all the world like a nervous dog trying to rouse his master, what with the antenna waving from side to side like a wagging tail.

After the other terrorists rode off we took stock. None of our party had been hurt, thank God. We picked our way down the incline and Peter made a quick body-count while Raoul and Gordon gathered up the dead terrorists' rifles and smashed the stocks against a handy rock. They were Russian-made weapons.

The rest of the afternoon passed without incident as we kept moving west at a fast pace. In camp that night all I could think about was the firefight. I reran the action in my mind, feeling again the tingle of excitement that went all the way to the very tips of my fingers and toes. I decided right then to talk Peter and the others into setting up a permanent team as soon as this mission was over. I was convinced there wasn't a better group of men to go into Cambodia or wherever else there might be victims to bail out. Being a member of a permanent rescue team was somewhat at odds with my independent nature. But this mission had provided a hint of things to come, and I knew if I kept at this rescue work someday I'd feel on top of the world, Himalaya-high.

The third day out we were still in Mozambique but moving west at a good rate and hoping to get to the border of Zimbabwe by dark. At noon we hit the peaked high country where the heat lost its heavy humidity. But we didn't have time to take in the scenery or dry out before we were ambushed. Lucky for us, our attackers weren't too smart. They must have been in a hurry, because they didn't wait long enough for our point man Gordon to lead the rest of the team out of the high grass and rocks and into the clearing. The first shot deflected off the strobelight that was attached to the front of his L-C harness and he dropped to the ground like the rest of us. He did a good impression of a sidewinder and joined the confab going on in the tall grass as we tried to figure out what we were up against.

There seemed to be twice as many enemy as there had been in the patrol the day before, and while their rounds mowed the field and splintered the rocks around us we returned their fire. Within seconds of our first burst the ambushers began yelling in a strange language which I didn't have time to try to decipher as they started charging us armed with long knives. We kept firing and dropping them in front of us with short bursts—standard operating procedure in a situation like this. The idea was to shoot the closest attacker and then hit the next closest and then the next until none was left standing. After that you were supposed to train your piece on the first fallen attacker and give him a head shot, then rerun the same action with the second and the third and so on. You never knew when a "dead" enemy was going to pull a Lazarus and play killer instead of corpse. In our case there wasn't any need to think about the second stage because the terrorists hit the ground so full of holes that if any of them so much as twitched it would have been a medical miracle. When it was over there were thirteen bodies scattered all over the ground, but not one North Korean. We weren't surprised. Roger said that five or six of them had taken off in the opposite direction when the Blacks charged. The North Koreans had left their black "comrades" to cover their own retreat.

We knew the Koreans wouldn't be coming back soon so we took some time out to assess the situation. We were still a ways from the border and a little over a third of our ammo was spent. We didn't expect an open-arms welcome once we crossed into Zimbabwe either. If anything, our situation would be shakier there, because the ambush we had just walked into told us Raoul's radio operator must have managed to broadcast before he bought the farm. We were sure to run into some more trouble between here and our rendezvous point near Salisbury. Still, our luck was holding in regard to casualties. Except for relatively minor cuts and scratches we'd received as a result of rock fragments being kicked up by the enemy's rounds, our only wound was still Glen's razor-wire leg-cut from the first morning. We were weighing our pros and cons when Gordon asked, "Where's Werner?"

Peter had told me that Werner was a real wacko who didn't fight for the money or the cause, but for the sick joy he felt in killing. I'd never seen a rikki before and didn't have any strong views about the breed. I always figured it took all kinds to make the world stop going around with terrorists. But this mission was a real education in rikkiism. When we found the missing Werner he was throwing the body of one of the terrorists over a cliff into a rock-filled gorge. Five bodies were already disposed of, and when the sixth hit the rocks Werner turned and slowly walked back for number seven. Raoul made a move toward him with the idea of stopping him, but Peter grabbed Raoul by the arm. The last thing we needed at this point in the mission was a row between the team members. Each man stifled the urge to vomit as Werner stabbed out the eyes of the corpses with his knife, then pissed in the empty sockets. After he splattered the rest of the terrorists on the rocks he took a long drink from his canteen to fill his bladder for Act Two.

Peter had warned us before we started the mission to keep our eyes on Werner at all times because nobody could be sure what the guy would do or when he'd do it. He sure wasn't firing with a full clip. But he had a long record in the bush and a knack for staying alive, and Peter said he was almost as tough as the Bird. So we held our tongues, if not always our stomachs.

When we made camp the night of Werner's bizarre show, the Bird did some pissing of his own that served a lot better purpose. Glen's bad leg was swelling and the supply of disinfectant was getting low. He was worried like the rest of us that Glen was going to slow us down. He might even have to be left behind, which would end in certain death if not in capture and torture. We were all talking about Glen's problem when the Bird stood up and walked over to put his arm on Glen's shoulder in a not-to-worry gesture. He explained he was going to piss on the wound because it was in a part of the leg Glen couldn't clean with his own water. He knelt next to Glen and washed the wound with a well-aimed stream. One of my warfare school instructors had told us that this was an old wartime tried-and-true cure. I never thought I'd see it put to the test, though, and I sure wasn't ready for the care the normally fierce Bird showed that night. Glen wasn't surprised, and later I heard him tell Raoul he was moved by the Bird's action. Feelings like that didn't surface very often during a mission. There wasn't much call for any kind of talk other than technical. But because these men had been together so long, they had great respect for each other's talent. On that foundation of respect and trust was formed a deep friendship. Depending on somebody to help you stay alive tended to do that.

In the middle of the night I woke up to the sound of somebody barfing and was surprised to find out it was the Bird. I asked Gordon, who was on guard duty, what was up. He just said, "He's taking his medicine and it doesn't agree with him." The medicine turned out to be a couple of canteen caps full of gasoline mixed with a little sugar. It was supposed to help the Bird deal with a bad case of worms he'd picked up from years of living off the land. His high-octane cocktails had him tossing till sunup, but after a breakfast of K-rations and a few hunks of bark stripped off a nearby tree he seemed good as new.

Some of Glen's swelling was gone too, so when we took off he was able to keep up pretty well. By noon we were hugging a rail line in rougher country than before, and just after we crossed into Zimbabwe with Gordon on point we sighted two of Mugabe's soldiers in a Land Rover. Fortunately we were able to slip behind some rocks before they spotted us. From our position a hundred yards from the Rover, Raoul and Topper picked off the driver and his partner. After we made sure we were alone with our new wheels, we put on our Zimbabwe cami copies with long leggings and long-billed caps and rode in style toward the west. Glen's leg got the rest it needed, even though there was no room for stretching it. The Land Rover was so full of team members it looked like a circus act, but at that point, clad in a fresh set of uniforms and wearing boots that were finally beginning to dry out after all the river crossings of the past two days, nothing could dampen our spirits. Knowing that there was half a tank of gas in the vehicle helped too.

Just before dark we killed a wild goat. It didn't look all that mouth-watering hung over the fire, but after half a week of K-rations it tasted good enough to give our little clearing in the African bush a five-star rating. That night by the fire I talked with Peter long after our goat was turned into a bundle of bones. The two of us had become close friends because the weaknesses we shared were strong bonds. He told me about the time he fought with the legendary Colonel Mike Hoare. "Ah, there was a fighter, Sam. He was absolutely ruthless in combat but one of the sweetest men in other situations. He was really quite charismatic. He's about sixty-five now and not as active as he once was. He talked me into forming a unit in the Seychelles island coup attempt. That mission nearly put me in jail and Gordon, who was along too, was caught and spent two weeks locked up. But for me the whole experience was worth it because of the feeling I had that I was contributing to a cause. That seems to be the only way I feel at peace with myself."

I continued to be amazed at how much Peter and I were alike. Like him, I had never known where to scratch the vague itch I suffered all my own life. But nothing I ever experienced before made me feel the hard ground under my feet the way this mission had, and I knew that after we rescued the Canadians I would have to find other missions like this to keep alive my sense of worth. As the campfire burned down that night I asked Peter if he would help me set up a permanent rescue team made up of eight or nine of the best men his connections could recruit. I wanted to call the unit Free Lancers because it would stand ready to take any rescue jobs that took daring and guts. I would back the missions with money so the men wouldn't need to look for other sponsors. Peter liked the idea and said he would get on it as soon as he got back home. "We only need someone to replace Werner to have the best bloody team we could hope for." Peter knew a lawyer in Pretoria who might be willing to act as our agent. There would be a need for a lawyer because of legal and insurance questions that needed answers. During my watch that night the only thing I could think about was the Free Lancers, and I decided to talk with Peter again about the recruiting during our morning march.

Midway through our fourth day we made the first radio contact with A-team, receiving a report that they had met the enemy as well and kicked some ass. A couple of their mercs were wounded, but fortunately both teams were ahead of schedule, so we could take our time getting to the rendezvous point. There was no word yet from B-team, but none was expected since they would still be pretty far away.

At one point, when we were coming down a pass, I was standing in the back of the Land Rover, probably looking like a seedy gun-bearer in an old Hollywood movie. From that height you could look out on the kind of scene everybody always links with Africa. Below us was a long stretch of yellow plains and somewhere in the distance native drums. The sound and the scene were in perfect sync. Right then I think I felt in touch with my own soul for the first time in my life. God how I loved this place and these men beside me. I hoped we would find the Canadians soon. I owed their rescue as another partial payment for all my useless years. But I didn't want this trip to end either. I blocked out everything but the scene and the sounds. Topper noticed my preoccupation and broke the spell by reminding me that we would probably get to our goal the next day.

We veered northwest in the direction of Salisbury and into the Tribal Trustland where you couldn't trust anybody. Terrorists used it as a holding area. Most of the C-team men had been in Trustland before and they warned me about the enemy units that could be expected. Glen gave me a lecture on the political scene as we rode. He was especially upset with some American newsmen who were calling the terrorists "freedom fighters." He told me all about how

Marxist Mugabe won an "election" through violence and set up a military police force that lived on terror and killed every pro-Westerner in sight. Thousands of deaths were blamed on his "special army." I didn't have any reason not to believe Glen's political preaching, but my reason for being in the Trustland transcended politics . . . I wanted to serve the clearest cause, whatever the politics were, and there couldn't be *any* excuse for kidnapping and killing innocent tourists, never mind the rationalizations. The important thing for me was that six Canadians were supposed to be somewhere in the center of the mess and that we were on our way to rescue them.

Just after the Land Rover got the dry heaves and we were forced to walk again, Werner started to get all bent out of shape. Somebody called Aloan had him screaming, "I'm going to get him, I'll stab his eyes out, I'll cut his nuts off, that son-of-a-bitch killed my friends. I'm going to get him . . ." I never saw so much hate in a human being as Werner apparently had for Aloan. When our rikki calmed down a little Peter dropped back and walked beside me for a few minutes because he could see Werner was riling me up. I asked Peter to tell me more about Aloan. He said it was true that Aloan had helped the terrorists by spying for them and giving them a safe-haven. A lot of people had died because of him, Peter said. "But there's one problem, Sam. Aloan is a priest." I was so shocked. I told Peter I didn't want anything to do with Werner or killing his priest, and he promised me he didn't mean to tackle that chore at this point. He said our goal was a few miles to the south of Father Aloan's "mission." I asked him how he was going to keep Werner from going all-the-way bonkers, and he said he'd handle him the same way as in the past. That meant giving him free rein till he was about to do something that put the team in danger or some innocent bystanders. "But he's crazy," I said. In a way Peter's answer was tough to argue with. "Sam, we all are."

The next day we were moving across flat country just a couple of hours away from our meeting with the other two teams. By then, we had established radio communication with both. A-team was running alongside about three klicks off our left flank. We were closing the gap because the link-up point was less than ten klicks away. All of a sudden we heard automatic weapons fire. Within seconds a radio call from A-team told us they had been ambushed. They were pinned down in a firefight by about fifteen of the enemy and were asking us to help. Before we could, though, another call let us know that half the ambushers had been taken out and the other half were hightailing it in our direction with a river between us. Peter immediately ordered us to position ourselves for an ambush. We took off on a dead run and made the river in time to set up on both sides.

The swift, narrow river ran between banks about ten feet high and we could see our guests would probably be moving up a path that ran out of the bush, then down the east bank and next to the river, and then up the west back into the bush. It was their easiest route. I was positioned with Topper and Ernie on the bank over the path and had orders from Peter to get the drop on the last three terrorists but not to kill them because they might be able to give us some facts about the Canadians. Raoul would back us up, and Peter and the rest would lay in wait for the others.

The plan couldn't have been sweeter. Soon we spotted seven of the enemy jogging along the path with their weapons at the ready. They were cooperating to perfection, because the last three were a good thirty yards behind their buddies. We let the first four pass, and they moved up the path and climbed the west bank. The other three were jogging close together. When they were right below us Topper and Ernie and I jumped for their backs. About halfway down it was clear there would be a problem. Topper's jump was perfect, but Ernie and I landed on the neck and head of the same poor bastard and killed him just like that. Lucky for us Raoul had us covered. Even so, the third terrorist was so surprised he threw down his weapon and raised his hands. Just then shots sounded up above the riverbank and we knew the advance members of the enemy party hadn't lived long enough to return fire.

Peter got the team together and started to question our prisoners.

He had been hoping to get three alive, because he wanted to use one as an example for the other two if they refused to talk. But he'd lost one of his would-be newscasters thanks to Ernie and me. And he was about to lose another one because he didn't have time to start popping questions at the two in our hands before our Bird in the bush, without so much as an "oh, by the way" leaped at the first prisoner and with a black-belt karate chop jammed his hand up into his rib cage and crushed his heart. The prisoner was dead before he hit the ground, and so much of his blood was everywhere I nearly threw up on him. I was gagging for minutes while Peter explained that the Bird recognized the prisoner from a firefight a couple of months back in which one of his cousins had been killed. I knew I'd spend quite a few sleepless nights trying to forget that image of the Bird squeezing the man's still-throbbing heart. I wondered, too, how much brutality could ever be justified. I tried to remember that the Bird had been concerned for Glen, but was that enough . . . ?

Thanks to Peter, whose screams managed to restrain Werner, our other prisoner was still alive. But unfortunately he didn't know the whereabouts of the Canadians. We'd have to rely on the intelligence reports we'd received before the mission started, unless the other teams had more success in finding an informant. Those pre-mission reports had placed the tourists at a tiny village called Urundi. Peter got all the facts he could about the place from the prisoner. Since we didn't want to leave him to roam the countryside searching for his friends, Peter ordered him tied up, and Raoul bound him 69-fashion to the corpse of the Bird's prey. I wondered later if he ever managed to get free from that hug or if his friends turned him loose or if the jackals made a meal out of him.

At dusk we got to the right coordinates to find A- and B- teams waiting for us. B-team had, in fact, picked up an informant. He was one of those low-lifes who made their living in the third-world countries by ratting on anybody whose troubles would bring a price. This one acted like he would sell his mother to the highest bidder. He told us we had the right village. The rest of the night was spent getting ready for an attack on Urundi, but the next morning we found the place empty. There were no signs the tourists were ever there. We headed out of the area to search for more informed informants when abruptly the snitch we had with us remembered seeing some soldiers dig a mass grave a couple of hundred yards to the east a few days earlier. He led us to the spot, where we found a long and wide ditch. At the bottom, covered by a thin layer of dirt, was the most grisly sight I ever saw. Torsos, hacked-off arms and legs and heads were covered with maggots. The bloated body parts gave off a stench that had everybody except Werner gagging. All of a sudden Werner stepped in front of Peter and before any of us could react he emptied his whole clip into the snitch's chest. It seemed to bloom like an orchid as blood and flesh and bone sprayed. None of us questioned the rikki's action this time, since at that moment we all thought our Canadians were in that stinking hole.

After we calmed down we did our best to confirm the dead were in fact the missing Canadians. There were six heads in the grave. We had information that one of the tourists had been missing a couple of fingers since childhood. Topper volunteered to check the hacked-off arms, but it was impossible for him to be sure because the butcher job was so complete. When we were sure we knew everything we could know, we left, and while Urundi slowly faded behind us I tried not to think about the terror the Canadians must have felt before the machetes stopped their suffering. Instead, I thought about how God could carve this beautiful scenery and then allow His creatures to foul it. Why had He brought me all this way only to meet failure?

We took our pre-planned three-hour exit route toward safety across the South African border. Thirty or forty kilometers from the frontier we spotted two trucks sitting on a road that ran through the fields we were traveling. Twenty-five or thirty workmen were busy putting in a pipeline. Since Glen's leg was still giving him trouble and a couple of the other men from A- and B- teams had wounds, we decided to commandeer the vehicles. We were a force of twenty-seven so the workmen didn't have much choice. I'd worry about the rightness of our action later...

Soon we were bouncing through the bush and staying off the main roads hoping not to be seen. Five minutes into the ride there was an explosion and C-team's truck tipped over, spilling us like tin soldiers out of a kid's Tonka toy. But this was no play war. I was spitting dirt out of my mouth and feeling a lot of pain in my chest and hearing people shouting, "Don't move. Minefields, minefields!" The other truck was way ahead of us, out of sight, and the teams traveling in it were too far away to know what happened to us, so I picked my slow careful way to a spot where the rest of the team crawled and we checked the damage. There were injuries, but none serious enough to keep us from walking the two klicks into South Africa.

Two days later my chest x-ray in Joburg showed three cracked ribs and a damaged chest bone, but my letdown from the failed rescue hurt more than my bones. I had wanted to top off the mission with the Canadians' release and I was down because it didn't turn out that way. But at least my C-team friends had more kruger-rands to keep them in food and clothing until we could get Free Lancers organized. And I had a few things as well, including more combat time and a line on some good fighters to sign up for future rescue attempts.

Once we got back to Durban, Peter started firming up the details for Free Lancers and I looked for a way to put together a purse to buy a ticket home. By this time my funds were at an all-time low and I had to get back to the States to raise money for hardware and to pay the men who'd be signing on for the Cambodian mission. Just to pay for my flight home my prize $2200 Rolex got a new owner for a 1000 rand—about 900 American dollars.

As soon as I touched down in Dayton I began to put together a POW-MIA fund. Raising the money got a little hairy. After all, there was no way to tell the investors what the money was for.

There were enough people around town, though, who were used to my borrowing money and the knew they'd get it back. Within a week three friends chipped in $48,000. Then my father's two-carat diamond ring netted me $5,500 and my gun collection brought another $30,000. After some real estate selling I had $92,290, enough to put together a skimpy budget for the attempt. The total budget package looked like this:

Weapons and ammo for mercenaries	$ 8,240
Transportation	
	22,000
Three radios.	600
Salaries for two Thai guides and eight Thai stretcher bearers/soldiers	4,000
Weapons for Thais.	6,000
Mercenaries' salaries	30,000
Medic kits	800
Stretchers (litters)	200
Mercenary training (team together for one week in Florida and three days at Thai base camp).	12,000
Cameras.	1,200
Insurance for mercenaries ($250,000 term on each man at $125 for three months for each man. Discount rate provided by Dayton friend)	1,250
Emergency funds.	1,800
	$92,290

Once my budget was set I needed to open a legit bank account outside the United States to funnel funds for the mission. The Cayman Islands seemed like the right choice for the account . . . one of my friends had a condo there that could be used as a base and the islands were way off the beaten track. From the Caymans it was on to Bangkok to buy weapons and info and set up a training site. The help of Sawee, my friend who'd worked for Thai CID, would be critical, so I called her at the "coffee house" right away. She told me that Wassana and Sawang were not only still alive but back in town and the flap over the broken Egyptian contract had been almost forgotten now. That was great news, because they could be even more helpful than Sawee in connecting me up with the right people. It's tough to trust people you don't know in the Far East, but I knew I could put my life in my three friends' hands. Sawee had ways to get the latest information through Thai CID about possible POW-MIA holding sites in Cambodia. Wassana and Sawang could point me in the direction of the hardware. They might even be able to put me on to a Huey helicopter gunship and a pilot who wouldn't ask too many questions.

I checked in at the Bangkok Palace with its carved teak wood display and its big crowd of jetsetters. After I unpacked I was joined by Wassana and Sawang and went straight to meet Sawee in the cocktail lounge. The four of us spent a couple of hours filling in the gaps since we had last seen each other. When the two travel agents said we should all go to dinner I voted for a place that served something blander than the local five-alarm fare. Wassana pointed us in the direction of a Korean place he knew and he ordered the least spicy items on the menu for me. While we were all attacking our Seoul food I told my friends why I came to Bangkok and what was needed from them. Sawee didn't show much surprise, but Wassana and Sawang were shocked and called me "crazy round-eyed fucker" the rest of the night. But all three agreed to help.

Wassana and Sawang set up a meeting for me with two of Bangkok's leading black marketeers. They told the gun runners they should be careful with Sam Hall, who was a well-known world-class badass who didn't have any second thoughts about getting even with chiselers. They went into a lot of make-believe detail about how Hall blew up the shop of one gun dealer who tried to cheat him. I was glad Wassana and Sawang gave me such a big sendoff, because the two arms dealers turned out to be tough customers. They looked like they were sent over from central casting to play the heavies in an Oriental version of "Godfather III." One was a sweaty type, so fat he made Pavarotti look like Don Knotts, and the other was Mr. Bangkok Cool decked out in lots of flashy gold jewelry and a silk shirt open to his sun-kissed navel. After an hour of bullshit I gave the two of them the order for the weapons and they asked if I were going to start a war. But they set the price at $50,000. I told them no way because there was $30,000 for the whole list. Wassana and Sawang acted as referees. We finally worked out the deal at $39,000. We gave them the weapons list in an envelope with a $2500 down payment to seal the bargain. The physical act of buying the weapons was carried out by Wassana and Sawang. They were more than willing since they owed me a favor for the $98,000 commission through the MFO in Israel.

We made arrangements to store the weapons and ammo in a Bangkok warehouse till we were ready for them. There were enough weapons for more than ten men, and two of everything, so we had spare parts just in case. The plan called for the rescue team to meet at a training site in Thailand to get to know the weapons and do some firing to make sure they were working right. The gunrunners offered the use of a three-square-mile rice paddy outside Bangkok toward the Cambodian border. I decided to take them up on it, because the paddy was near the Stung Houei Sai River. A boat could be used on the river as a backup if we couldn't connect with a Huey pilot.

After the two days in Thailand the team was to spend a week together in Florida to go over the plan and make sure everybody was in shape. Even though the rescue team would be comprised primarily of the men I'd soldiered with in South Africa, I didn't want to leave anything to chance. Things were shaping up when word came from Wassana and Sawang that they had a French pilot who was willing to fly us into and out of Cambodia.

Sawee would be the key person in the next phase of the operation. She was going to be a real pen pal over the next couple of months. Using her contacts with intelligence, she would give me the latest scoop about locations of POW camps. She would also keep me up to speed about the progress of the weapons deal, not to mention Wassana's and Sawang's success in buying the right medical supplies and other musts. Our letters had to be in code, of course, but while I was in the Air Force in 1961 I had gotten enough code training to design a system that would work. Knowing the towns and the climate of Thailand and Cambodia was the key to the code. If a code-breaker didn't know all those things he couldn't possibly succeed unless he had plenty of time. I wasn't about to give him any.

Sawee and I each had a copy of the weapons list, and we agreed she would write to me in the States once a week with a report about buys along with any info she picked up on the POW camps. The code matched a kind of weapon or piece of equipment with a city or village in Thailand. Here's how it worked:

1	Mergui	M–14's—2 each
2	Ye	M–16's—20 each (A–1 burst control)
3	Tavoy	M–16's—2 each (with .203 grenade launcher)
4	Ban Pong	45 automatics—5 each
5	Samut	M–79—2 each
6	Mae Sot	High Standard .22 cal. mag. with silencer 75 RDS
7	Tak	Radios—2 each (either the PMR 2000 or the PRC–10)
8	Rayong	LC–1 Combat harnesses—15 each (each with 3 M–16 magazines, pouches, K-bar [knife] and canteen)
9	Khon Kaen	Medic bags, general type—2 each
10	Uttaradit	Night scopes—2 each
11	Chiang Mai	Night scope detectors—2 each
12	Nan	Case of Laws rockets—1 each (6 per case)
13	Lamphan	Case of claymore mines (with trip wire, detonators and cord)
14	Si Racha	Case of M–39 grenades—2 each (30 to a case)

15	Chiang Rai	20 pounds of C–4 plastique
16	Inthanon	Case of HE (Heavy Explosive for M–79's—11 each)
17	Phrae..............	Case of 203 grenades—2 each (30 to a case)
18	Cha-am............	1500 rounds of .308 (unbelted for M–14's)
19	Hua Hin	2000 rounds of .308 (unbelted for M–14's)
20	Sara Buri...........	25,000 rounds of 7.62 x 51 mm
21	Sisaket	25,000 rounds of 5.56 mm x 45 (.223 ammo)

Each item we'd probably have trouble buying was linked to a city or village with a high elevation. The easier ones to come by were pegged to valley towns and villages. That meant the High Standard .22 Cal Mag with silencer was lined up with the town of Mae Sot. Mae Sot is a town in the mountains. The silencers would be hard to get. The next part of the code was tied to the relative humidity in a city or town. Except that it dealt in fake readings. Sawee would write that the humidity in Mae Sot was 0%, which meant that our gunrunner couldn't find any silencers; or she might write the humidity in Mae Sot was 47%, and that would mean the gunrunners found one silencer. If the humidity reached 96% we were now the proud owners of both silencers.

Word started coming in this way that the order for weapons and hardware was slowly being filled. I was choosy about the types and numbers of weapons. I asked for twenty M–16s because I didn't know if the gunrunners would find new or old ones. The team was planning to practice with each one and take the best ten. We'd strip the other ten and keep the bolt-action carriage for replacements. In the past that part was the curse of the gun. The Laws rockets were hard to find, so I asked for as many as turned up. They're very light bazookas that can take out a communications hut or a guard tower. To the average person the list of weapons I'd drawn up might seem long, but it represented the limit of what we could

carry. Even at that, our supplies would dry up in twenty-three minutes if we got involved in a fight that caused us to fire at a steady
rate. We knew we were ready when Sawee's coded message said
that ninety percent of our shopping was done and the goods were in
the Bangkok warehouse.

The most important information in Sawee's letters had to do with
the probable locations of POW-MIA internment camps. To keep
these secret I used a code that was based on one my uncle had used
in his letters to my family from the Pacific theater during World
War II. He couldn't tell us where he was at any given time, but
when he arrived in Iwo Jima he wrote us a two-page letter. The
first page had three paragraphs with first letters of first sentences
that spelled IWO. The second page had four paragraphs with first
letters of first sentences that spelled "Jima." My uncle's was a
good system, but it needed to be changed a bit so any crypto clerks
out there wouldn't crack it too easily.

Sawee's letters with site information were disguised as love
notes, and if she had information about three different sites she sent
separate letters. If she wanted to get information to me about a
good site like Siem Reap in northeastern Cambodia, she named the
country by changing my middle initial in the address on the enve-
lope. If it was a Cambodian site I was Sam C. Hall, and if it was
Laotian I turned into Sam L. Hall. But that still wasn't enough to
confuse a good cryptanalyst. My uncle's system needed one more
turn of the screw, because, after all, I was playing with fire.

Since Siem Reap is two words, Sawee would send a two-page
letter. But we changed my uncle's 1944 system by counting four
letters (if there were four paragraphs on the first page) to the left of
the first letters of each paragraph. The first four letters on the first
page might be TEIV and the first four letters on the second page
OIMW. Since the first letter was T we would count four letters to
the left and get P and then counting four letters to the left of E we
would get A, and so on until we got the letters PAER MEIS. The
next step was to reverse the letters to get REAP and SIEM, then
one more reverse and the Siem Reap message would be clear. To

tell me how far the POW compound was supposed to be from Siem Reap, Sawee would write something like "Tuesday of last week I went to visit my relatives up country in a small hamlet twenty miles southwest of Lop Buri." What I was looking for was "twenty miles southwest." Reversing the numbers and the directions again gave me what I needed, as in this case where my target was two klicks northeast of Siem Reap. Sawee did send two letters naming a couple of possible sites in Cambodia, so we were just about ready to swing into action.

The plan called for me to jump into Cambodia on my forty-sixth birthday with two Thai ex-soldiers. We wanted to take pictures of the sites with long-lens cameras. The idea was to drop in with the cameras and light gear to scout the terrain just before the real mission. We were supposed to leave our staging area that was a rice paddy up-country east of Bangkok and drop in three klicks from the site so we wouldn't be detected. We needed to move around the campsite as much as possible to get some pictures from different angles. I was hoping somebody would donate a powerful camera with a good scope. We were supposed to walk the seventy-five miles out of Cambodia after we had our pictures. There were around 200,000 troops in the country, so the chances of our getting captured weren't that slim. Once the whole team dropped in for the rescue there was a strong chance we would have to walk out again. That made a trial run to get pictures all the more important.

We needed to have at least a couple of possible sites too. Sawee had come through for me on that score. If one site didn't work out we could try the other one later. The intelligence reports Sawee sent about the two sites rated the risks about the same. I picked our target by flipping a coin and kept the other site in reserve. The trial run would let me check on my Thai scouts while I made sure about the compound and got to know the French Huey pilot. If he didn't work out I'd have to change the plan and line up a junk to take us in by river. I gave the overall mission the code name World Series. The scouting jump was dubbed the play-offs and the two suspected POW sites were named Mantle and Maris.

Once we found our POWs and MIAs we'd have to get them to an "escape and evasion" zone. We had designated three such zones northwest of the camp. Each site was named for a member of the most famous double-play combination in baseball history—Tinkers (color-coded red), Evers (color-coded white) and Chance (color-coded blue). If we met up with a large number of enemy troops at the campsite we were to break into two radio teams (code names Ruth and Aaron). Each team would be in touch with the other and with the Huey pilot back at the rice paddy in Thailand. The pilot would go back to the base after dropping us off. We would remain in constant touch with him, telling him when we would hit the POW compound and when and how we were coming out. If one team had more troops pursuing it than another, the popular team would act as a decoy while the other one headed for the closest escape zone. One member of each team was picked to go to the zone and set off a smoke canister to guide the Huey pilot. If our radios failed we would use canisters of color-coded smoke to mark the night escape-zone. We couldn't get strobe lights in our harness rigs, but we had flares in case we needed them for any reason. We planned to come in from the Laotian instead of the Thai side, just to confuse the locals.

An ex-Navy Seal friend and one of America's most decorated servicemen helped me put together a sweet escape plan. The Huey was to set down in the middle of a designated landing circle with 340 degrees full of Claymore mines. The other twenty unmined degrees, marked with canisters of green smoke, would be the path our guys would run through with the POWs to board the bird. My friend would have an hour to set up the reception committee of Claymores but he told me he wouldn't need over twenty minutes to blow up 340 degrees of the circle as we ran through the other twenty. He planned to use fifteen mines. They would sound like the Fourth of July so our trackers would probably think we were a regiment and a half.

We had a river route plan too in case we couldn't find a chopper and a pilot we could trust. It called for some Thais dressed like peasants to stand on the deck of a junk while the nine team-members hid under a canvas tarpaulin. Getting the junk would be easy enough, but it had to be customized with a hot motor. Wassana and Sawang were keeping on the look-see for one. I planned to grease the motor so it would look well-used. I wanted it to be the floating equal of a rusted '69 Corolla with a brand new but greasy Targa engine. But whether we traveled the river depended on whether we could get the French Huey pilot.

All the details were eventually covered, including the pilot sign-up, and we were ready to put the plan in motion when I was hit with one of the worst blows of my life. It was the first week in March, just before my birthday, and the knockout punch came in the form of a newspaper article. A retired army colonel named Bo Gritz had been arrested in Thailand, the article said, for planning a mission to rescue American POWs in Laos. I was devastated and went straight home to think things through, but the more I thought the more unsure I became about what could and should be done. The flap caused by Gritz's gaffe might provide a cover for our own mission, but it also might induce the Feds to start checking into reports of other missions, which would result in our plans being discovered.

All night I tried without success to puzzle it through. The next morning a friend who was in on the plan called from overseas with some follow-up news. "Scrub it," he said. "The pressure is on in Washington and the Far East." I tried arguing that all the fuss would provide a ready-made cover-up. "Are you crazy?" he said. "The mission has to be aborted. Do you think the Vietnamese and the Cambodians haven't heard the news? To go in now would be suicide. It's a lot quicker and less expensive to slit your wrists." I slammed the phone down but it wasn't until a couple of hours later that I realized just how much I was hurting inside. I couldn't stop thinking of the wasted work, not to mention the time and money. Twelve thousand dollars had been shot on trips to South Africa and Bangkok. Twenty five hundred down had been paid to those two gunrunners. Five hundred had gone to the Huey pilot that couldn't fly for me. And there was a growing bill for weapons that might never be fired unless somebody decided to attack the warehouse where they were stored.

What really bothered me, though, was that I had been convinced my team would be able to bring back the first POWs and MIAs from Cambodia. I had been looking forward to sitting in front of my television set and watching the reunions of the rescued men with their families and friends, all the while thinking of how pleased my dad would have been by what I'd achieved. Now that dream was blasted.

As I sat around my apartment reflecting on what had happened, I felt increasing anger toward Colonel Bo Gritz. Because of him all my hopes—and the hopes of a number of POWs and MIAs as well—had been deep-sixed. If I could have found the good colonel then I would have used a rocket launcher to fix him up for a singing career with the Vienna choirboys. Anyway, his arrest effectively put my mission—and maybe others as well—into cold storage and forced the Reagan administration to blast publicly all such civilian freelance attempts. On May 12 Richard Childress, the President's National Security Council Advisor, gave a talk to a group of Vietnam vets in Virginia. He argued that Colonel Gritz's would-be rescue mission had dealt a setback to the talks the government was conducting with Laos to resolve the POW-MIA problem—whatever that was.

Eventually I came to the view that old Colonel Bo deserved a lot of respect. I knew we had the same idea of helping end the Vietnam war once and for all—for the brave men still in enemy hands and for their loved ones suffering back home. And we both had tried to do the job. I've never met Colonel Bo Gritz but I eventually decided I would be proud to serve with him in combat anytime. Colonel, someday maybe the two of us can get together with the rest of the Free Lancers for a rescue mission, and if so I can tell you where there's a bundle of cash plus some warehouse weapons. Not to mention a waiting pilot. With you along we'd make quite a terrific team of ten.

SIX

WHEN I scrubbed the Cambodia mission I knew I had to immediately find another compelling cause to get into. My new life had me hooked harder than drugs ever had, but the effect was just the opposite. I felt better about myself than ever before. My physical shape was the best since the Olympics. Most important, I was ready with my training to help people in trouble when and if they could be found.

The key to finding them turned out to be a stranger who was about to play a big role in my life. The surprise visitor was Commander Francis Douglas "Red Dog" Fane. By then retired, the commander had headed up the United States Navy's Underwater Demolition Team and was a one-time master and navigator in the merchant marine, plus a former correspondent for Mutual Broadcasting. He was also the hero of a 1957 MGM movie called *The Underwater Warrior*. I was sitting in my Dayton hotel room thinking about Cambodia when Commander Doug Fane knocked on my door. When I opened it he introduced himself and said he knew all about my work in Israel and just about everything else I'd been up to lately, including my POW plan and how it was too bad Gritz got his ass caught in the wringer, or words to that effect.

I was bowled over, but I managed to ask how the hell he knew about all that. He said he couldn't tell me that but he could tell me where I should go next. Like maybe Central America, where he said he had some connections that might help. Before long we were talking about everything from underwater demolitions and weapons and tactics to the goings-on in Israel and El Salvador. He was one of the easiest men to talk with I'd ever met and after the first ten minutes I felt he was my friend for life. Before he left late that night he said, "Buy yourself a New York *Times* and read up on El Salvador while I pull a few strings to get you some action with the government troops down there. You'll have to get past the American brass in your own way." I said I'd study the papers and wait for his call. The idea of going to El Salvador appealed to me because it would allow me to judge the accuracy of what was being said in the press. You never knew whether reporters were getting the facts straight.

In a week the commander called and said, "Everything is set with my contacts. They'll look after you if you find a way to get close to the military."

"Sounds like a challenge I'd like," I told him. In another week I was ready to go.

My busted Cambodian plan called for a look-see jump in the neighborhood of a targeted POW-MIA camp on March 10 of 1983, which was forty-six years to the day from my first butt-slap. Thanks to Red Dog, that cakeless, candleless birthday was spent rolling down the runway in El Salvador's capital, San Salvador, instead. The airport taxi driver briefed me on the whereabouts of the American advisors and the press corps. Since I was pretending to be a reporter, I needed a base of operations at a hotel close to the military, but not so close that a lot of questions would be asked. The press was staying at the Camino Real and the advisors at the Sheraton annex. Both buildings were patrolled at every entrance and exit by Salvadoran soldiers armed with sub-machine guns. The perfect spot for me then seemed to be the main building of the Sheraton, close to the military and away from most of the reporters.

The morning after check-in I went to the American Embassy with my wallet stuffed full of laminated fake ID cards and asked to see somebody about writing up the war from the field. A pretty secretary told me some second stringer would see me in about an hour. Time would be wasted that way and my request could only be okayed by a top dog anyway, so I said, "You look a lot like Morgan Fairchild", with appropriate embellishments. Five minutes later I was getting a special closed-door briefing from the government press attaché in El Salvador. By showing him pictures of myself in combat gear in Lebanon and at some of the warfare schools, I convinced him that I was qualified to handle the action that came with covering the story. He then introduced me to a higher-up who conducted a second closed-door briefing. The bigwig had a letter typed up that intimated I was a close personal friend of his. It described my mission to the defense minister of El Salvador, who name was Captain P. A. Luis Mario Anguilar Alfaro. Alfaro gave me a second letter that would get me wheels or wings or props to take me to any combat area in Central America. The permission authorized me to train with the troops and join in as much action as I wanted. I wondered if Captain Alfaro was one of Red Dog's contacts.

For the next couple of days talks with a lot of people gave me the lay of the land. At a press corps meeting the reporters questioned me about my fabricated "midwestern magazine chain," Washington Centre Publications.

"It's a new outfit. Started by a guy who used to be a reporter for UPI in the old days."

"What's his name?"

"Gee, I can't remember exactly. It's an Italian name. Gambini or Bambini. Something like that."

"Never heard of him."

"Well, he's really on the make, wants to make a name for himself."

"Oh? Well, good luck getting the story."

Some high-powered press people at the Camino Real gave me some good information about the relative strengths of the government troops and rebels. I didn't press them too much, though, because I didn't want to call attention to myself. Evidently *someone* took a particular interest in me, because my room at the Sheraton was broken into twice and some papers and pictures stashed in my Gideon Bible came up missing. Fortunately, I had stashed most of my important things in a safety-deposit box in the hotel.

After only a couple of hours walking the streets of San Salvador, I found out the ripe old age my life insurance predicted for me would be a joke if I wore my camis on the streets, as I had in Israel. There was a civil war going on here between, roughly, the right and the left, and you couldn't be sure whose side the guy walking next to you was on. The best bet was to try to fade into the crowd. On my first morning's walk three gunshots up ahead had me running for the spot. A government soldier was lying in a pool of blood with a crowd of civilians checking him out. Just then the camis I was wearing underneath my civilian clothes began to feel pretty tight, so I ducked inside a clothing store and walked out twenty minutes later dressed like Juan Valdez on his way to check the coffee crop.

One of the reporters I met the first day in town gave me some early advice about the mail service. He warned me not to trust any important papers to the El Salvador postal system. The mailmen there could be stayed from their appointed rounds by rain and heat and gloom of night. Not to mention government snoops or bribes or siestas or margaritas or senoritas. I'd have to find a way to set up my own private mail service for the stuff that my lawyer needed to keep me out of trouble—papers listing everybody who gave me the okay for this and that. Eventually I found the courier I was looking for—a hooker who hung out at a whorehouse frequented by U.S. embassy personnel. It turned out that she made a couple of late-night plane trips a week to Miami to take care of business details for her pimp, and she was willing to act as a mail person for Americans. She proved to be a reliable conduit, not only for me but for many others.

Once my study of the country's political and military setup and the role of the press was finished, Operation El Salvador was in gear. I knew that my IDs and letters of introduction would be useful persuaders, so on Friday morning of my first week I took a cab from San Salvador to what used to be the international airport but was now a converted government military base at Ilopango. Over the next few weeks I flew every day from Ilopango to different

Central American combat zones. But before joining the fighting I did some training with Salvadoran equipment.

I was already requalified as a paratrooper but I wanted to work with the local gear, so a Huey gunship took me to A'huachapán on the border of Guatemala. A'huachapán was an intelligence corps area. Some training was going on there, and I made three static-line jumps from an old "Goonybird" that was a World War II relic. All the equipment was so old it seemed new to me. Taking commands in Spanish was new too, so on one jump I misunderstood an order and left the "goony" too soon. That landed me on top of the lead jumper's billowing white chute. The only thing missing the first third of the way down to top off the effect was a white robe and a harp.

Back at Ilopango I spent a couple of days training with mortars, running obstacle courses, jump practicing from a stationary tower and joining in maneuvers. I was assigned to a Special Forces officer. He made sure I did everything, within reason, that I wanted to do, which included the Salvadoran army commando routine. There were five Salvadoran brigades and the first three were trained at Fort Bragg in the States. The newer troops got their lessons at Ilopango, though, because Fort Bragg turned out to be too expensive.

After two days of tough training at Ilopango I climbed into the belly of a C–123 cargo plane loaded with weapons and ammo. The classified goal of my first Central American combat mission was a dirt landing strip around the Quartel of Usulatan, where we were supposed to join up with a commando unit. They were hard-up for our supplies. As it turned out, though, we didn't make the delivery or the hookup, because the government troops were already overrun and pushed out of the area by rebels who were waiting to grab our load of ammo. We first discovered that when we tried to land and got surprised by small-arms fire. I was wearing ear plugs to muffle the sound of the engine, so I didn't know what was going on till one of the flight crew turned to me and pantomimed the message that the plane was hit in both wings. The rebels only wanted to force a landing with the ammo cache, so they went for the wings and not the fuselage. When I realized what was happening I knew what a mallard must feel like that has the bad luck to fly over the blind of a sharpshooter set on winging him to keep his breast and drumsticks puncture-free and juicy for the cook. I had perfervid visions of the plane being forced down and carried away in the jaws of an oversized water spaniel to the rebels' hiding place. But our pilots managed to zigzag their way out of danger and we flew to another classified spot to dump our load.

At this site we were faced with a rerun of the first landing attempt—more small-arms fire from rebels who had overrun the government troops' position. Again we took some rounds in the wings, but this time I was pretty calm, even though I knew that if the fuselage took a hit we'd have bought it. The pilots were terrific, and in spite of flying low between high hills they managed to maneuver our mallard out of the rebels' range. Eventually we landed safe back at Ilopango and a detachment of government troops took our ammo and delivered it prosaic fashion, on foot, to their buddies who'd been overrun.

Thanks to my passes and letters I soon found myself moving into all of the military hot spots and climbing into or out of helicopters around the clock. At one point a Huey gunship took me from Ilopango to a jumping-off point near a mountain river where three companies of Fort Bragg-trained Salvadoran commandos were getting ready to assault a guerrilla stronghold. This would be my first time in combat with such a big outfit. I didn't know what to expect because there were over four hundred and eighty men in the combined unit, and I was the only American. All my combat before had been with groups of nine men and fewer. I was looking forward to this sort of Cecil B. deMille production just for the sheer spectacle of it. As soon as the copter dropped me off among my temporary comrades from the Salvadoran 5th Brigade it circled the area in search of the enemy. Thirty minutes later we heard the two M–60s aboard the Huey open up and the crew radioed, "Enemy

spotted . . . coordinates are . . . They're on horseback heading down
the mountain and into the jungle." Shouts and cheers went up and
we moved out on-the-double up the mountain to meet the enemy.
Nobody seemed worried that we were on foot while the guerrillas
were on horseback—these kids, whose average age was fourteen,
were hungry for a fight. They were trained by the best—the instructors at Fort Bragg—and this moment had been a long time
coming.

Nothing was going to stop these boys from meeting the enemy
head-on, so we were walking at what seemed like the pace of a
miler at a track meet. That was unbelievable, because the countryside was so rough. Months before, in Mozambique and Zimbabwe,
the marches had been made a lot easier by long stretches of flat
bush country. But in El Salvador the land was mostly peaks and
valleys and your only break came when you struck a thick jungle or
a roaring river. It was up and down and up and down and then chop
and slice and then ford and then up and down again. The rivers
were difficult to deal with because they flowed so fast. They were
particularly troublesome for the smaller Salvadorans, who were
sometimes caught up to their necks in the foaming water. During
that morning we only stopped for breath twice—each time for no
longer than five minutes. At noon the maps and my watch told me
we had covered forty-one klicks in seven-and-a-half hours. My
blood was pumping so fast I could have walked another forty-one
in the afternoon, but we made camp and got some food into us. I
took off my shoes and my two pairs of socks to look at my feet.
With all the blisters and bruises, they looked like relief maps of El
Salvador. There was no time for a geography lesson, though, because we were off again.

The Salvadoran officers kept all 480 men bunched together. This
was partly due to their lack of leadership skills and partly due to
the fact that their smaller units took so many ambushes. Not once
during the day did we split up. In the afternoon there was a brush
with the enemy. We had two minor firefights, captured three guerrillas and flew them to Ilopango for questioning. Nobody was

killed in spite of, or maybe because of, the muddle on both sides. The government troops were willing and eager to do a good job, but their leaders just weren't very capable.

Before the day ended I got bent out of shape over the lack of polish in the officers and the troops. We were each carrying one canteen of water on this long day. During our few breaks a lot of the young soldiers were drinking from ponds of full stagnant water alive with larvae. They just didn't know any better. I pulled as many back from the edge of the ponds as I could and yelled, "No, no, no!" I was so ticked off at the Salvadoran commander that I chewed him out for letting the kids drink the crawling slime. He at last seemed to agree with me, because he too started yelling at them when they tried it again.

A lot of troops were running without the safeties on their weapons locked too. What a great way to end my life. Shot by some babe of a soldier on the same side of the war. At this point there was no question in my mind that the best kind of fighting was with a small, highly trained unit equipped with the best of weapons. Why had I let Red Dog talk me into this godforsaken war anyway? I was free to pick my own spots.

We made camp once it was clear that most of the rebel force was still ahead of us. It looked like it would be a long time before this unit saw any action, so I decided to head for a more promising combat zone. Within an hour I was on my way back to Ilopango. The next day I flew to Morizon, which was an even more mountainous region that promised still worse marching, but more action too. Nicaragua supplied the Salvadoran rebels in Morizon with enough guns to control the sector. Another government unit there showed me the same lack of leadership skills I had witnessed before.

At one point we were closing in on a group of rebels, hoping to catch them napping—when a couple of hundred yards short of catching them one of our boys who wasn't more than fourteen couldn't resist the fun of blasting a three-foot-long iguana out of a tree. I blew my stack and went back to the boy and slapped the rifle out of his hands and yelled at him in English that the goddamn iguana wasn't the only one out of his tree. The commander, who was no more than twenty-two or twenty-three himself, kept nodding, kept shouting, "Estupido," but it was never clear whether he was talking about the kid or me. Do I need to tell you the rebels by then were long gone?

On this Morizon march I also observed fourteen-year-olds carrying so many weapons and so much ammo that they could barely move. One boy was carrying an M–79 with an M–16 on his back and two bandoliers of ammo strapped to his chest. While most of the army was under-equipped here was this one human arsenal on foot, and that just didn't make any sense. The boy and his buddies had a lot of guts, but their leaders were failing them.

At Morizon the Salvadoran mañana attitude was also something that tended to get me steamed. No wonder this war was so hard to win. Late one afternoon we met up with the rebels again and we were within 500 yards of them, hoping for some action. Just as I was getting set to draw a bead, the commander announced it was five o'clock and time to head back to the base. I couldn't believe it and I told the commander he was out of his coffee-picking head. He paid me no mind, and everybody went home because they weren't trained to stay out in the jungle overnight. It was strictly a nine-to-five war for the government troops. On the way back to the base I half-expected to see Jane Fonda and Dolly Parton double-time past us.

The rebels fighting against this rag-tag army were just about as mixed-up themselves. Most of them were not quite as young, and were peasants with no more than seventh grade educations. Even if you were a bright high school grad in El Salvador you had very few choices. You could, for example, work in the sugar cane or coffee or tobacco fields for a dollar and a half a day. Or you could be a rebel and join 800 buddies against the government for what looked like good money. With those picks it wasn't any wonder why so many wanted to be "doughboys."

* * *

After Morizon I hopped a Huey back to Ilopango. As we got near the landing pad a big group of civilians was waiting for us on the ground. There were a lot of cameras and what seemed to be some VIPs in the front row. It looked like they were going to waylay the pilot and crew, so when we landed I started for the officer's club to get a couple of "cool ones." Instead of tailing the others, a bunch of important-looking types started following me. When they caught me, an embassy aide grabbed my shoulder and said, "Would you come with me, please. Congressman Oberstar would like to meet you." My first thought was that my cover was blown and my ass would soon be in a sling. When I got back to the bigger group, a middle-aged-looking gent stepped up and said, "I'm Congressman Oberstar and I wanted to meet you. Congratulations on the job you and the other military advisors are doing."

Now I was sure I was in trouble. To make matters worse, before anything else could be said a burly captain in the Salvadoran army who was a liaison officer and interpreter popped me a starched salute and held it for me to return. How could I, since I was really a civilian? There I was looking every inch the camouflaged commando and trying to smile through jungle makeup that would have made Max Factor proud. If the Congressman only knew this "unarmed adviser" was in possession of three knives, including the one taped to his bicep, plus a 45 automatic hidden under his cami blouse and two grenades in a pouch where his magazines were supposed to be.

I stood there trying to keep cool and feeling like each second was a lifetime. Finally I said, "How do you do, sir. My name is Sam Hall and I'm a correspondent, not an adviser. I have permission from the Minister of Defense of the government of El Salvador to look at the troops in the field and report on any firefights. I might add, sir, that the troops were damn good." The Salvadoran captain lowered his arm in slow motion and a surprised smile broke over the face of the Congressman. The crowd of reporters began moving toward me. I was in for a lot of flak unless I thought fast.

Congressman Oberstar gave me the opening, saying something about me being an aggressive "young" reporter.

"Young reporter," I said. "I'd say this forty-six-year-old body that just dragged in from the field after a forty-five klick march is probably older than yours." All the talk from then on was about how I stayed up with the troops. We just kept yakking and the photographers kept snapping.

The next night my Dayton lawyer, Jack, called to tell me I'd been on the NBC Nightly News. I was alarmed at first, thinking that I'd been identified, but Jack explained that there was no sound from the site. The pictures were used as a backdrop to a report by Roger Mudd.

Though my greasepaint makeup would probably prevent anyone from recognizing me, I asked Jack to check the wire services to make sure my name hadn't been used in any way. If it had, I might turn up next on the rebels' hit list, and that wasn't the one topped by "Malaguena." It was a known fact that the rebels' death roster already included some correspondents and U.S. embassy officials.

Jack had some other interesting news too. He told me that Brian had called from Pretoria to say that all the details for Free Lancers had been worked out and that a contract with the French government had been set up. The French wanted to rescue a priest who had been kidnapped in Angola. Jack asked where I would be and I told him I'd be going to Belize for the weekend, then coming back to El Salvador to stay until I heard that all the Free Lancers had been rounded up. I asked Jack if Brian had heard anything from Peter about the Mozambique action and Jack said no, that it had been close to a month and Brian had heard nothing.

When Jack hung up my own worries started. If Peter and the others were in trouble or, God forbid, even worse off, we'd have to cancel our first contract and that might be enough to sink the Free Lancers before we sailed. But there wasn't anything to do but wait for word, so it was on to Belize.

The Belize scenery was relaxing and the slow pace was perfect for forgetting the grimy little war just over the horizon. I rented a fishing boat from an old man whose services included relating a history of the place. We talked so long it was late afternoon before I got the small boat out to sea. When I got back I window-shopped in the village marketplace, even though there weren't any windows. I wasn't interested in buying anything anyway. I just wanted to meet some of the local people. A lot of them spoke English. I got a good taste of the place and liked the flavor. That night I sampled the local food and made the rounds of the bars. Back at the hotel I had a message from Brian that there was no word from Peter but that I should get some hardware together for the Angola mission. The French wanted us to go the next week. I cancelled my second day in Belize and flew to Florida, where I felt I could get the intelligence we needed. That's when I got Brian's cable informing me that Peter and the others had been captured. All that could be done was wait for word about the ransom, so I went back to El Salvador while the wheels made their slow turn in Africa.

From San Salvador I was airlifted to a spot on the border between Honduras and Nicaragua—a staging area for the Nicaraguan Contras, who were supposedly armed and trained by the CIA to fight the Sandinistas in the northern part of their country. I felt if the CIA was really supplying the Contras, William Casey should have been ashamed. Their stuff was miserable all the way from their ragtag uniforms down to their ancient Chinese type-56 assault rifles. I was eager to see the Contras in action and the chance came at my next stop. The area was inside Nicaragua, just north of the city of Esquipulas near the province of Nueva Segovia.

The Contras were based at eleven different places in Honduras and they had three leaders—two in Honduras and one in Costa Rica. When I linked up with the rebel forces in Nicaragua I saw that my jungle camis looked out of place—the Contras fought in olive drabs. But I wasn't the only person to stand out. The other sore thumb was an American newspaper reporter dressed in civilian clothes. The fact he hadn't been packed back to the States in a pine box long before said something about the slow tempo of the fighting. Some Nicaraguan militia were looking for this group of Contras, though. In fact, the enemy found us the next day. A firefight broke out but it didn't last long. One or the other unit could have wiped out the enemy if only they had some decent leaders. The young peasant next to me seemed to be shooting at some strange target in the trees, because the leaves and limbs across from him were getting ripped apart, as though he were trying to bury the Nicaraguans under the branches. For no good reason our young commander gave the order to draw back, and then the Sandinistas, for no better reason, retreated too. What was this war all about?

When I walked the twenty-one klicks back into Honduras with the Contras I was able to check out their arsenal. Besides their ancient Chinese weapons they were carrying some M–79s and 60-mm machine guns, plus a few Laws rockets and M–26 grenades. They had American radios but none of the stuff looked new or taken care of.

After a few more days holed up with the Contras I went to a village called San Carlos in Honduras. It was a small patch of huts that served as a hideout for peasants running from Sandinistas in Nicaragua. The airstrip was overgrown with weeds and even small trees. Later, after my visit, CIA backing and money made it a going operation. I spent a couple of hours talking with the refugees and found out that most of them were Indians who had always been treated like dirt in their own country. They didn't have much food and their clothes were a mess. One old man asked me to tell somebody in charge that his wife was sick. He was afraid she'd die without medicine. On my way out of the village I pointed out the man to the Honduran officer in charge. He said he would take care of him, but I wondered if he ever did.

After San Carlos I flew about seven miles to Mocoron. It was much bigger than San Carlos and the saws were buzzing there to make a new hospital. It would be staffed by volunteer doctors and nurses from the States and Europe who were part of a group called "Doctors Without Borders." Each medic was supposed to serve a couple of months' hitch in Honduras.

Back in El Salvador I was airlifted again to Usulatan, but my missions with the Salvadoran troops rarely led to any firefights. The government needed arms and ammo as well as replacements for broken and worn-out parts. The average weapon there had a cracked stock or a broken trigger guard or both. There were no cleaning rods or bore brushes and no solvents. A lot of the rifles had oil in their gas systems. The M–60s were a disaster and the fifty calibers were in even worse shape. There weren't any spare parts anywhere. The weapons were so old their cases were always being sent back to get repaired.

But the Salvadorans needed more than supplies. If their weapons were in bad shape, their tactics were even worse. They stored explosives and detonating caps in the same containers, and there wasn't any flank protection so the troops always bunched up. One grenade could take out a good part of a platoon or more. They set themselves up for ambushes all the time. Over and over they gave out open invites.

Once I was with a couple of companies of government troops in a truck convoy headed for a rebel camp in the hills. The six open-bed trucks filled with forty men each were rounding a bend in the dirt road when a barrier of tree limbs and boulders stopped us. The rebels had been doing some landscaping. If the five of them were a little smarter or better equipped or thought to bring a few more of their buddies or had two grenades apiece instead of one they could have wiped out over fifty percent of three Salvadoran companies. As it was, we took some injuries before our fire sent them hot-footing it back into the hills. When everything calmed down the commander of our convoy explained to me why he didn't have a few jeeps scouting the road ahead of the trucks. His reason was tough to argue with: he didn't have any jeeps. We left the trucks behind and walked the rest of the way in a single column. We were lucky to be alive to have our talk.

The Salvadoran army made a lot of other tactical foul-ups. For example, they never had first light or last light stand-to's. Half of the troops at any given time could be living it up in Acapulco for all the commanding officers knew. Also, the Salvadorans never set off smoke canisters to signal landing zones for their helicopters. In a guerrilla war that was like supplying the enemy with gift choppers. And the boy staggering along with an M–79 and an M–16 turned out not to be the only one carrying an impossible load. There were many others like him carrying a disproportionate amount of equipment.

The list of deficiencies went on and on. The Salvadorans didn't have any night-vision devices. Even if they could be talked into changing their banker's hours they still wouldn't be able to fight after dark unless a lot of owls enlisted. They didn't have any training in plastic explosives or Claymore mines. Fifty percent of their blasting caps were so old they were duds, and only about thirty percent of their stick dynamite would explode. There weren't enough medics. It wasn't any wonder they weren't winning the war.

When I got back to Ilopango from Usulutan a telex from Red Dog was waiting. In it he laid out an idea he wanted me to put into action. He said that a year or so before, a Texas news hound named Mike Luhan spent some time with the Salvadoran rebels and wrote their side of the war story. Luhan just walked into a guerrilla camp and was accepted. In his time covering the rebels he lost thirty pounds, and he had to be fed through tubes when he got back to the States. Red Dog said Luhan had made a good try at figuring out the rebels, but he was a reporter, never had any military training, at least not the kind that gave one the ability to make knowing military assessments. I did. So Red Dog thought if I could get myself captured by the Salvadoran rebels I might be able to pick up some meaningful information about them that his contacts could use.

I was pretty sure a meeting with the rebels could be pulled off. I wrote a letter to Donald Hamilton, who was the U.S. press attache in San Salvador, asking for permission to try to get the rebels' side of the story. I'd met Hamilton at a cocktail party in San Salvador the first couple of days there. We didn't talk much at the time. That was largely on account of the New York *Times* reporter whose press badge said her name was "Sylvia." Believe me, her figure across the room made it hard to focus on anyone else. Anyway, I made it clear in my letter that the mission would be at my own risk and that my motive was just to get the story for Washington Centre Publications. My plan called for buying my own parachute and then hiring a plane and jumping at dawn near a known enemy rebel hangout. I hand-delivered the letter mapping my plan on April 2nd and asked for a reply by the 11th in Dayton, where I was headed to visit my kids.

Donald Hamilton's response didn't get to me until weeks later, dated April 16. The delay could have been a Salvadoran postal screw-up, or Hamilton could have been responsible. Anybody in his spot would tread carefully. He might have thought I would make the jump if he didn't write me, and so he did presumably decide to get in touch. The first paragraph of his letter said that he couldn't give me clearance for a parachute drop. It was too dangerous. But the next paragraph reminded me you didn't have to parachute in anyway, because journalists could make contacts with the rebels just by walking into their camps around the Guazapo volcano. Hamilton reminded me about Mike Luhan's case too. It warned me against any contact with the guerrillas without first getting clearance from one of their international support groups. Right or wrong, I read "go for it" between the lines.

Donald Hamilton's clearance wasn't really a must anyway, I felt. I'd already decided to go with or without his permission, figuring Red Dog could probably get me out of any trouble with the government. On the phone the day after I sent Hamilton the letter, Red Dog told me I probably wouldn't get cleared, a mission like that would be labeled too dangerous. He pointed out that the guerrillas might know me by this time, but I told Red Dog I was going to go for it anyway.

The idea of finding the rebels on Guazapo volcano instead of by parachuting into their hideout came to me long before the attache's letter. Travelers were always being stopped on the roads near the volcano by guerrillas looking for loot. So it really was possible to make contact at least.

After a quick flight to San Salvador and a night resting up at the Sheraton, I grabbed a taxi the next morning. Two hours later I left the cab and started walking up a mountain trail. I was wearing chinos with a blue shirt that flashed my correspondent's ID. I also carried a pad and a pen, plus a camera. After walking a bit the old sense of danger started to settle in my gut. The rush was back too.

About half an hour into my hike three young boys carrying brand new M–16s stepped out of the trailside tangle of trees. They were wearing rebel uniforms and they seemed as scared as I was. I raised my hand and hoped they wouldn't squeeze those mean-looking triggers. In my best Ohio Spanish I said, *"Me llamo Sam Hall. Correspondiente. Necesito alguien que hable inglés."* I had been practicing those words and a couple of other sentences for days. I wasn't sure until that minute that I wouldn't goof and deliver the only line I knew for sure from years of use—*"Yo quiero un bourbon Canadian Mist con Coca Cola, por favor."* I had visions of a slip-up like that and the captain of my captors, who might have learned English as an exchange student in East London, spitting out in cold cockney, "This bloody bloke wants a bourbon and coke. Shoot the bastard."

I must have said the right thing, though, because the rebels hustled me off. An hour later we finished a two-mile walk. They introduced me to a band of about twenty rebels. I asked again to see somebody who could speak English. For my trouble a couple of rebs stripped me of everything except my shirt and socks. When one, who seemed to be in charge, grabbed my disc camera I yelled, *"Me gustaria sacar algunas fotos."* I was either going to lose my camera or my life. If Sam Hall's name had ever made their hit list it would be my life. When the guerrilla smashed the camera with his foot I was so relieved I nearly jumped on the damn thing myself.

For the next three hours they made me squat next to a corrugated steel-roofed hut that was one of the five buildings in the camp. The sun was beating down off the steel, and I was *sweating*. Fear sweat always had the special smell I smelled that day, and it reminded me of a goat I shot once at about eight-thousand feet up an Hawaiian mountain. There was hardly any vegetation and no water that high up, so the goats drank their own urine. It took six months for the mounted head of my goat to reach me in Ohio, but when it did the thing smelled so bad that for six more months it hung in the garage while it got treated with Lysol doses. Even after bringing it into the house we had to spray it every week for fear it would take over the place. During those three hours outside the rebels' hut in El Salvador Sam Hall smelled as bad as that goat. If the rebels planned on killing me they'd have to bury me twelve feet deep.

All the while I was crouching half-naked in front of the hut, soldiers were passing by in pairs talking to each other. I wished the whole time I could remember my Spanish lessons from high school. I imagined them saying anything from, "The captain has established his CIA connection" to "Look at the dingo on that gringo." I must have checked out okay, though. When the three hours that seemed like three weeks passed they gave me some water and a little rice in pita bread. Then one of the rebels showed up and gave me my underwear and pants, but I noticed he was wearing my shoes.

After a while some rebels took me to an English-speaking Cuban who seemed to be *honcho numero uno*. His first question was: "Why you no go through official clearance like other writers?" I told him I had to be back in the States in five days to make my deadline and I didn't have time for red tape. Thank God I expected that question. After a few looks the Cuban told me, "You ride with us to observe operations." Apparently he believed I was a reporter and the rebels must have wanted their side of the story told. They gave me a horse and for four days I rode with them from camp to camp on what seemed like a morale boosting tour.

All the while the Cuban honcho rode next to me on the trails he never said much, but since he took me to be a writer it was no problem wandering the camps without an escort. I made mental notes on everything I could for Red Dog. The older guerrillas had better uniforms and weapons than the government troops. Some of their M–16s were brand-new. But the younger rebels had very few uniforms and they carried antique Colt .45 automatics. Their shredded sandals told me why my shoes were such a prize. In spite of the setup and the fact they weren't organized very well they seemed to be in good spirits. And they showed a lot of gusto about their cause.

At one of the camps I found a rebel who spoke English, and we had a talk about the war. He was sure the rebels were going to win. Here's the way our exchange went:

"Our cause is just and the government is corrupt."

"Why do you take orders from the Cuban honcho?"

"The Cubans are heroes to the people of Latin America because they stand up to the United States and the other fascist countries. The rebels recognize Cuba has the best fighters and the most advanced military equipment in the Caribbean, so it's natural to accept help from them."

"But can you win the war?"

"Some day our flag will fly in Mexico City."

That night I asked the English-speaking rebel to translate the campfire conversation for me. If you could believe him, the group spent the night blasting the government and praising communism. Seemed sort of pat to me, but maybe they were putting on a show for the Cuban. Hard to tell.

The Cuban honcho had a girlfriend in every port. When we got to each new mini-garrison he would disappear inside one of the huts for an hour with a camp follower. He must have had quite an Havana cheroot burning inside his cami pants. I confess I wanted to help him out in this mission but the women didn't look like the sort to mess with; they were well-armed to fight alongside the men.

I know it sounds old-fashioned, but it bothered me to see women fighting too. Women make great doctors or lawyers or politicians or teamsters or just about anything else you can mention. Someday we'll probably have a woman president, because we've been wasting women's talents too long. But when I go into combat I don't want any women along. Not that they aren't strong enough for combat. If they can stand childbearing, they can stand just about anything. They can stand tall with their feelings too. No question.

Take for example a story I once heard about a Vietcong officer dragging a boy to his house to force his mother to identify him. The boy was caught shooting at the Cong and the mother knew if she pointed out her son her other kids would be killed. She stood without a flinch while her son was shot in front of her. The soldiers even left his body outside the woman's hut, hoping she'd come out for it. While the Cong waited in front she slipped out back and took her other children with her. She sacrificed her son for the rest of her family.

Deep strength like that proves women can be giants, but I still don't like the idea of them in combat. They shouldn't have to see a body torn to pieces. They shouldn't have to be so afraid they lose all control of their bodily functions like men do and rarely admit. They shouldn't be blasted apart by mines. I want women beside me at the office or in my arms on the dance floor or in most any other part of my life, but not in a foxhole.

During my horseback tour of the back-country with the rebels we slept on the ground. The first night I didn't get much shut-eye because I still wasn't sure they wouldn't kill me. Later I could focus on the notes for Red Dog. The rebels' food supply was really low, so we ate mostly rice and beans. I tried to joke with my hosts so they'd be more open with me. The food itself was a joke and I wondered how many rebels would have gone over to the government for a good meal. I found out the first morning of our ride that the Cuban had a little sense of humor, so I started kidding him about the food. The rebels seemed to be totally under the Cuban's thumb, so they laughed if he smiled and they roared if he laughed. As we sat around the fire one night the Cuban left his mess kit full of food while he checked the horses. My little joke was to take his beans and hide them under a bush. The rebels looked shocked and angry. I thought, What a mistake that rib-tickler was. But the Cuban came back and chuckled when he found out about my little prank, whereupon the rest of the rebels cackled like a television laugh track.

On my third day's ride we were coming down the side of a mountain in thick woods when an explosion blew me and three rebels off our horses. My first thought was that the Cuban or somebody acting on his orders had tossed a grenade at me. One of the rebels landed on top of me and two more were twisting in pain next to me. If I was supposed to be the victim, the attackers were pretty sloppy, and moreover the unhurt rebels along with the Cuban were all on the ground with rifles at the ready checking the woods for government troops. The fact that no attack followed the blast made me doubt government soldiers were to blame. The blast first hit my belt, so that most of the blow was deflected. Some small fragments were lodged against my rib cage, judging from the look and feel of the wound. Only one of the three rebels hit was really hurt with a horrible gut wound. Also one of the horses was killed by the blast and another one had to be shot.

After one of the guerrillas fixed up his gut-wounded buddy the best he could, he cut the biggest metal fragment out of my side. There was no sulfa or antiseptic, so after he drew out the bad blood with moss he packed the wound with mud and a leaf from one of the trees. Another rebel tore off a part of my shirt and wrapped my side with a tight tie. The gut-wounded guerrilla and his two nicked buddies and I were allowed to travel on horseback while two men walked until we could replace the mounts we lost. I was left to try to figure out the source of the explosion as the horses and men headed toward the next camp. The Cuban didn't volunteer any explanations and neither did anybody else. I figured the guerrillas wouldn't sacrifice some of their own men just to get at me. Arab terrorists would do something like that, but not Salvadorans. Anyway they could have just shot me any time they wanted. My best guess was that, like the government troops, they were carrying their explosives and detonating caps together and the saddle pouch on the horse next to mine probably just blew.

After a few hours rest at the next camp all of us, except the gut-wounded rebel, mounted up and headed out again. Despite the pain in my side I rode with the rebels for two more days while I sized up their strength and tactics. We didn't meet up with any government troops . . . the Cubans must have been trying to avoid them. At one point we spotted a big column of soldiers when we were coming over a rise, and the Cuban signalled his men to rein in the horses and wait for the troops to pass in front of us. These boys wanted to pick their own time and place to fight. They either didn't want me to see them in action or their plans didn't call for any during my time with them. Like rebel troops everywhere, they lived by the sneak attack followed by a quick cease-fire. That way they could figure the firepower of their enemy and either launch a second attack or fall back into the hills.

On the fifth day we came out of the mountains near the same spot where I went in. I thanked the Cuban for the chance to get my news story with about a hundred *graciases* and shook hands with the man who patched me up. As I walked to the highway I still wasn't sure I wouldn't be shot in the back before I got to the road. I breathed a very long sigh of relief when I finally flagged down a car headed toward the airport. When I got there I took my ditty bag out of storage and bought myself a t-shirt. It didn't do all that much for me. I looked like a skid-row bum with blood all over me and a week's worth of unshaved whiskers. I got a shock when I checked a mirror in the airport john and thought for a minute I was staring back at a wounded, hungover clone of Yasir Arafat. Gorgeous Sam, you bet.

I was also beginning to run a fever caused by a low-grade infection around the wound as I left to board a plane for Miami.

When we landed I immediately called Red Dog to give him a verbal summary of the full report I'd written on the plane. Then I grabbed a cab for Fort Lauderdale and stayed there for a week and a half at a hotel while a doctor visited me in my room. The mystery of the "hand grenade" that blew me off my horse at last got cleared up. The doctor took out quite a few pieces of metal that worked their way to just under the skin. When he sent them to a local lab the report told us the metal was brass. That argued against grenade fragments, but not against the kind of blasting cap used to trigger plastique. A cap must have gone off accidentally in one of the saddle bags when it was jarred on the mountain trail, just as I'd suspected.

A call from a friend in San Salvador advised me how lucky I was to have survived my visit with the rebels. Four days after I came out of the mountains a commander of the Navy Seals was killed on a street in San Salvador by terrorists connected with the rebel forces.

About a month later, and feeling better, I dropped in on Commander Fane outside Fort Lauderdale. We fell into a relaxed talk that reminded me how much he was like a father to me now. He wanted to know *all* the El Salvador details, even though he already had my long written report. He asked what I'd do next and I told him I was waiting to see my if my lawyer in Pretoria could arrange for my friends' release. In the meantime I wanted to put my thoughts down on paper—maybe in the form of a letter to my kids—and explain everything I'd been doing lately so the record would be straight if I ever got myself killed.

Red Dog thought the writing idea was a good one, but suggested that an even better idea would be to write a book. I told him I didn't have time for that and besides, all I ever knew about writing was that you had to keep your participle from dangling and your infinitive from splitting. Red Dog encouraged me to give it a try, though.

We talked on and on while the sultry summer afternoon stretched through the humid night and into the small hours of the Florida morning. We both had more to say to each other than time to say it in. I invoked John Kennedy's 1960 notion that America was the "watchguard at the gates of the world" and said, "My biggest ambition, and I hope it doesn't sound too vainglorious, is to be the best damned watchguard against terrorists." Red Dog asked, "Why do you feel so strong about terrorism, Sam?" and I answered the best I could. "Because I've had this need for a long time to give back something to this country. Kennedy said, 'For those of us to whom much is given much is required.' I believe that. I've been blessed with money and some athletic honors and a million other things and now I'm at least beginning to pay America back. I've just started to live by the Olympic creed after all those wasted years. You know that creed, Commander. 'It's not the triumph but the struggle that counts.' "

All my strongest feelings flowed out to Commander Fane. I was always leery of people who wanted to know what was going on with Sam Hall. That was none of their business. But the commander brought me out in a surprising new way. When I left for Mozambique to help rescue my four captured buddies, Red Dog started looking for somebody to write about the experiences that led to the Free Lancers.

SEVEN

THE BACK-TOGETHER Free Lancers hit Pretoria two days after Peter and the other three prisoners were sprung from Mozambique. We called Brian right away to get the lay of the land. He said, "The French have confirmation their priest is dead. The Angola mission is off." That meant our first contract was broken. We were all frustrated, but there was nothing we could do except go on about our business till Brian found another client. After we said our "so longs" we scattered.

The first day home in August a friend of mine who worked in the television business and knew of my new interest, thanks to Red Dog, in possibly writing a book called to say that two writers might be available. The best part was that I wouldn't even have to leave my hometown to work with them. They both lived in Dayton. That was a real break. I could give the kids some time while my story was getting told.

That night I called the writers to set up a meeting for the next morning. But I was nervous about the deal. My TV friend said both writers were college professors, and that might mean trouble. Somebody once said that professors live life to the limit from the neck up. I was afraid these two might not be able to relate to my story. But when we met, the good vibrations beat the Beach Boys'. The female half of the partnership was quick and bright—hell, she was one of the better marathon runners in her age group. I liked the fact that she could relate military training to the grind of her sport. Her job was to get the details of my story on tape and note cards, then put the whole thing in some kind of order to set up the flow. You sure wouldn't mind working with her if you saw her, a diminutive blond beauty. The taping sessions could be looked forward to.

Her male partner was her opposite number. He had an uneven beard that couldn't figure out whether it was supposed to be Richard Nixon's five-o'clock shadow or a Grizzly Adams soup-strainer. He was to do the writing. I felt better when I found out he once did a military hitch. He seemed to respect me and even understand my new line of work. We also hit it off because he told me the days he spent at the university using his gray matter were followed by quite a few nights of more erotic pursuits. A man of parts. He told me the one about the Oxford don who got asked where he wanted to die if he could choose. The prof shot back without missing a beat that if he had his druthers he'd give up the ghost at a faculty meeting. That way he wouldn't notice the passage from life to death. A non-academic academic. I figured I could work with this man.

Within a week the three of us were working away—and great friends, too. But that didn't make the chore of getting myself recorded on tape and paper a piece of cake, and when Red Dog called halfway through the first draft with a new assignment, I was really relieved, although my collaborators weren't thrilled about my leaving with the book unfinished. They perked up some, though, when I promised them some fresh stories—good, bad and ugly. So in late November I left them and headed south.

After a month of gray midwestern cold and cooped-up taping sessions, the steamy south Florida sun was a welcome change. Red Dog met me at the Ft. Lauderdale airport and we bounced to his house by Bronco. On the way he filled me in on his latest doings. When I was settled in I asked him what he had for me. He smiled and said, "Not yet," then launched into a long talk about terrorism. Hey, he was a walking handbook on the subject. That night as he talked a lot about ways of dealing with kidnappers, I kept wondering what my new job would be, but I knew Red Dog would only tell me in his own good time.

We talked deep into the night till he finally complained about the sleep he wasn't getting thanks to me. On his way to brush his teeth he mentioned the terrorist Carlos, and that kept the conversation going for another four hours. Carlos interested me so much by this time that he played the lead in most of my dreams. If there was only a chance to make him pay for his crimes ... especially for the massacre at the Munich Olympics. Red Dog seemed excited when I told him I might take the Free Lancers to the Middle East to hunt Carlos down if I could get a lead on him. He then gave me all he had on him. Carlos' real name was Ilich Ramirez Sanchez, a Venezuelan in his mid-thirties linked to Germany's Baader-Meinhof gang *and* Italy's Red Brigades *and* the Japanese Red Army *and* Turkey's neo-Nazi Gray Wolves *and* the PLO. By the time Red Dog finished his bio the morning sun was about ready to bake the beauties on the beach. The Commander collapsed into the sack while I went out for a walk.

Back in an hour, I found Red Dog wide awake and attending to a skilletful of egg yolks. While we destroyed the eggs we talked about how lucky we felt we were to be friends. Especially *I* felt. He treated me like a son, and that morning over breakfast he said he thought of me as a sort of young clone of himself. I felt damn flattered. Our dialogue as I remember it was something like this:

"I was always after thrills when I was your age, Sam. Life without them is pretty hollow."

"You've had a life and a half, Red Dog."

"But it was never enough. I wanted more and more of the same."

He was seventy-four now, but he was still passionate about the war against communism and terrorism. Even after three heart attacks that had left him wearing nitroglycerin patches instead of camis, he lived a fuller life than most men half his age. He seemed to understand my love of danger and my need to put together a slate of accomplishments to hand to my Maker.

"I worry about meeting God myself, Sam. I always wonder if my life's been up to his standards for us."

"I know mine hasn't measured up," I said. "It's been too much booze and drugs and waste—till the last year."

"Well, I think He'll take kindly to what you've tried to do in Israel and Africa. Not many of his people in this country do too much for their fellow man."

He saw quickly how I could fall into a slough of dashed hopes and have no outlet for the strong feelings building inside. He also could appreciate my high for the last year. We laughed over the picture of my old suburban self trapped in a gray flannel business suit and a station wagon. Then Red Dog said, "I want you to do some working out before I tell you why you're here. This afternoon I'll take you to a training site I know about in the middle of the Everglades."

As we bumped along a dirt road on the way to the site the commander told me he knew about the Free Lancers' broken Angola contract. But he couldn't tell me how he knew. He must have sources in and out of governments all over the world. But now the training he had waiting for me was at the front of my mind and his connections didn't matter. The climate in the Everglades was Africa's, so the training would help if Brian called about a new mission. And Red Dog's spot deep in the swamps was the perfect place to test myself.

For the next two days the commander was the director and I was the star, sort of, of our own Tarzan movie, swimming across lakes clogged with weeds and plowing through thick jungle and wading into stinking marshland. Red Dog was ruthless . . . a five-minute break was terminated with an "off your ass," followed by hours of running or wading and swimming. A shorter break than the last one would end with a "hit it" and a return to the mushy stuff. For added misery Red Dog would toss a couple of small TNT charges at my feet and pepper me with rocks. By dusk on the second day my camis were soaked with enough muck to dry up the Everglades. My body was bloodied. I was *beat*. One time while I was collapsed on a rotting log Red Dog screamed, "Up, you miserable fucker." Which was enough playing Tarzan for me. I grabbed the commander and wrestled him to the ground and pushed his face into the soft slime. A couple of minutes later he staggered to his feet. With a wide grin on his face he spit out, "Sam, you're ready." At first I thought he meant for the firing squad. Except he probably could have done the job himself. A very tough, and wonderful, man, never mind age.

When we got back to his place the commander told me about the investigation he was heading up and how he needed my help. He was trying to find out what caused a couple of frogmen to drop out of sight on a secret mission. He knew about my underwater diving, so he figured I'd be interested in his attempts to puzzle out what happened to the frogmen. He was sure right about that.

The next night I got to Red Dog's on schedule for a drink and found him with a second guest. Doctor Dimitri Rebikoff turned out to be a Paris-born Russian known for inventing underwater gadgets and vehicles. He used his mother's maiden name because his father was killed by a KGB assassin. During World War II the Germans kidnapped him and forced him to work on their scientific gizmos.

We spent the first night at Red Dog's talking nonstop. I asked all about his work, but he wanted to know everything about my 150 hours of dives all over the world too. It went like this:

"Since you've done so much diving, Sam, you'd probably be interested in my latest project. I'm going to try to raise the *Monitor*."

"You mean the old Civil War battle boat? You can't be serious. Boy, would I love to help you with that one."

"Well, we'll see if you can when we're ready to go."

I also thought his questions about my dives might have something to do with the commander's investigation. He promised me a trip to his lab the next morning.

True to his word, at dawn next day Dimitri, with Red Dog, showed up in front of my hotel in a panel truck and we were off to the lab, which turned out to be a waterfront warehouse crammed full of Rebikoff's toys. The one that especially caught my eye was a one-man underwater unit that looked like nothing I'd ever seen before.

"That gizmo over there is a real beauty, Dimitri. What do you call it?"

"I think it's the best thing in its class. Would you like to see how it works?"

Half an hour later I was being trained to use the 266-pound underwater machine called "Pegasus." The surface control system and navigation aids in the cockpit, plus the "dashboard" with gyro compass and artificial horizon and depth-indicator, made it perform like a dream airplane. Dimitri explained the machine could be used at a depth of 6,600 feet if remote-controlled. I was allowed to test it out in one of the laboratory's tanks.

Later that day Commander Fane and Dr. Rebikoff talked over some possible reasons why the frogmen could have disappeared. Just listening was a terrific kick. Here were the leading heads in marine technology and underwater demolition talking over their theories with a novice waterbaby.

Quite a few gin-and-tonics later, Red Dog finally let me in on the secret mission, which went like this:

"Sam, how would you like to fly down to the Bahamas with Dimitri and me?"

"Whatever you need, Commander. What will we be doing?"

"I want to find a spot where we can pretty much duplicate the conditions the night the frogmen were lost. We'll pick up another diver on the way and the two of you will try to pull off a mission to simulate the frogmen's."

"Let's give it a shot."

Red Dog got right on the phone to a diver he knew and then was calling weather stations to get a reading on conditions for the next couple of days.

Next morning I found myself buzzing over the Keys in a twin-engine Beechcraft with the Commander and Dimitri and my new diving partner, whose name was Paul Merritt. We were headed for one of the offshore islands in the Bahamas where the forecast said the right weather was waiting.

Once on the ground we loaded our gear in a pick-up and drove half a mile to the harbor and boarded a private launch. After lunch the commander let Paul and me know about the weather and the seas the night and morning of the frogmen's mission. The frogmen had been on a pre-rescue recon operation when they hit a light squall and a three-knot tradewind. Swimming against that for any distance would be like double-timing up Mt. McKinley. We'd have a strong wind for our mock-mission too, although we wouldn't be jumping in at night with paratroop gear like the frogmen.

As Red Dog gave us our assignments we went over aspects of the frogmen's mission. Their load would be heavy, including either German Draegger tanks or oxygen-rebreathing outfits. The commander produced both systems. Paul was supposed to use the Draegger and I got the rebreather. Red Dog told us the Draegger had been used in another experiment three days before. He checked it then for white powder. One explanation was that the frogmen might have been chemically poisoned, he said. If there was a residue it could have been oxides of aluminum, *supposedly* harmless but . . . which rang a bell—years before in Okinawa a buddy of mine had nearly died from exposure to oxides of aluminum.

My own rebreather used pure oxygen instead of compressed air like the aqualung. The oxygen was filtered and the carbon dioxide was cleaned after each breath and recycled back to me. The problem with the rebreather was that below thirty-three feet the pressures over twice atmospheric could poison you. The rebreather had great advantages, though. For example, no air bubbles were released, so you couldn't detect it on the surface. Along with our "skins and fins," we would also each carry a Casio shock-tested alarm chrono and 45-automatic "Hushpuppys" fitted with silencers. Plus a holstered C-Lite II—one of the world's brightest underwater lights. We each carried a packed assault rifle and a pouch of explosives.

Commander Fane would drop us in the launch's rubber dinghy

two-and-a-half miles offshore. Our job was to swim in in darkness after testing ourselves against the wind and the current. The goal was the launch where Red Dog and Dimitri would wait with our reward, which was probably enough booze to float three more boats. Before we collected we had to explode a beat-up aluminum rowboat tied 200 feet off the stern of the launch. Paul and I were supposed to attack the anchored antique before Red Dog or Dimitri spotted us. If one of them did spot us he would fire a red flare.

Paul and I would split up while commander and Dimitri were watching our floating target and, no doubt, sipping a little bourbon and branch water. Paul would put a charge under the rowboat and I'd swim bubble-free wide around the launch and tie a half-pound charge on the coral reef twenty feet behind it. When my little charge blew I could get some revenge for the Everglades where Red Dog's mini-bombs exploding at my feet had made my Tarzan performance look more like the lead in "Flashdance."

At 2030 hours that night the four of us moved out in the launch from the harbor to the far side of the island. There weren't many people around, which was good. We set a course for a spot two-and-a-half miles out to sea. When we reached it Paul and I were lowered into the rubber dinghy, where we sat waiting until 2130 hours. By our figuring we would be up against two knots of current, which would make two hours swimming with half-an-hour to set the charges.

Just after sundown we started talking about the sharks that would be swimming between us and launch. My imagination was running. It went like this:

"I'll bet these waters have some big mothers in them, Paul."

"I was down here last winter. Not more than a hundred miles away. Some of the biggest sets of teeth I ever saw."

"You're a real comfort, fella."

"Well, Sam, you look like you'd make good roughage for a big Mako."

"If I spot a big Mako tonight I won't ever need any roughage again." Nervous joke.

We weren't using any repellent and the only one you could trust anyway was a live grenade. We'd be swimming in the dark, so if Jaws was nearby at least we wouldn't see him. With luck we'd pass in the night.

At a quarter to ten we made a final check of our satchels and went over our equipment one more time. Then we spit in our masks and held a couple of thumbs up as we flipped backward over the side of the dinghy. We swam side-by-side in the direction of the island, keeping an eye out for the launch. Our plan called for us to swim with our heads above the water till the last quarter mile. Then we'd zig-zag toward the launch. The water was warm, but no bath-tub ever had such a bitch of a current. Instead of rubber duckies we had the heavy satchels in tow behind us, and the two assault rifles each didn't help. Two exhausting hours later we were treading water and eyeing our targets about fifteen hundred feet away.

We could see Red Dog and Dimitri framed by their deck light and the moon tucked behind the clouds. We were in luck. We switched to our breathing gear and dropped under the surface. If everything worked out the rowboat would be in orbit in twenty-five minutes. And Red Dog would be drenched and surprised a moment later.

My role was human torpedo, cutting toward the launch from the front. Twenty-five feet down was a spot just below the launch's bilge keel. I tied the satchel's line to a piece of coral. My charge was planted six or eight feet behind the aft of the launch to produce a tidal wave that would add sea water to Red Dog's bourbon and branch. I was enjoying myself when I heard my chrono's beep signal that Paul had started his fuse burning. All I had to do now was wait underwater. As soon as Paul's explosion sounded I pulled my tab and then swam like crazy to the port side of the launch and broke water to watch the show. Red Dog was yelling out to the spot where the rowboat just took off stage left. "Good show, you two."

Dimitri added it was a great job, that he didn't see a thing before the explosion. They didn't see me right below them either, so I yelled, "Thank you, sir," and startled them for a split second before they got the big shower from the second blast, which had the launch rolling in its wake.

Back on board, we stowed our gear and downed some rum to warm us up. Red Dog and Dimitri checked our equipment for any clues that could help solve the frogman mystery. There were different maybes, such as oxidation or lime poisoning from the tanks they were using. But those theories didn't make sense in four cases at once. The men could have been captured—that was one chance in a million. The local sharks might have got them. That could've been. My own theory was that they must not have hit their parachute pins in time, so the squall dragged them back and down and hooked them on some coral. When Red Dog and Dimitri finished checking our equipment I asked them what they thought. They just gave me the old Mona Lisa. I never got any more from them.

When we all got back to Ft. Lauderdale a message from Jack was waiting for me. It said to call Brian about a new contract right away. When I did, he told me, "It's a rescue attempt in Angola. Four nurses were kidnapped a couple of weeks ago. Everybody's waiting for the word from you." It sounded like the kind of job we were after, so I said, "Get the papers signed and I'll be there as soon as I can grab a flight."

I said my good-bys to Red Dog and Dimitri, who said they wished they could come along with me to Angola, then called my writers to let them know the rest of the taping sessions would have to wait a little longer. They were used to my leaving them by now so they just said be careful.

Twenty-one hours later at Jan Smuts International Airport in Joburg my butt was numb but my stomach was churning because I was going to see my old Free Lancer buddies again. I wasn't sure if anybody would be at the terminal to greet me, but as I walked down the rolling steps I spotted Peter and Raoul at the edge of the tarmac. Even from that distance they looked fit and restless. After the bear hugs the three of us grabbed a cab and headed for the bar where the other Free Lancers were waiting.

My curiosity got the best of me on the way and I asked Peter what he'd heard from Brian about the mission.

He said the team was to board a bus outside our hotel at 1900 hours this evening and head for a dirt airstrip just north of Warmbath where we'd be given our uniforms and test-fire our weapons. R–4s.

My ears pricked up at "R–4s." I had some experience firing that South African rifle, but this would be my first time in combat with it. It was put together like Dr. Frankenstein's monster, using the best parts from a lot of different weapons. The synthetic mischief-maker turned out to be quite a piece. It was a nine-and-a-half pound gas-operated beauty with a collapsible stock and fifty-round magazine capacity, plus a night-sight that gave you instant high noon. Not to mention the weapon's terrific durability. The R–4 could also do a lot of damage when it was linked up with the HE rocket launcher using M–26 grenades with fins. It came equipped with a bipod that could cut barbed or concertina or razor wire. There was even a bottle opener under the breach block.

Peter laid out the rest of the details: "We'll each be issued dexedrine, salt and balazone tablets. We'll take along small double-gauze bandages and burn dressings as well as morphine and syringes and an antidote for nerve gas. Our service support will be eight meals and two canteens each for water. The only other source of food will be 'on the hoof,' as you Americans say. Once our supplies and equipment are loaded into an old Dakota left over from the war in Biafra, we'll board her for a four-hour flight. Over our target at 0615 hours we jump in T–10 chutes at one hundred meters."

The low jump-point would make a reserve-chute useless. Peter reminded me that in spite of all the planning everything and anything could happen once we hit the ground in Angola. If all went well we were supposed to regroup at the north end of our landing zone and move out as a splinter group of UNITA (United Forces for Free Angola), the U.S.-backed Angolan rebels whose home base was Namibia, a country on Angola's southern border. We would be up against SWAPO terrorists too—the South West African People's Organization set on taking over South Africa. Meanwhile, it seemed to make them happy to shoot up Angola.

Peter went on to say: "UNITA command wants us to operate independently and maintain radio silence except in certain situations. If we spot MIGs or T–54 tanks or helicopter gunships we break radio silence and report in. We'll be one hundred and fifty kilometers in front of the main UNITA advance, so we run less of a risk of discovery." Peter finally got to the reason for our mission, which was why Free Lancers had gotten the job: to find and bring out the four missionary nurses who hadn't been heard from in eleven days. He pulled out a typed sheet of paper that gave the information on the nurses. They had been kidnapped from the hospital they ran in Alto Zambezi Province. Two nurses, Norah Draper and Florence Wilson, were Canadians in their thirties. The other two, Emily Roundtree and Eva Warke, were Northern Irish in their mid-fifties.

Peter pointed out that we would be doing our bit without UNITA's official sanction. The organization would disavow us if we were discovered. But they gave him specific instructions for the mission. We were to wear cami shirts and shorts and red berets so we could be spotted by UNITA aircraft. Once a day we could make radio contact with UNITA command. They could then relay our position to friendly forces in the area and tell us where to meet our Dakota on the way out. UNITA even promised a completion bonus, which was a needless incentive for getting those nurses out.

When we got to the "Zodiac" the other Free Lancers were holding our table. The three of us joined the group and we all fell into the nervous kidding that always led to more serious talk just before a mission. I asked the Bird, "Are your worms still acting up? I suppose you'll keep us up every night drowning the damn things in super unleaded." He shot back, "Those little buggers will make capital fish bait on the Zambezi. You'll think again if we run out of rations and I'm the only one who can save us with a stack of fresh filets." By now I was able to bring out the Bird in a way the others never had. He would kid with me but always pull back if I tried to get really personal.

Topper gave Raoul a hard time for losing the world combat shooting competition again to Jimmy Sorgenfeli from Durban. "I don't know if we should take you along, mate," he was saying. "It looks like you're over the hill, the way you lost to that South African." The title was always changing hands between Raoul and Sorgenfeli. We were waiting for Raoul's excuse this time, but he just smiled a fuck you with that Crest-smile of his.

When the drinks were served the subject changed to women, as it usually did sooner or later. Gordon got us started with his word-picture of his latest love. "I met her on a Blue Trine last month. She's part Swede and part Danish. Name's Sonya. She writes for the university down in Capetown. She's too bright for me but I've got to get her back in bed as soon as we get back to Angola. She's the softest and the prettiest woman I've ever met."

Roger couldn't resist giving Gordon the speech he gave most of us too many times a day. The one about finding one woman and sticking with her. "I hope this is the lady you'll settle with, mate. I was as bad as you moving from one to another for a while and I had plenty of good times, but I was never really content until Saunden." We all knew Roger was in love with his wife for keeps, but none of us ever seemed to find our own Saundens.

"We're going to build a new house as soon as I get some *rand* put away. Working toward a goal like that can really bring two people together. Saunden says. . . ."

While he stopped for a breath in the middle of his speech I actually thought about some of the things he was saying. His idea about finding one woman forever was what I wanted too. I wondered why sticking with one woman for very long was so tough. It seemed like men and women were either going in opposite directions or at best were tooling along at different speeds.

But what Roger was saying about finding the right woman made some real sense. Especially since my third wife was it for a long time and maybe still could be. I was fooling myself, though. It was over for her and I couldn't get serious about anybody and stay in my line of work. I'd have to take comfort from short flings.

When I came out of my reverie Roger was well into Part Two of his sermonette. This part was always about how we all paid too much attention to a woman's flesh and not enough to her other parts. He was telling Gordon, "At least you say Sonya's bright, but it's almost like that's a footnote. Haven't you heard physical beauty fades? You ought to know by now a body can't love you. There's a person inside who's got a spirit and feelings to explore and those are the things that make a relationship work. Saunden says...." Gordon wouldn't let him finish. "Come down out of your tower, mate. We've all seen Saunden's picture and we know she's got a hell of a lot more than a soul. Count your blessings."

Roger shrugged and gave up, but I confess I kept thinking about what he said. I knew that the best times I ever had with women were when we talked over the things we dreamed about doing and let our strongest feelings come to the surface. But getting all the way to the core of a woman would take a lifetime. Even the ones that were supposed to be shallow were pretty tough to figure sometimes. But men like Roger were able to focus on one woman and they even seemed to like the straight and narrow. That was why Dagwood had his Blondie and Archie had his Edith and even Shakespeare had his Avon lady. But I knew where Gordon was coming from too. Women were too attractive to me to be satisfied with just one. And there was no question that I had to be really turned on to a woman's face and form before I could ever begin to connect in the deep way Roger urged. He was right when he said every perfect ten was headed for a countdown. Still, all things being unequal, it was better to start subtracting from ten than three.

About the time our dinners got to the table, I asked Peter and Roger and Raoul what it was like being locked up in Mozambique.

"You guys know what to expect if we get taken. I've always wondered if I could hold up under that kind of strain."

Raoul was the first to volunteer. "Sam, you don't know from one day to the next if you'll be able to get through it. Your mind starts to play tricks on you after the first few days. You can't remember much about the time just before you were locked up. But you begin to remember things from way back. From your childhood. Things you never remembered since."

Roger added a few notes. "Raoul's right. There were times when I wished they'd kill me and get it over with. And I was so sick after a while I was afraid I'd live. All the while what kept me going were the faces of Saunden and the kids. I kept seeing them clear as day."

Then Peter brought it home. "You'd better hope it never happens, Sam. You've got the sort of makeup that wouldn't fare well in prison. Better to give yourself a round in the head."

Which pleasant note got us talking about death. Peter asked if we knew that as many as nine of the A- and B-team members from the Zimbabwe mission just a couple of months back would never fog a mirror again. Three were killed fighting with the Pathfinder company in Angola. Four were missing and presumed dead in Zaire. One died of cancer and another of alcoholism. That was a grim box score that got us all thinking about how slippery our own footing was. Roger said his friends said he had a death wish. "I just have to do what I do, I get frightened sometimes though." Topper's comment was he was too busy living to think about dying.

I believed Peter felt as I did. We had talked about death before, and he told me getting it in combat was as good a way as any, and better than a lot of others, to leave this world behind. Watching my father fall apart day after day from all his diseases had taught me that a long time before. I knew I didn't want my kids to see me like he was in those last years. On his deathbed he told us, "You and your brothers promise me you'll never lay on your backs and accept fate. Always make the effort to stand and face it." I knew I didn't have the death-wish Roger's friends accused him of having. Life was way too good to want to check out. If I had to die I at least wanted to go out like a lion not a lamb.

But before I could tell my comrades how I felt, Peter was making the same point in that well-bred British way of his. As I recall it: "The way to die flows out of the way to live. You must try to experience both with the greatest possible intensity. You can find capital prescriptions for living and dying in the great British writers. Walter Pater had the perfect formula for living. He wanted all his days to 'burn with a hard gem-like flame.' God deserves no less from us for the gift of life. When it comes to how we should die, Dylan Thomas had the last word. He warned us not to 'go gentle into that good night.' There isn't any question that I would prefer combat to a coma as my way out of this life. I want my world to end with a bang, not a whimper."

I could relate to what Peter was saying, even though I'd never read the writers he liked to quote when he talked about life and death. I felt so close to him and all my Free Lancer friends that night, I just had to lay out my own feelings in my own way. "I know where you're coming from, friend. I haven't read any of those writers you're always quoting, but they sound like they'd understand one of my heroes. He's a baseball player you might have heard of. Name is Pete Rose. I saw him play his first major league game back in the early sixties when my dad took me on one of our regular trips down to old Crosley Field in Cincinnati."

Roger knew a little about baseball from talking with Americans and he'd heard something about Pete Rose. "He's the one you Yanks call 'Charley Hustle,' isn't he?" I couldn't resist the chance to tell the group why Rose was such an example to me for so many years even though I'd always failed to measure up to him. "You could tell he was going to be one of the great ones from the very beginning. He was just a brash kid with a crew cut, but he played the game with more fire than probably anybody in the whole history of baseball, including Ty Cobb. He used every ounce of the ability God gave him and he went all out every inning of every game day after day and year after year. He's in his forties now and he's still going with every drop of energy and love he's got."

Peter understood right away why somebody like Rose would be special to me. "I know what you mean, Sam. A person like that is a constant goad to your conscience. The two of us have wasted so much of our past lives that someone like your baseball player makes us sorry for our sins and inspires us to make the most of the time we have left to us." Peter was right about that. Thanks to the Free Lancers, Commander Fane and the people he represented, I was living my life to the max now and I wanted to keep on living it that way up to the last breath. I wanted to crash into heaven the same way I pictured Pete Rose making his entrance—all out into that last home plate with a heart-first dive. Corny? So be it.

Still, I didn't know how much longer I could keep up the pace of my new life. Doing 2000 pushups a week got tougher all the time, and drawing a bead on a terrorist through bifocals told me I couldn't keep at it forever. If I didn't get killed on one of these rescue missions I'd have to find some other way soon to play out my option. When I had time to think about doing other things I always came back to the idea of signing up as a missionary when and if I got too old for fighting. That way I could keep working for people who maybe needed me in the same parts of the world.

After the waiters had cleared the table, Peter pulled out a map of Alto Zambesi. He ran through the details of the mission again. The new adventure was only a few hours away now. Peter finally broke up the meeting by asking who wanted to make a last-minute visit to one of the local knock-shops. Everybody was too keyed up for that, though, so we all headed for our hotels to wait for our zero hour.

I was on the bus waiting for my buddies ten minutes before it was time to pull out. A couple of hours later we reached the Warmbath airstrip, where Ernie and Chippy were waiting for us. We tested our weapons and checked our supplies and equipment, then grabbed a couple of hours' sleep in a small building by the runway.

At 0200 we were rousted out of bed and by 0215 we were airborne. I sat next to Peter on the four-hour plane trip to our drop zone in Angola, and the noise from the engines was so loud we needed the old closed-captions. Peter wanted to tell me about his divorce. He told me that he didn't feel for her anymore, and then he admitted that he'd numbed himself to stop the hurt. He felt safer that way. I was fine-tuned to what Peter was saying and I even knew what he was leading up to because I'd been through the same. He started blaming himself for the break-up with his wife. "Maybe if I'd tried harder I could have stayed away from the Beefeaters and left all of those cruel things unsaid. Maybe if I'd been a better father to my children I might have won her respect." A dozen more maybes followed but they didn't do a thing to change what was or to cheer him up. After Peter poured out his maybes I found myself talking about my third divorce too . . . "She tried her best to understand what I was all about, she even told me when I got my walking papers, like I said, that she knew I had to be free."

"It must truly punish a woman to love a man like you or myself, Sam. How could they ever tolerate us? Our restlessness . . ."

I thought about Janice and that last big scene between us when we split for good. Was she hurting as much as me or was she relieved to finally be getting me out of her life?

Halfway through our flight the subject changed to mercenaries and what made them tick. Peter contrasted the typical government soldier with the typical merc. The soldier, Peter pointed out, was paid and trained by his country's military. He depended on it completely. He accepted everything it gave him, its ways and beliefs and orders. I reminded Peter that his view didn't do justice to the elite units like the U.S. Army Special Forces, Rangers, Marines and Navy Seals. And Peter himself was once British SAS. He said he was talking in generalities and would except the special units. But the average soldier, even though he might be a good soldier, couldn't compare to the mercenary in morale, professionalism, independence, initiative and efficiency. The merc, he said, chose the fight that could call up his loyalty. He was usually a better fighter because he could operate a wide variety of weapons and could improvise much more creatively. He didn't rely on support like the ordinary soldier because most of the time there wasn't any support. He was able to go up against greater members of enemy with their often superior weapons. And the most attractive thing about a mercenary, he felt, was that he fought for ideals of his own making, not the assigned slogans of a particular government. Which was why mercenaries made such formidable enemies. They were dedicated, deadly and beyond influence of any kind. The morale for a standard soldier could be broken by the tyranny or incompetence of his leaders, or by the press, as during the Vietnam war. Not so the mercenary. But there was one unique problem the mercenary faced. He had to win. If he didn't win he didn't eat. He even smiled when he said that last.

We were within fifteen minutes of the point where we were supposed to make our jump. I asked Peter if he was afraid. He said there are some questions you should never ask a man. But he launched into an answer anyway. "Fear is like a whore, and because I'm a man I repeatedly go back to her. She's evil but I keep going back to her and after I've conquered her another time I feel nauseated and I shake and I say that's the finish. That's the last time. But I need her. I hate her but I need her. She makes me feel alive. I'll keep going back. And so will you, Sam, because you're just like me."

Peter was right. I've known Lady Fear all my life. I've seen her teasing me from the bottom of the Olympic pool. Felt her cold clutch in shark waters all over the world. Tasted her kiss in the booze and drugs. Heard the rustle of her skirt when I scanned my dad's heart monitor. Smelled her cordite perfume in Lebanon and Mozambique and Zimbabwe and El Salvador. Peter was right. She made me feel alive too. I loved her. I hated her. I needed her. I'd change my life if I could fall in love and stay in love. I've never liked sleeping alone. Better to be touching somebody. Being touched. Those were the joys. Being with somebody you felt good about. Somebody you didn't want to throw out of the place right after the sex. But there was never a real woman who could turn me on like Lady Fear. That's why I was crouched now in this old airplane. Tensed for our latest tryst.

EIGHT

HALF AN HOUR LATER Peter climbed over crouched bodies and reached the cabin door. We heard the order "Hook Up," stood and clipped on center line and faced the tail of the plane. Peter stuck his head out the door to check the geography. We were flying only thirty feet above the ground to avoid radar detection. Peter was satisfied with the look of the land, signaled the pilot to take us up to 350 feet.

Raoul was closest to the door. After his equipment check he stuck up a thumb. Seven other thumbs shot up one after another. Then my own signal from the back of the line. My left hand squeezed the T–10 clip. White knuckles. At last Peter gave the command go. Raoul was out the door, followed by Chippy and Topper and Roger and Gordon. Then Ernie with the RPG rocket launcher bound by a twenty-foot life line. Then Bird, yoked to four rocket tubes. I didn't realize I was out till the blast from the prop hit me. Below me I saw my big feet and then the Bird's billowed green chute. Then my own canopy popped. "Thank you, chute packer, whoever you are."

The low altitude didn't give me time to check if my chute was okay. I didn't have a reserve anyway, and the ground was coming up fast. I put my knees together and kept them bent. When I hit I did a roll while I pulled the pin and slammed my fist into the quick release. Then I shook out of the harness and headed for our form-up point.

The drop zone was in bush that was very flat, except for ant hills up to four feet high that pimpled the plain as far as you could see in the early morning light. In a few minutes the Free Lancers were grouped around Peter, listening to his last-minute talk-through. Our primary mission was to find the nurses. Our secondary mission was to detail sightings of enemy strongholds, supply depots, ammunition dumps and gun emplacements. We were expected to report on the makeup of enemy units, establish whether they were SWAPOs or FAPLAs, Blacks, Cubans, North Koreans, Bulgarians or Russians. Did they seem dull or alert? Were they young or old? What kind of protective detachments were up front and at the rear?

Raoul and Roger were carrying twenty-five pounds of C–4 plastique to take out any key rail lines or small bridges. Peter started the ritual that was second nature to us now ... "Raoul, check the rest of the team for any objects that might make sounds, make sure all metal surfaces are blackened." Peter didn't want any ID on us, but he knew we all carried a tag in one boot. Mine said B-negative Presbyterian, so some terrorist who took the time to riddle me with rounds could rush me to a bush blood bank, one that had a full-time chaplain. "... Empty pockets of anything valuable to the enemy, burn any letters or pictures or printed material." I got rid of everything except a couple of articles by French and Austrian reporters about terrorists butchering natives all over Africa. If I got killed I could at least make like a magazine rack to let the bastards know the world was catching on to them.

Our landing zone was about two hundred klicks into Angola, and our plan was simple. While the UNITA strike force was heading north we were starting south toward the Benguela railroad that divided the country. The missing nurses' Land Rover had been last seen just south of our position and headed farther in that direction. The four women might already have been killed. A Portuguese missionary priest had been found mangled a few weeks earlier near Nampula, so we thought we might find another open grave like the one in which we found the Canadian tourists in Zimbabwe.

During the day we weren't likely to meet up with the enemy. Because of the heat and the attacks of the South African Air Force, night was their time. But our mission didn't give us the luxury of holing up during the day, so we walked south in a column, Raoul on point, Peter and Chippy checking the radio for any useful news.

Two hours into our march I was sorry I was so free with my "insect dope bath" earlier in the summer morning. My forehead was a burning river of sweat and bug spray that washed into my eyes. Besides the sharp sting and the blurred vision there was the old fear-smell. Nothing that flew would dare come near me. Not even a MIG. I finally had to stop and wash out my eyes with my canteen water. A few hours later God finished the job for me. In the middle of the rainy season afternoon the skies fell in, and we were swamped. The rains surprised me, because there had been a severe drought for the past five years. But occasionally it did come down hard, and when it did you didn't move for a while. There wasn't much vegetation, so the hour-and-a-half downpour blinded us and soaked the mud and sand, bogging us down in a sea of muck. In weather like this it was better to have a horse or donkey than a Rover or halftrack.

When we got going again we started to see a lot of zebras and other big game. Peter pointed to a couple of easy-going elephants off to our left. Then Ernie spotted a fresh set of rhino tracks curving in from our right and now leading us on our own path. At dusk, just before we hunkered down for the night, I spotted a giraffe at his favorite acacia tree. The night was filled with African bush sounds that made your soul shake. If death found us on this mission, he couldn't have picked a more perfect spot for the meeting.

The next morning about ten we struck the rail line and followed it east toward Zambia. Half an hour later we found what looked to be a fairly well-travelled dirt road that crossed the railhead. Peter decided this would "bloody well make a fine ambush spot," not to mention an inviting place to rest. Raoul helped Roger pack about ten pounds of plastique under the rail line. The rest of the team got ready for any visitors.

Within half an hour we were all stretched out on the ground with rifles at the ready. The silence was complete except for the crackling now and then of the radio. To ease my nerves that made more sweat flow, I went over and over the lessons from my training. Lie still, as deep in the sand and dirt as you can get. Sink your knees further into the ground. Rest your body on your arms and legs. Pull in your ass. If and when a firefight started I would need to fling out my elbows and extend the R–4 to let its butt absorb the sudden pounding that could leave me breathless. Roll fast if I needed to roll. Crawl like a baby, not wriggle like a snake, if I had to move. Watch where the rest of the team was and shoot anything else that twitched.

About the twentieth time through the review my focus blurred. A humongous thirst told me to turn over on my side and pull my near-empty canteen out of its dirt-caked case. After I unscrewed the top, I rolled the water around in my mouth like it was vintage Paul Masson, then swallowed and let it rinse its way down my gullet. I shook the canteen and the silence told me I was in for a long dry spell until the afternoon rains hit. God would send no water before its time. (Dumb puns like that helped ease the tension a little.)

He did send our team an army of bugs to take our minds off the thirst. I tried to count the different kinds to pass the wait. There were beetles and roaches and mites and sand fleas and every kind of tick. The mosquitoes looked like Russian Backfire Bombers with swarms of fat gnats for fighter escorts. I was warned before the mission to be on the lookout for scorpions, but they must have all been scoring with each other somewhere else. I hoped when I met some they wouldn't be as big as the Sinai variety.

All of a sudden Ernie jolted me back from my day dream. "Look alive, look alive, I see dust." Peter jerked to his knees and trained his binoculars on the road to our right, then warned, "We have company. There's plenty of time. They're a distance away. I can't tell what's headed toward us. It may be the missionary's white Land Rover. Sam and Raoul, give it a bloody look from your angle."

When I got to my knees I almost went over backward from the rush I felt and my loosened leg muscles. Once my glasses were trained on the dust cloud I couldn't identify the source either. But it was coming on fast. Inside my stomach the jerky we had for breakfast was living up to its name.

Raoul weighed in, "I'm looking at three, maybe four military vehicles but I can't be sure yet." I called back, "I spot four." Then he confirmed four, and Peter said they'd be on us in no time. He told Raoul he wanted him to blow the rail line under the first vehicle while Ernie and the Bird hit the second with the rocket-launcher. If time would let them, they were to reload and take out the third vehicle. Chippy was supposed to use his grenade-launcher on the third in case Ernie and the Bird didn't get reloaded. My job was to rake the trailing set of wheels but leave it working so we could use it later.

Peter confirmed the makeup of the convoy. "I read four vehicles. In the front is a Saber with what looks like a 7.62 mounted MAG. Next is a twin MAG-mounted Saber. The third is a bloody deuce-and-a-half [two-and-a-half ton supply truck] with a mounted Soviet heavy machine gun. The last one's an AML–90 with a 7.76 mount."

Raoul double-checked Peter's reading. Peter reminded the backups to spray the turrets with semi-automatic bursts. But not the bed of the deuce-and-a-half that might be hiding our missionaries or some high explosives that could spread our own body parts along with our visitors all over the bush.

The vehicles kept coming. Every thirty seconds seemed like thirty years even though they were doing about forty mph and not suspecting a thing—we were, after all, far from the front lines. Raoul was on his back cupping the detonator in his hands. When he tripped it the explosion signalled the rest of us to get to work. I raked the windshield of the AML–90 just as the loud woosh of the Bird's rocket sounded. Chippy's grenade-launcher found the deuce-and-a-half. The gas tank on the lead vehicle blew up, and a second woosh from the Bird sent the deuce-and-a-half into a ditch next to the rail line. Chippy pulled the pin on a grenade and threw it through the windshield of the big truck. At the same time a scared soldier, who looked to be Cuban, jumped out of my armored vehicle and headed for cover. Roger cut him down before he made it. Then two Orientals in back climbed over the dead driver, who had been thrown back of the front seat. They had ideas about returning our fire just before a burst from Gordon's R–4 ended their thinking days.

All of a sudden the firing stopped. The smell of cordite filled the pall of smoke that stung our eyes and fogged our sight. One of the terrorists was framed in flames, running in circles and screaming. Raoul put him out of his misery with a short burst. The Bird was standing over three stunned Cubans lying on their stomachs with their hands clasped behind their heads. Ernie had a couple of Blacks he caught running from the bed of the deuce-and-a-half. Then there seemed to be a delayed reaction. Two or three soldiers who were being cooked in the flames of the first Saber began screaming. My mind flashed back to the burn-victims crying in the water tanks at the Dayton hospital where my father was getting physical therapy. But this was much worse. Why didn't somebody do something to stop the wailing? We were all standing still, too stunned to respond—all except the Bird. He walked up to the burning Saber with that cool calm of his, called for a grenade and pulled the pin. There was an underhand toss through a broken window. After the explosion the sobbing stopped.

Ernie started questioning the Black prisoners in Zulu. He was trying to find out if there were other enemy patrols nearby and whether they had any news about the nurses. The rest of us stockpiled the weapons and ammo from the back of the wrecked deuce-and-a-half. The caravan had to be on its way to the front with all the firepower it carried, and Peter decided that the cache was too big to let it fall back into enemy hands.

"Shall we break radio silence and get a helicopter, Raoul?"

"It might be risky, Peter. We could stir up some unfriendlies. Better take a vote."

We all voted to try to get a chopper to pick up the shiny new weapons and equipment we'd captured. In the hands of the right parties they could do heavy damage to the wrong parties.

Peter got through to a French accent who put him on OPS channel three for a clearance check. We knew this wasn't UNITA Command, but it might be a friendly force working in the area. When Frenchy asked where we were Peter would only give him coordinates for a close flyby. Peter told him he hoped we could be chums. If not, he said, our captured hardware included two 7.62 mags and a 14.5 mm that were operative and trained upward. In a few minutes we heard the familiar whap-whap whap-whap whap and spotted two unmarked Puma helicopter gunships overhead. Peter got on the horn and asked them to set down on the road just south of the railroad tracks.

When the gunships set down, two officers from each got out and headed our way while we kept them covered. They were French out of Zaire and they drooled over our booty. But they didn't want to take our prisoners with them. They were headed for a secret site and didn't want to bother hauling enemy troops. Peter told them it was all or nothing and that Command might not like to hear that the French refused to bring a captured Cuban officer back for questioning by G2. He threatened to have his team blow up the weapons if the prisoners weren't included in the deal. The French officers promptly agreed.

We all pitched in and loaded the gunships, and when we were done the Bird escorted the prisoners on-board one of the choppers while Peter talked with the pilot. Afterward Peter told us the Bird had made sure the prisoners would get back to headquarters. He borrowed one of the French pilot's wire cutters and used a wire cable to tie up the captured Blacks and Cubans in the copter's cargo-bay. They were in a circle around the prize Russian heavy machine guns we'd inherited. The Bird ran the wire through the machine gun trigger housings and the pin circles on three grenades. He kept the wire cutters so the French couldn't disentangle the weapons and the prisoners in mid-flight without blowing themselves out of the air.

After the gunships lifted off, Raoul and Roger put a one-pound charge under the engines of each turned-over vehicle and blew them all sky-high. Not all the king's men or even Mr. Goodwrench could put those suckers back together again. When the parts were scattered we loaded our gear and ourselves into the AML–90. We knew the smoke signals still puffing up from the other vehicles would lead another enemy unit to us if we didn't make tracks. Besides that, the aroma from the burning bodies had us gagging. The rains were due any minute, so fast as we could, we started rolling south cross-country to continue the search for the nurses.

Half an hour later the rains hit. For two more hours we huddled under our ponchos, watching God fill our canteens to the brim. When the rain slacked off and the ground dried we dropped our water-purification tablets into our canteens and boarded our battle bus. Ernie and Chippy sat on the fenders, using the tracking talent God gave them. But we had no real plan beyond driving in a wide arc and hoping we'd be lucky enough to pick up the nurses' trail. There were no radio transmissions coming through to help us. Three hours into our search the AML–90 coughed to a halt. The Bird wired a grenade to the carburetor to make sure it made the KIA list. When night came on we made camp without a fire and set up a watch.

The next morning we did calisthenics to work out the stiffness, then slurped down some canned peaches and headed south on foot. Two hours hard walking later we'd still had no luck. Peter decided to break radio silence again to try for some friendly with information, and just before noon a squeaky voice that called itself Med-Vac Blue answered his calls. When Med-Vac Blue switched to our channel three we figured they were friendly, but Peter wasn't taking any chances. He asked them for a positive ID, and while he was trying to get it Raoul guessed who "Med-Vac Blue" was. "They're probably one of the units of the 'Flying Doctors' out of Lesotho, a band of South African medics who volunteer their time and skills by flying into combat areas to perform surgery." Raoul thought it was one of the South African ideas that might help lead that country back into the United Nations. And some respect in the world, in spite of the hated apartheid.

In a few minutes Peter double-checked Med-Vac's ID by making them give him the nickname of "Moeketsi." He was their driver-bodyguard. The Med-Vac radioman said he had heard Peter's chit-chat with the French choppers the day before and checked with UNITA Command in Namibia for us. There wasn't any word on the nurses. But Command did pass on the information to Med-Vac that SWAPO or FALPA (Angolan Army) forces were in our neck of the woods with nineteen native kids stolen two days earlier from Botswana. The radioman said he informed UNITA's 32nd South African Battalion about the kidnapping. They were tied down in heavy fighting near Kaokoland, and besides, the "5 by 5" he was hearing from our transmission meant we were a lot closer to the terrorists than the 32nd anyway. Probably a flew klicks northeast of them.

Peter put Med-Vac on hold and called us all over for a huddle. He wanted to change our direction a little, to help our chances of picking up the trail of the kids and the terrorists. But he wanted our feedback too, because we'd be putting our lives in the line for a mission we hadn't planned on. Also, medical help would be unlikely since Med-Vac said the fighting at the front was fierce.

We didn't want to give up on the nurses, but we were all for going after the kids. Especially Chippy and Ernie, who had a special hate for terrorists who snatched innocent children to use as hostage-shields in combat. That happened all the time in Africa.

Finally Peter went through the motions with me. He reminded me that Free Lancers was my idea, and did I really want to look for those children? I told him it was a question that answered itself.

"We may not be able to locate them, and what about the nurses?"

"We might stumble onto the nurses too. What are we waiting for?"

Peter got back on the air to ask more about who made the snatch of the kids. He wanted to know how they were traveling, as well as their last known coordinates and the general direction they were heading. Med-Vac told Peter information was sketchy but it looked like four squads of SWAPOs in desert camis took them. They'd been last seen twenty hours ago headed in our direction.

After Peter got off the radio we all grouped around him for a think session and to check our maps. We decided to make a sweep to the southeast, with Ernie and Chippy on point, Raoul and myself on the flanks. Peter would walk in the center of the formation and we'd keep a hundred yards between each team member.

We walked that way the rest of the day but didn't find any trace of the terrorists or the kids. At dusk we camped, and I pulled the first three-hour watch with Roger. The guard-duty suited me fine, gave me a chance to relax after a day spent behind enemy lines expecting to be spotted by Russian MIGs or T–54 tanks. Roger stood and then sat back-to-back with me, talking in whispers about our own families. The Botswana kids' trouble naturally made us think about them. Roger was going to be thirty soon. He was one of the few Free Lancers still married and was like a kid brother to me by now. I guess I felt something special for him because he was the one team member I'd recruited myself; the rest came in a package along with Peter.

Roger had a ten-year-old boy and an eight-year-old girl back in Durban, and they were both musical wizards. He couldn't explain why, because he was tone deaf and so was his wife. For two hours he matched my bragging about my three with tales about his Robin and Eliza. Then he told me how much he loved his wife Saunden. I knew from her pictures that she was a beauty, but that night in the African bush Roger went on and on about her soul. He wondered how she put up with his job. He said the worst times she ever had were those weeks when he was locked up with Peter and the others in Mozambique. He also thought maybe his need for the Free Lancers was related to some deep guilt about the racial situation in South Africa, that perhaps if we could rescue these children he might be able to face himself. "It's strange, Sam," he said. "I don't lack the balls for combat but I've never had the courage to stand up against apartheid."

I told him I thought I understood where he was coming from. Martin Luther King and those marchers of his needed as much guts as any soldier, maybe more, I said.

"I'd like to stand with the whites who want to overthrow the system someday. I very much respect the few who speak out."

I told him that was a fight I'd be glad to join him in. I also told Roger I could relate to guilt as motivation. For me it was the waste of so many of my years . . . When we roused Topper and Gordon for relief I was sorry our watch had ended. All the team members were closer to me than my own brothers by now. We needed each other in ways few others did. I went to sleep that night feeling better than I had in a long time.

Raoul and the Bird woke us up at dawn, and after a little canned fruit we moved out, heading southeast. Three hours into our trek Ernie, on point, jerked up his arm and waved us to form on him. When we reached him, breathless, he pointed to the trail he'd found. Plenty of deep heel-and-toe marks made by military boots and small bare feet. They looked to be just a couple of hours old.

Ernie and Chippy stripped to their underwear without being told, grabbed their R–4s and took off on the run in the direction the tracks led. The rest of us moved out at a fast walk, and the tension started to build. Following the clear spoor was like tracing a herd of buffalo and their calves moving through the spring snow.

But later we were wondering how far Ernie and Chippy could run. There'd been no sign of them since they'd set sail, bent over and following the tracks. I couldn't run three hundred yards at a half crouch, but they'd already been gone two hours.

I noted over my shoulder that the clouds hadn't formed yet, which meant we had three hours or more before the rain washed out the spoor. Peter checked the sky too, then said, "Ernie and Chippy must be two hours ahead. We need to pick up the pace to close up the distance before the downpour."

He took off on the run, paralleling Ernie's spoor. We all followed, but twenty minutes later we dropped, exhausted. A five-minute break perked us up, and we were off again. The Bible line, "Thou shalt walk and not faint" came to me, but there was no verse about running with combat gear. I prayed for Jesus to help me keep up with Peter, who was flying along at a killing pace. Then I started cursing him for showing me up.

Another short rest. Just enough time to ask Peter to give a forty-six-year-old a break. We were off again. Now he was setting an even faster pace. I was breathing so hard I couldn't mouth the curses I was wishing on the limey bastard. I thought he must have read my mind because all of a sudden he slowed up, and then I saw Chippy up ahead with a small form at his feet. It was the body of a child.

We all grouped around Chippy, who still stood over the Black boy of four or five. The boy's head had been bashed in by the bloody rock lying next to him in the spoor. His leg was badly cut, too, which slowed the main party down and was probably why he'd been killed. Chippy didn't say a word, just knelt there and rubbed the dead boy's cheek. Then he too a swig from Raoul's canteen and took off on a dead run to catch up with Ernie. None of us said a word, but Peter understood we had to unleash our feelings—our pent-up hate could make us foolish. The Bird's eyes were flaming. We all knew he was ready to swoop for some SWAPO meat, but Peter sensibly told us, "Remember, we need to control our wits, we're probably close."

We piled some rocks on the boy's body, and just as we were about to start after Chippy he came running back to us with a message from Ernie. "The terrorists are less than half an hour ahead now and they'll be stopping soon because the rains are coming." Chippy put his camis on and we all walked at a good clip toward a meeting with Ernie.

Fifteen minutes later we heard what sounded like a tornado, and Peter called out, "Look alive, zebra, zebra." The SWAPO squads must have stirred a herd in front of us—about a thousand head that seemed like five million were headed straight for us.

Everybody but the Bird dove for the nearest rock while that incredibly fearless bastard just stood there daring the zebras to run him down. When they were no more than fifty yards from him he picked off the three leaders with his R–4. The sound made by the rifle was completely drowned out by the thunder of the zebras' hooves as the herd abruptly changed direction and passed off to our right. When our way was clear again the Bird grumbled, "God-damn it to hell, those striped sons-of-bitches will wipe out the spoor." But Chippy said, "The herd's passing between us and Ernie. When we find him, he'll know where the kids are."

We took off on the run again, knowing we had only a few minutes before the afternoon downpour and wanting to link up with Ernie quickly. Ten minutes later we still hadn't reached him and the rain hit. Again we huddled under our ponchos, wondering where or if we'd ever see Ernie again.

Once the rain let up Chippy ignored the slippery footing and set out to look for Ernie. We followed as fast as we could, trying to surprise the enemy force by slip-sliding our way through the sea of mud. Up ahead was the end of the clearing we were crossing and the beginning of a huge kopje that in the misty gloom looked like a castle. Then, all of a sudden, Ernie and Chippy were running back toward us waving their arms.

Which meant the enemy was on the kopje. Our Black buddies were probably framed in their gunsights. I was praying they could cross the two hundred yards between us without any trouble, but halfway home, with Chippy in the lead, the firing from the kopje started. Just as Ernie opened his mouth to yell something, he was pitched forward on his face like he was punched by a big fist.

Chippy ran back to drag him behind a small rock while the rest of us opened up on the kopje. Peter broke the team into two groups and told us to circle the kopje from a safe distance. There was pretty good forest cover. Then Peter and I got to Chippy. The three of us managed to get Ernie behind a bigger rock. He had a shoulder wound, but at least the blood flow was stopping. He told us the captured kids weren't on the kopje. The main terrorist group had split with them. Only eight men were left behind as a stopper force to face anybody who might be following.

Peter told Chippy to skirt the kopje and tail the main force while we took out the squad above us. Roger and I were to work our way around to one side while Raoul and Bird took the other side.

The kopje was flat on top, without much cover or room to dodge grenades. The terrorists firing in our direction thought they had us pinned down, but in the half light they couldn't really see where we were moving. They also didn't know we had launchers.

The plan called for Roger and me to lob two grenades from one side of the kopje, while Raoul and the Bird sent them two more from the other side. Peter told us to be sure not to overshoot or we'd have to abort the mission for a Free Lancer funeral. If the terrorists decided to pull up stakes under our barrage they'd run right into Peter, Topper and Gordon's R–4s. Everybody had twenty minutes to dodge the SWAPOs fairly aimless but steady fire and set up our party. We were ready in ten, and when Peter's shot signaled us to open up, we plopped the four grenades right on target.

There followed a series of blasts and rock fragments were flying everywhere. Then Roger yelled, "Two running our way." Before I could fire he hit them himself with two short bursts from his R–4. Their flung-out arms closed as if they were hugging the rounds that knocked them head over heels.

Then everything went quiet and we picked our cautious way up to the top of the kopje to check the damage. The Bird took the IDs off the dead and switched them around when he put them back. Only one terrorist was alive, lying on the ground, dazed from a grazed head. When the Bird got to him he took out his knife and sliced both the man's Achilles tendons to keep him from getting back to his buddies. Horrible but effective. Raoul and Roger broke the captured weapons against a rock.

When Peter was satisfied we took off to find Chippy. His spoor was running next to the terrorists'. We were going full stride when we spotted another child's body ahead. When we stopped the Bird knelt down and touched the one cheek the boy had left. One side of his head and his jaw were missing. The Bird picked up the dead boy and put him under a big tree. We didn't have time to cover his body with rocks, we had to keep running alongside the spoor. While I ran I literally prayed for the strength to get to the SWAPOs before any more of the children lost their lives. Somebody had to pay for this, and as though hearing my silent thought, Raoul called back, "They will pay." Just about then we came out of the canopy of trees onto the open plains and stopped for a short break before what we hoped would be a final run for the terrorists.

Peter asked me if I would take the point. I was too tired to do anything but nod my head, and after a two-minute rest we took off again. I didn't have any trouble picking out Chippy's spoor. We couldn't be far behind him, I decided. And twenty minutes later I spotted him running back toward us out of some high elephant grass, his body drenched in shiny sweat mingled with blood from brush- and rock-cuts and scrapes.

When he got to us he caught his breath and told us, "They're on the other side of the grass, not making good time on account of the children . . . There's a long deep dent in the earth up ahead of them that will make an ambush if we can get to it . . . If we keep up a good pace we might be able to get in front of them but we have to hurry, not much time before we lose daylight."

Nobody said a word but we all started running through the tall grass behind Chippy. My adrenaline was again so high I didn't even feel tired now. Some of those kids were still alive and close by, which made me feel super-alive myself. The Bird was flying high too, despite the weight of the two rockets we had left. Even Ernie with his shoulder wound was keeping up with the killing pace. The death of those two kids was spurring us all on.

Every few minutes Chippy would run up a small rise and check on the location of the SWAPOs to see how far we needed to go to set up the ambush. Finally he motioned us off to the right and to slow down. We were going to pass the SWAPO party. When we came up next to them in the tall grass about fifty yards away we couldn't see them but we could hear them talking and some of the kids crying. Pretty soon their voices were behind us. We kept running at full speed until ten minutes later when Chippy spotted the ditch off to our right. It looked to be right in the terrorists' line of march, so we veered off at a forty-five degree angle and ran straight into it.

Within two minutes Peter had us in position to spring our ambush. He reminded us to place our shots as accurately as possible to avoid hitting the children and to take off those red berets. As we peered over the lip of the ditch I remember thinking to myself our position was too easy, almost like sitting in a duck-blind. I was wrong. Just as the terrorists were coming within range, there was a commotion at the rear of the group . . . one of the terrorists had pulled a screaming boy from out of the pack and thrown him in the mud and kicked him. When he stepped on the boy's back and pulled his revolver out of his holster Chippy let out a yell on my right and Raoul fired at the same instant. I watched the man's head implode and then the little boy, bloodstained, was up and running in our direction. By now everybody else was firing. Ernie and Chippy were yelling in Sindebele (the language of the Matabela tribe) that the children should drop flat, but the noise was too much, and all of a sudden the rest of them started running toward us. Ernie and Chippy stood up, still trying to tell the kids to hit the dirt but they still couldn't hear—and Chippy took a round and fell back into the ditch.

We stopped firing then out of fear of hitting the kids. The terrorists didn't stop, kept raking our position through the fleeing wave of kids and a seven- or eight-year-old boy was hit in the spinal cord and the neck bone. He fell like a rock. Raoul jumped out of the ditch and ran toward him, but a round ripped his chest, driving him backward into the mud. And then Peter was out of the ditch. I ran after him with the Bird beside me, the three of us with the same idea—drop on top of the kids. I felt like I was running in slow motion. I remember thinking my number, as they say, was probably up and just hoped I wouldn't get it in the stomach. And then I stopped thinking, because only a few feet from the kids it was *Peter* who dropped from a gut shot. Peter down, God . . . no more time for shock as a bullet slammed into the breech of my weapon and buckled the loading handle for the slide, deflected and lodged in my right cheek bone. A second round went through my neck, a third through my shoulder. My legs had gone to rubber from the sharp pain, and it was down for the count just as I reached two of the kids.

I couldn't have been out more than a minute when I was brought back by something moving under my chest. It turned out to be one of the kids. Then something else moved under my legs, and there was another one there, but my numbness was losing to an awful pain. I didn't have the strength to look up at the faces of the team members, but I could see the empty shell-casings spraying from their breeches. I heard the old woosh of the Bird's rocket-launcher and the explosion of grenades. The cordite stung my eyes. There was a lot of blood. I just hoped it wasn't the kids'. There were hundreds of metallic blue flies all over me. They were sucking my blood, but my head was still swimming and my face was beginning to throb. I couldn't hear out of my right ear or see out of that eye, but the Bird was yelling something, trying to get me and the kids into the ditch.

I must have passed out again, because the next time I opened my eyes I was lying on my back in the ditch and Gordon was dressing my cheek and neck and shoulder. Some firing was going on behind us and my vision was getting better. My hearing was almost back to normal except for a steady ring. I asked the Bird, crouched next to me, how bad we were hurting. It was a dismal report: "Raoul's dead, Peter's got a bad gut wound, Ernie's shoulder's still bad and now he's got a hole in his hand too and Chippy's arm and rib cage are ripped and Topper's woozy from a head wound."

Remarkably, the Bird himself looked almost none the worse for wear. He started to help me up, but I noticed that something seemed to be wrong with my left hand. It was then that I realized a little girl was holding it. A large group of other kids was huddled in the ditch, where a little boy was actually playing with my canteen. He had a hole from a round through his right calf, but that was patched up now and he seemed in good spirits. At least he was free of the terrorists. When I got my sea legs back I moved over to the lip of the ditch to check things out, the little girl trying to go with me till the Bird grabbed her back.

The view I had showed about ten terrorists and the seven- or eight-year-old boy sprawled in grotesque positions. Gordon was keeping the live terrorists pinned down with a burst every few minutes. Some sporadic return-fire was coming from behind a couple of rocks. In the gloom of the dusk the orange tracers from Gordon's weapon crossed the terrorists' green ones. I couldn't tell how many of them were left untouched or wounded behind the rocks, but my guess was they would pull back as soon as it got dark. I planned to do the same when we were able to move.

Bird told me to take a look at Peter, that his teeth were clenched in pain and his gut looked terrible. When I got over to him I didn't think he could make it. He didn't think so either. We would have to carry him out. There was no way we could call for medical support until the next morning, at the earliest. I asked him stupidly how bad it was, and he just said between his spasms, "Sam, don't bury me in this godforsaken country unless you have to . . ." I promised I'd get him back home, somehow, then injected a cc of morphine into his thigh. I tried to blank out the reality of it. Peter down. Peter . . .

I called the Bird over and asked him to make a check of our ammo supply. Roger volunteered to get a litter ready for our trek. I went back to the lip. Topper was directing some short bursts to keep the enemy's heads down. He was Raoul's best friend among the Free Lancers, so I asked him if he wanted to bury Raoul. He said it would take him thirty minutes, and he would say a prayer. Gordon took over his position. The Bird had thirteen children bandaged and attacking our rations in a way that said they hadn't eaten for days. Everywhere I went in my pain, then numbness, then pain, my little girl friend followed me. The little boy, who turned out to be her brother, was still playing with my canteen and he still wasn't complaining about his calf wound.

When Topper got back from burying Raoul it was almost dark. Roger brought the litter he had made out of Peter's poncho, and I called a meeting around Gordon so he could hear while he kept the enemy pinned down. I told them, "We'll move out in thirty minutes if we get decent cloud cover. Ernie will be on point heading for home. We'll follow on a one-hour forced march, then bed down for the night. Gordon and Roger will carry Peter's litter. I'll carry the boy who's got my canteen. Bird you carry that little girl. She's only got a couple of scratches from rock fragments but she's too scared and weak to walk. Chippy, you cover our rear." I'd taken over, at least for the moment, without even thinking about it, and the rest seemed to accept it, maybe because they knew how close Peter and I were . . .

Ten minutes before we started out I checked on Peter again, found him conscious but moaning in pain. I knelt next to him and broke open another ampoule of morphine. Before I gave him the shot I asked him if he wanted to tell me anything. I didn't know what the hell else to say. He just said, "Take good care of the men and those kids. And you were right all long, I still love the bitch . . .Oh, God, Sam. It hurts. Oh sweet Jesus it hurts . . ."

I held his hand and said a prayer before I jammed home the needle.

Gordon made sure each of the kids got an antibiotic and a salt tablet. Then Bird came over and asked if we could use the grenade-launchers to give our friends beyond the ditch a curtain call.

I asked if he was sure there weren't any more kids over there, and he said yes, he'd accounted for all of them during the firefight.

"Let's get those bastards."

That sounded like a good idea, even though we might need the grenades later. Our last chance to make sure we got them might be the grenade-launchers. While the orange-and-green tracers kept passing in the dusk Bird and Roger and Chippy each took a launcher and aimed for left, center and right of the terrorists' position.

Just as I was about to give the order to fire, Peter started moaning and reciting, "Hail Mary, full of grace, blessed among women." I tried not to look at the dark blood and the collection of bugs trying to get through his soaked gauzes. It was too soon to give him another shot, so I forced myself to try to ignore his moaning. My mind flashed back to nights in the past when I would sneak into the garage while my wife and kids were watching TV and shoot some Demerol into my tricep to ease what I thought were my big problems. What an asshole. But now, looking down at Peter's face, I considered for a moment my new turned-around life . . . here I was, *leading* seven of the best men I'd ever known. With Raoul dead and Peter so badly wounded, the Free Lancers were looking to me for their orders. Quite a switch for a former junkie. I couldn't let them see how scared and unsure I really felt. If I hesitated it would be goodby respect. That was the quickest way to lose control.

I turned away from Peter's litter and checked with Bird and Chippy and Roger. They had their launchers ready. I gave the order to fire. When they did, the explosions sounded like D-day. All hell broke loose, and there were some frankly gratifying screams from the terrorists.

Then silence.

Five minutes later we headed for home, Ernie on point, Gordon and Roger carrying Peter's litter. The rest of us herded or carried our thirteen adopted kids, with Chippy bringing up the rear, walking alongside two beautiful little girls. The going was tough but some moonlight helped us see where we were. My shoulder woke up and felt like it was on fire, but at least I could walk all right. After a few short breaks Ernie picked out a spot under an acacia tree to bed down for the night. Everybody helped feed the kids and dress their wounds. One little boy couldn't stop crying, but Ernie

finally got him settled down with a couple of stories about a small
child who grew up to be a great tribal chieftain. As for my two
little wards, they just sat and stared at me without giving me any
clue they were going to sleep. If I didn't make it through this
mission I wanted to love them like my own David and Samantha
and Kelly, who might never be with me again. I tried smiles and
hugs to reach the little girl and boy, who of course had no idea
what they did for me, making me forget some of my own pain.
And not just the pain in the shoulder. I pulled them as close to me
as my shoulder would let me and looked at their faces, which
already knew more trouble than most luckier people do in a lifetime. There wasn't much doubt their parents were dead. The terrorists in Africa usually saw to that before they grabbed kids like
these.

When Ernie came by I asked him to find out their names. it
turned out the boy was five-and-a-half and his English name was
Cedric. His little sister was two-and-a-half and hers was Penelope.
But Ernie found out she wanted "Morano" to call her "Dineo."
When I asked Ernie who Morano was he said, "That's you. 'Morano' means chief." I told Ernie I liked my new name. Then he
added with a pearly smile, "It means black chief." "Right on, bro,"
I said, trying to smile, and set out to teach the kids how to say
"right on, bro," but when they tried it kept coming out "ret on
brew." As I looked around the camp I saw the Free Lancers were
doing everything they could to make the kids comfortable, including Bird, washing a little girl's face.

When I checked on Peter he seemed to be deep in a coma. And I
was thankful for that. I gave him another shot in case he could still
feel pain, and forced myself to face the unthinkable, that he might
not make it through the night . . . I pulled off my gear and spread
my mosquito netting and poncho so the kids could be wrapped next
to me for the night, and the three of us lay on our sides in an
S-formation, with Cedric holding onto my back and Dineo in my
arms.

Three hours later Roger poked me awake for my watch, but I

had to walk around a while to take some of the soreness out of my neck and shoulder. Fortunately the pain had lessened, but when I checked on Peter he was awake and moaning again. He asked for some water and another shot. I plunged the needle into his bicep once more and held his hand while I waited for the drug to take effect. He dropped off and I heard myself saying a silent goodby.

At the end of my watch I returned to my canvas and net-womb for a few more hours of sleep with Cedric and Dineo.

When the sun came up and somebody shook me it felt like my whole body was lying under a lead weight. There was a terrific soreness all over and my wits were very slow coming back. When my eyes finally opened there was a shadow of a small person next to me, and for a couple of minutes I thought I was back in Ohio battling drugs with my daughter's hallucinated helping shadow. But the searing pain and soreness set me straight. When I did manage to sit up I found out that Dineo was the owner of the shadow. Cedric was sitting next to her, pretending to drink from the can-teen. I couldn't actually see Dineo herself for a few minutes, then I twisted my creaking body around and found her kneeling just be-hind me with a big rock in her hand. I put my own hand down to help myself to my feet and found the reason for the rock. An inch from the spot where my head had been a few seconds before there were two smashed scorpions. Sometime during the morning they must have been making their way toward my blood-soaked ban-dages when Dineo did them in. I hugged her the best I could with the soreness. Cedric promptly crawled over when he saw his sister getting some attention, grabbed my sore shoulder to get inside my arms with Dineo, and the mixed joy and pain were almost too much to handle.

After breakfast of canned pears we got the kids ready to travel, and I checked on Peter and thanked God he was unconscious. We then all moved out, with Ernie and Chippy on point.

Within two hours a blistering sun was baking the flat land. I wasn't able to raise anybody on the radio so I kept checking for damage but couldn't find any. I wanted to contact some friendlies who could evacuate Peter and the injured kids. According to the map, we were still about thirteen hours from safe territory.

Peter let loose with a soul-wrenching scream when we stopped at noon. I ran over to his litter. He was only an hour from his last shot, but the morphine was starting to lose its effect. He was twisting in blood and soaked with sweat. The flies were eating at him and the morphine supply was down to a couple of shots. I gave him another one anyway.

I realized the chances of raising some help were slim . . . we were still without any radio contact and we seemed to be the only humans in that flat, treeless part of Africa. We walked on for another forty-five minutes until the rains hit and this time two house guests joined me under my poncho—Cedric and Dineo, who sat in front of me in the sled-positions my kids used to take on snowy days back home. I spent the rain-soaked afternoon thinking about those days, wondered what my own kids might be doing at this very minute. Cedric broke my mood when he started crying. His calf was hurting him. I did what I could for it and tried to explain to him that he needed to stay off it as much as he could. Ernie noticed my pantomime and talked to him in his dialect.

Finally the rain stopped, the afternoon sun started to harden the mud and I got back on the radio. No audience. Then with Cedric on my back and Dineo holding my hand, we followed Ernie and Chippy trying to lead us to safety. As I looked back at the litter, I prayed God would take Peter soon to end his suffering. He was screaming now each time Roger or the Bird slipped or even stepped into a dent in the earth. I gave him the last of the morphine and he quieted down, but I didn't know for how long. Again I tried the radio and this time actually picked up some conversation, but still nobody was hearing me.

At sunset I called a meeting and told the group, "Since it looks like we'll get a clear night and a bright moon we should keep going—cover as much ground as we can before we run out of luck and stumble on some unfriendlies." Peter was moaning, and all agreed to push on. Our food was almost gone by now, so only the kids ate that night. After they were fed and their wounds were redressed we started out again. We'd have to be careful. We knew the terrorists moved mostly at night to stay away from South African search planes.

About one in the morning we were taing a break in some high elephant grass, with Ernie detailed to stand guard while the rest of us set up a temporary camp. Just as we were ready to crawl under the ponchos for some shut-eye Ernie came running with some bad news. We had company. A small caravan of vehicles was headed in our direction and there was no chance they could be friendly, so Ernie used his best dialect to keep the kids quiet and Roger had to tie a bandanna gag over Peter's mouth to muffle his moaning. We all then moved back further into the elephant grass to assess the situation.

If the caravan was small enough we could ambush it and drive a couple of wheels across the border into Namibia. I walked to the edge of the grass and looked about a mile-and-a-half across the bush where two sets of headlights were pointed straight at us. We had a few minutes to set up. The vehicles would pass right in front of us from our right to our left. I wanted the Bird next to me with his launcher and the one rocket we had left. The lead vehicle would make a tough night-shot if I decided to let the Bird go for it. My other men were deployed to my left at fifty-foot gaps. Big terrorist convoys were known to travel with only the lead vehicles' headlamps lighting the land ahead. It was common for an armored car with a mounted machine gun to trail a night caravan without using its lights. Should the Bird blast the front of the convoy as soon as the second vehicle's lights came within range? The men on the left could open up as soon as they heard the woosh of the rocket-launcher. I told the Bird I would give him the signal only after I checked for gunships bringing up the rear. If we hadn't had the children the choice would have been simple—take out the convoy. That would give Peter the slight chance that we wanted for him to make it. But we couldn't risk a firefight that would put Cedric and Dineo, not to mention the other kids, in serious danger.

As the convoy got closer the Bird was telling me to go for it, to scrub the firefight for the kids' sake was to give up Peter's life. But there was no more morphine, and he might not live through the day even if we managed to grab a vehicle... Now the first one was passing in front of us at about thirty miles per hour. Then another. They were both Sabers with machine guns mounted up-front. I put my hand on the Bird's shoulder, which was the signal to fire, felt his muscles tighten. But just as he was about to squeeze the trigger I looked to the right and saw another vehicle. I couldn't make it out clearly because I was still a little blinded from looking into the headlights of the two Sabers...

With the roar of the engines in our ears I yelled for the Bird to abort the attack. When the third vehicle passed, we all fell back in the tall grass. The Bird lay down beside me while the other men left their places to join up with us. Nobody said anything. We all knew we'd just signed Peter's toe-tag. But there was nothing any of us could do and still be sure the kids would be safe.

We headed back to Peter and the kids. I went over to the litter and took out Peter's gag. I looked down at what was left of him and listened to his weak moaning and sterterous breathing. "I'm sorry, friend. I played God with your life." When I turned to the kids my misdirected rage boiled over at them, to my shame... "You goddamn little fucks, I just killed my best friend because of you." Not surprisingly they looked scared, and Cedric started crying. I managed to control myself enough to kneel down and put my good arm around both of them while my own spasms shook my body. Control has its limits.

We made camp then and tried to get some sleep. In my case exhaustion took me deep into the escape of blackness until a bright sun woke me the next morning. As I rubbed the sleep from my eyes I heard a sudden hideous cry—shrieks of some sort of laughter rising and falling. I wondered if I was hallucinating. I stood up quickly, flinching from the pain, and looked over at Roger, who simply said, "Hyenas." They were making a racket out on the plains. There were no human sounds. Roger pointed silently to my

left, where the Bird was sitting with his head in his hands next to
Peter's litter. The Bird didn't look up when I bent down and flattened my palm against Peter's chest, hoping to feel a beat or a
flutter or a throb. I felt only damp sweat and blood. I used my
bandanna to flick away the flies, then draped the cloth over his
head.

Tears were now streaming down the Bird's face. The fierce Bird.
I never thought I'd live to see that. "There won't ever be another
one to take his place, he was the most man I ever met," Bird was
saying. I swore to myself there in the light of the bush morning to
visit Peter's ex-wife and children back in England to tell them
about what he'd achieved and the love he told me he had for them.

In the late afternoon, before the rains hit, we crossed over into
the free state of Namibia. Right over the frontier Ernie pointed out
a beautiful shaded spot near a small stream. In the afternoon gloom
we buried Peter under some big rocks. We were finishing up when
the rains came, and I sat with Cedric and Dineo under the poncho,
staring at Peter's makeshift grave.

When the sun came out and dried the mud we said our last
good-bys to Peter and were on our way. Just before nightfall I
raised UNITA Command on the radio and they directed us to an
open spot of bush two hours further on. When we finally got there
the Dakota and a bus from a Catholic mission were waiting for us,
along with Med-Vac and a representative of the International Red
Cross. The doctors shot us full of pencillin and we even got our
wounds patched up without showing our Blue Cross cards.

To tell the truth, in spite of everything, we were damn glad to be
alive, and even a little proud of what we managed to do. Not even
Peter's death could spoil that feeling and I tried to remind myself
how happy he'd been on his last few missions. For both of us, it
was more than most people got in a lifetime.

Roger lined up the kids to board the parked bus and we said our
good-bys to all of them. The men wanted to see that each one had a
couple of souvenirs to remember us by. I gave Dineo my red beret

and Cedric got my knife and canteen. After one last painful pull into my arms, I held them for several minutes. When they boarded the bus I knew I'd always be wondering how my two very special kids were doing.

The Free Lancers then boarded the Dakota for the flight to South Africa. As we lifted off the bush I leaned my forehead against a window and let the glass cool it. I took one last look at the mission bus as it bounced along below me. Was that Cedric or Dineo waving to me, or just my imagination? I was sure I could hear them both saying, "Morano, ret on brew."

Commander Douglas Fane and I planning a mission in 1984 which would take place in Central America.

From right to left: myself, Commander Fane and Dimitri Rebikoff, inventor of the one-man underwater vehicle known as "Pegasus."

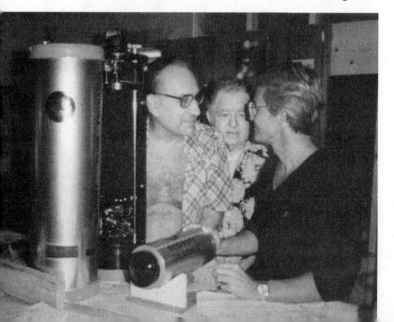

COMITE DE PRENSA
DE LA
FUERZA ARMADA
DE EL SALVADOR

DEPTO. RR.PP

SECCION COPREFA

R. LMAA , mra

ARCHIVO

San Salvador, 28 de Marzo de 1983

Oficio Nº 228

Señores
Comandantes y Jefes de Cuerpos Militares
Presente.

    El señor SAM NESLEY HALL ————— quien desempeña funciones para WASHINGTON CENTER PUBLICATION con sede en WASHINGTON. U.S.A , siempre que no vulnere las normas de Seguridad Militar, a su criterio puede desarrollar sus labores periodísticas.

    Para tal efecto se le extiende la presente, con ruegos de darle las facilidades convenientes.

Atentamente,

COMITE
DE
PRENSA

CAP. P.A. LUIS MARIO AGUILAR ALFARO
Comité de Prensa de la Fuerza Armada

Letter given me by the Minister of Defense of El Salvador that enabled me to travel anywhere within the country's borders and to use any transportation I needed.

Myself and Cedric, one of the children my commando team rescued
from terrorists in Angola, saying a prayer for Peter, a fellow
commando who has just been buried. (Note: I always took a camera
along with me on these missions so that I could supplement my reports
with photographs.)

An Israeli press pass that
enabled me to go to
Beirut, Lebanon.

It was always easy to get passes giving me access to restricted areas. At various times, I've been identified in passes as a tool-and-die salesman, a British subject, a teacher, a coach and (in this case) a correspondent.

United States Information Service
Tel Aviv, 71 Hayarkon Street, Tel. 654338

EMBASSY OF THE
UNITED STATES OF AMERICA
Tel Aviv, Israel

November 18, 1983

To Whom it May Concern:

Sam N. Hall is an American freelance correspondent doing research for stories. Any courtesies extended to him will be appreciated.

Very truly yours,

Arthur S. Berger
Press Attache

Bathing with my two wards, Cedric and his little sister, Dinero, in Botswana— semi-friendly territory.

My daughter Samantha and I reunite after my return from Africa in 1985.

```
  341367 CTAL IL

  7775ELTEL IL
  IT IS RAMADA CONTINENTAL ?~~~~~~~~~ YESJ+.
  OK PLS PASS MESSAGE



  SAMUEL HALL
  ROOM 1106
  PROPOSITION SOUNDS INTERESTING .
  NEED MORE INFORMATION . WE REQUEST YOU RETURN ISRAEL AT YOUR
  SOONEST .
  ENJOY S.A KEEP HEAD DOWN .
  ARI
  7775ELTEL ILO
  341367 CTAL ILO
```

Telex sent to me by an aide to Israel's Minister of Police. The "proposition" it refers to is my plan for the Phoenix Battalion, a unit intended to combat worldwide terrorism.

Inspecting troops in El Salvador, 1985.

Air support for Salvadoran army units
about to take on rebels.

Training with an elite unit of the
Salvadoran defense forces.

For the next six months I licked my wounds and then, slowly, worked myself back into shape. I knew I'd never find anybody like Peter or Raoul again so I decided not to try. Free Lancers was history without them. Nineteen-eighty-four was half gone by the time I felt strong enough to put in a call to Red Dog for work. He set up a couple of African missions for me and one in Central America, but it wasn't until November that he sprang the big one.

He knew by then that there was something special going down in Washington, had heard rumors in the late summer about a new counter-terrorist policy. When the talk heated up in the fall he called one of his contacts at the Pentagon, a navy captain named Bill Hamilton who was Director of Special Warfare for the Joint Chiefs.

It turned out that Hamilton was apparently interested in speaking with me, or so Red Dog said. When I finally got up the nerve to call the Pentagon I couldn't have been more surprised when Hamilton got on the line and began asking what seemed friendly questions about my stint in Central America. The captain, it seemed, had been doing some homework. When he asked me if I could come up to Washington on November 20th I answered with a most enthusiastic yes.

The 20th was only seventy-two hours off, but by the time the day finally came it felt as if I'd waited seventy-two years. The cabbie who drove me from the hotel to the Pentagon wanted to know who I was going to see at six-thirty in the morning, which was tough to answer sensibly since the place didn't open for official business till eight and my own meeting with Hamilton was scheduled for nine-thirty. By the time the guards let me in I'd

245

paced the taxpayers' sidewalks circling the five sides of the huge building some fifty times.

At nine-thirty Hamilton's executive assistant led me into the second floor office next to the Secretary of the Navy's. The Special Warfare Director looked bigger than the room and wore enough ribbons and gold braid on his uniform to deck out Mr. T. I mean no disrespect. I was impressed.

What followed was three hours of questions from Hamilton about my experience and training, including who my contacts were in Israel, whether I'd ever talked with Bo Gritz about POW rescue attempts, how well I knew the merc network in South Africa . . . I was amazed at how much Hamilton already knew about me.

The captain must have been satisfied by the answers I gave him because he ended our meeting by telling me he'd make an appointment for me at CIA headquarters that afternoon. I was supposed to meet a friend of his who'd have me fill out a questionnaire and sign a form.

That afternoon at Langley I was directed to Hamilton's friend. After a brief chat he had me speak with his associate, Roger Martin. We didn't talk very long before Martin put the promised questionnaire in my hand and told me to take it home with me. He also asked me to sign a paper headed 'Warning Notice." The paper talked about the need to keep your lips sealed if you were hired for any covert ops by the Agency. Once I signed the loose-lip warning, Martin told me to stay in touch with Captain Hamilton at the Pentagon, then he gave me a quick heave-ho. I got the idea he didn't want to keep me down on the Farm any longer than he had to.

Back in Dayton it took me three days to fill out the CIA info sheets. By the time they got mailed, I knew twice as much about myself as I did before. Six more days and Bill Hamilton called to say my security clearance would take a while but he wanted me to check in every day in case.

The next day I pointed my Trans Am south and when I hit Atlanta I dialed Hamilton's number. The captain told me to go immediately to Doug Fane's place and call him from there.

The record time from Atlanta to Ft. Lauderdale by car got broken that day. When I roared into Red Dog's driveway I had to hit the brakes hard for fear of crashing into his garage. Inside, I got on the two phones along with Red Dog and called Hamilton in Washington.

The captain explained the reason for calling from Commander Fane's place. (The commander's phones had been secured.) Then he hit me with a question I hadn't anticipated—would I be interested in organizing a counter-terrorist military unit? I waited for more, and Hamilton explained that the job called for someone who liked to work alone—somebody who knew how to operate more-or-less outside the system. When I asked him what size unit he was talking about he staggered me by saying big enough to wage war on terrorists world-wide. Hell, that meant a battalion, maybe even a whole division.

Hamilton told me he was sending me a list of names—people in the private sector with money—and that I'd have to approach them to get funding for the project. The unit was to be made up of four strike forces, each stationed in a different country. The Middle East, the Far East, Central America and Europe were likely staging areas.

The first step would be to set up an organizational chart for the unit. Commander Fane would have knowledge of men who could provide leadership in certain key positions. When the paperwork was finished I was to go to Israel—where most terrorist attacks were taking place at the time—and talk to my contacts about getting the government to loan us a site, then start lining up a team.

After Hamilton rang off, Red Dog and I talked about the government's apparent new get-tough policy toward terrorists. This unit Hamilton was talking about promised to get results and I confess I was proud to have been asked to organize it.

I spent the next four days putting together a battalion-size force on paper. There were phone calls and letters going back and forth all over the world. Some were to foreign intelligence contacts, some to arms dealers, some to mercs. And, of course, many were to the private individuals on Hamilton's list who could help us start a kitty—people like H. Ross Perot.

Perot was the kind of patriot I really respected and still do—one who didn't just talk but *acted*. His top veep, Merv Stauffer, asked for Captain Hamilton's secure phone number so he could check out Red Dog and myself. And we were to furnish him with our bios as well. Our letter to Perot went like this:

Dear Mr. Perot:

This letter and enclosures will serve as an introduction of Sam N. Hall of Dayton, Ohio, and of Commander Douglas E. Fane, USNR (Ret), now of Fort Lauderdale, Florida.

On 28 November took the initiative of contacting your office regarding an opportunity to meet with you, having heard of your experiences in the field, and upon the advice of my former Executive Officer, Captain William Hamilton, U.S. Navy.

The subject of the intended meeting is relative to the future continuance of plans for the rescue of persons captured and imprisoned by Communist forces inimical to the ideology of the Free World.

In the past two years, Hall has penetrated areas of Africa and Central America in surreptitious operations, fighting to bring out Canadian tourists, Irish nurses and young Blacks whom the Communists intended to indoctrinate in Marxism. Hall entered Angola and Mozambique with armed patrols, successfully releasing several South African troops who had been subjected to cruelty. In Central America a mission for the abduction of a suspected terrorist wanted by allied authorities for interrogation also succeeded. I worked with Hall in his training in the Everglades swamps for this deed.

Hall organized teams of select ex-military veterans recruited for their experience in Commando-type maneuvers, parachuting and use of automatic weapons. These men, all volunteers from civilian life, were motivated by hatred of the Red regimes, and they were imbued with a desire to aid helpless people who could not depend upon any other means to help due to the restrictions placed by diplomats upon our regular military deployment.

Both Fane and Hall have had face-to-face encounters with Red guerrilla and regular forces in various geographic areas, and have planned operations and commanded units involved in surreptitious attacks.

Therefore, having heard of the experiences of Ross Perot and upon a rather enthusiastic suggestion from Washington, we have taken the liberty of contacting you and offering our services, particularly hopeful of obtaining support for future independent anti-terrorist operations.

Hall's extensive experience in air-borne deployment into the hinterland plus Fane's conduct of sea-borne reconnaissance and demolition operations provide a combined background of experience which should round out the leadership requirements for the intended good works.

We trust we will have the chance to discuss this proposal further with you at your convenience, and are ready to travel to Dallas at any time. The growing threat of terrorism imperils the way of life of all right-thinking men and is the inspiration for our desire to deliver righteous people from bondage.

> Most sincerely yours,
> Douglas Fane
> Sam Hall

When the four days of letter writing were over, the commander and I were exhausted. But we still didn't have any working cash, so I called a friend in Dayton for a loan and he signed a bank note that put the first $10,000 in our pockets. I picked up the money at Western Union and Red Dog drove me to the airport for a flight to New York. From there it was TWA to Tel Aviv.

On the flight to the Middle East so much was running through my head that there was no way to relax. I tried to make like Lucy Goosey, swapping my shoes and hat for the airline booties and sleeping mask. But when I settled back for the long trip the project was the only thing I could think about. I reasoned that something of this size and scope had to have clearance from the top. Only one person in Washington knew about it as far as I could tell for sure— Captain Hamilton, a navy four-striper. But that didn't altogether add up. Hamilton had said something about helping "us?" I figured that the idea for the outfit probably went considerably farther up the chain of command. Wouldn't Weinberger, for example, almost have to know? And the National Security Council? And maybe President Reagan himself?

Whatever, Hamilton's orders made it plain that none of the members of the new unit could have ties to any government. And all the monies would have to come from the so-called private sector. Everything had to be handled to try to make sure the public would be on our side if and when the news ever broke. That didn't seem like much of a problem to me, even granted my lack of great political sophistication. Once John Q knew we were out to put terrorists six feet under, he'd be cheering us on. Period.

The plan I worked out at Red Dog's place called for a battalion instead of a division. Hamilton's timetable wouldn't permit me to think much bigger—I'd only been given a couple of months to work everything out. And it would be a while before the money started flowing in. I'd have my hands full lining up friendlies who could help with logistics and sanctuaries, not to mention training sites. The battalion could be fattened to a division later.

The training sites wouldn't be difficult to get hold of. If the Israelis came through, for example, we might get one in the Negev. I already knew we could use the one near Durban, where I'd first met Peter and the Bird. And Red Dog had a good piece of land pinpointed. One of his friends had been the late movie producer, Ivan Tors, and his surviving sons had an 11,000-acre ranch in Namibia that we might be able to use.

I also wasn't worried about getting good men for the battalion. There were plenty of independents around with lots of combat time behind them. The unit was going to be para-military, all airborne commandos. I didn't plan for an engineering company, there wouldn't be any time to clear mines or build bypasses anyway. We had to be able to move in fast, strike hard, move out.

Moving out was tougher than moving in and striking hard. The Free Lancers had made combat jumps knowing there would be no air-support for getaways. That usually meant walking out unless we could find easy credit-terms on some enemy vehicle. We leaned on captured snitches to give us the latest word on mine fields in the area and other relevant info. Those were good enough ploys for a small team, but now the plans called for exit air-support from un-marked planes. I understood from Hamilton that that wouldn't be a problem. I once asked him where we could get 500 to 1000 T-10 parachutes and he said not to worry, that I'd get what I needed. Another time I wanted to know how we'd line up in a C 5-A or a couple of C-26's to drop us behind enemy lines and he said not to worry. Right or wrong, such assurances did suggest to me that the White House was somehow behind the project.

Once I landed in Tel Aviv my first contact after check-in was Mike Amir, the owner of a catering service and a friend who gave me some help with the parties I threw for MFO brass in '82. Mike had been in Israeli intelligence during the 1948 war and was still part of the inner circle. I didn't know just how to approach him with my proposition but I figured a gin-and-tonic would at least smooth the talk. We met at a little outdoor bar near the Ramada, and I noted that the streets were crawling with Israeli Defense Forces and that security seemed tighter than ever.

In the middle of my sales pitch Mike asked why it would make sense for an independent counter-terrorist team to raid terrorist camps when Israeli commandos could do the same thing. I re-minded him that every time the Israelis launched a strike to one-up the terrorists they got raked over the coals by much of the world press. And, of course, the Arab-slanted UN General Assembly.

When I was through pressing home the rest of my points I couldn't tell whether Mike was going to swat me on the back and tell me to sleep it off or turn me in to the MOSSAD.

Finally a big smile spread across his face and he told me to stay in my hotel room for the next couple days and wait for his call.

As it turned out that call came the next night around seven o'clock. Mike wanted to set up a meeting in an hour, and at eight we were sipping gin-and-tonics in Mike's favorite watering hole. He told me the response had been favorable but that he wanted to ask more questions. We went at it for the next two hours, and I could tell we were being watched the whole time. During the thirty-six hours between our first talk and this one, the MOSSAD must, I felt, have been checking things out. I knew the Israelis had a file on me. No doubt it was getting fatter by the minute.

One of Mike's chief concerns seemed to be how far up in the U.S. government the counter-terrorist plan went. I told him that, as far as I knew, only one man in the Pentagon was behind the plan, but my voice must have betrayed the fact that I also thought there were more people involved.

When Mike asked me specifically what we wanted from Israel I told him that we needed a training site—ideally, some place in the Negev desert; unmarked transportation, including evacuation choppers; commandos who could speak Arabic; and as many Uzis and Ghalils and Ak-47's as we could get our hands on. Most important, though, was intelligence. We would be depending on the MOSSAD to give us a line on the people we wanted to put out of business.

Mike took an itemized list of equipment from me and excused himself to make a phone call. Fifteen minutes later he was back, telling me to go back to my hotel and wait for a call, but before we parted he revealed who his contact was.

It turned out to be Haim Bar-Lev, Minister of Police for the state of Israel, who had served as a general in the IDF during the 1973 war. Mike told me he'd saved Bar-Lev's life in '48 and they'd been good friends ever since.

As I got up to go Mike caught my arm and asked me what I intended to use as a code name for the project. I told him I'd been calling it "Bill Hamilton's project" all along, but agreed with him that it needed a better moniker. "Let's call it Phoenix," I said.

Three hours later I answered a page at the hotel and met a man who called himself Ari, who it seemed was Bar-Lev's rep. After three more hours of questions and answers Ari told me to go to the Sheraton in Eilat to wait for word.

After two days there staring out a hotel window I started to get worried. I was due to fly out to Joburg the next day. So I left the room long enough to send a telex back to Tel Aviv. Mike telexed back right away, saying I'd be contacted that day at the Sheraton or the next day at the airport before I left South Africa. That night Mike called to assure me that everything was in order but that I should go on to South Africa as planned, since the bureaucratic wheels were moving in their typically slow fashion.

In a week Ari's telex found me at the Maharani Hotel in Durban, and I felt the message was encouraging: "Proposition sounds interesting. Need more information. Request you return Israel at your soonest. Enjoy S.A. Keep your head down."

Forty-three thousand miles and six weeks later my sales tour was over. Nearly everywhere I'd been I'd met enthusiasm for the new Phoenix Battalion. Especially among the mercs. The British and Dutch wanted in. So did the Portuguese. And the South Africans couldn't be kept out. Ready now to give an upbeat report to Captain Hamilton, I sent him a cover letter along with the plans and headed home.

The battalion set-up looked like this:

CHAIN OF COMMAND

Battalion Commander (non-combatant)
Capt. William Hamilton U.S. Army
Captain Hamilton will retire April, 87. Until that time Interim leader will be appointed. (recommended rank, Colonel)
Battalion Warrior (combatant)
Sam N. Hall, U.S. Air Force (recommended rank, Lt. Colonel or Major)
Battalion Admin. (non-combatant)

PHOENIX BATTALION

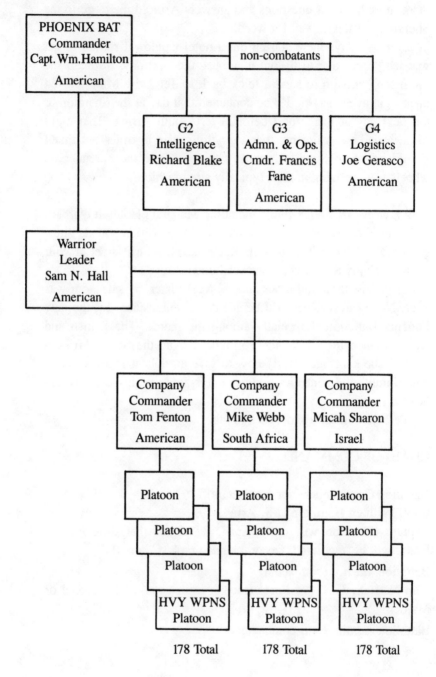

PHOENIX BAT
Commander
Capt. Wm. Hamilton
American

non-combatants

G2
Intelligence
Richard Blake
American

G3
Admn. & Ops.
Cmdr. Francis
Fane
American

G4
Logistics
Joe Gerasco
American

Warrior
Leader
Sam N. Hall
American

Company
Commander
Tom Fenton
American

Company
Commander
Mike Webb
South Africa

Company
Commander
Micah Sharon
Israel

Platoon

Platoon

Platoon

Platoon

Platoon

Platoon

Platoon

Platoon

Platoon

HVY WPNS
Platoon

HVY WPNS
Platoon

HVY WPNS
Platoon

178 Total

178 Total

178 Total

Cmdr. Douglas Fane, USN, retired (recommended rank, Lt. Colonel or Major)

Battalion Logistics (non-combatant)

Joseph Gerasco, U.S. Marines (recommended rank, Captain)

Battalion Intelligence (non-combatant)

Richard Blake, Marines, retired

Company Commander, Tom Fenton, U.S. Rangers (recommended rank, Captain)

Company Commander, Mike Webb, South African Special Forces (recommended rank, Captain)

Company Commander, Micah Sharon, Israeli Defense Forces (recommended rank, Capt.)

Instructors at training site
Sam N. Hall *American*
Mike Webb *South African*
Ron Shaneyfelt *British*

12 Platoon Leaders and 12 Platoon Sgts appointed on merit

Recommendations:

1. Purpose/Mission
Preemptive strikes against terrorist training sites.

2. Warrior Qualifications
All candidates must have prior combat experience. Commando trained and jump qualified. Must pass G2 checks from their respective countries (CID, MI5, etc). Be in excellent shape and of sound mind; possessed of sound morals, a high sense of honor and a deep sense of personal responsibility to themselves, their country and to counter-terrorism.

3. Training Site Preference
First preference, Negev Desert, Israel; Second preference, Tors estate/ranch (11,000 acres) Namibia, South West Africa. Third preference, Everglades or a large Texas or South African ranch.

4. Length of Training
4–6 weeks of training before mission. All warriors are seques-

COMPANY BREAKDOWN

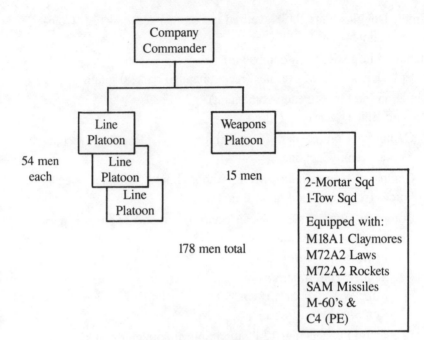

54 men each

15 men

178 men total

Line Platoon
Line Platoon
Line Platoon

Weapons Platoon

2-Mortar Sqd
1-Tow Sqd

Equipped with:
M18A1 Claymores
M72A2 Laws
M72A2 Rockets
SAM Missiles
M-60's &
C4 (PE)

PLATOON BREAKDOWN

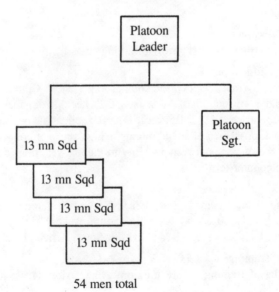

Platoon Leader

Platoon Sgt.

13 mn Sqd
13 mn Sqd
13 mn Sqd
13 mn Sqd

54 men total

tered (quarantined) for the duration of training, for security reasons. Also, all candidates not being able to keep up pace of training (washouts) will be held until after mission is under way.

5. Type of Training

   Each warrior will be re-trained Commando, Airborne with T-10's, air assault, weapons, explosives, field first aid, hand to hand, land navagation, recon, patrolling, ambushes, night operations, camouflage techniques, escape and evasion, raid team exfiltrating, and chemical schooling with use of M17A2 series mask.

6. Weapons Training

   I recommend that all warriors be trained on a variety of weapons. Where we strike and where we train will vary. For example, most of our preemptive strikes will take place in the Middle East, so familiarization by firing is paramount. Also recognition by sound of weapons being used against us. Therefore, all warriors must be familiar with the Israeli Uzi and the Ghalil, AK47 and the GermanG3. Each warrior must qualify with the side arm .45 or the 9mm; and also qualify with their main weapon, M16A1, Ghalil or AK47. All warriors will carry side arms as well as 6 Grenades (m-67). All will practice with M203 grenade launchers, the M60 Machine gun, some will qualify with the M72A2 laws rocket and surface-to-air missiles, also the M-79s. Most of this firing will be with the heavy weapons platoons. (Note... because of the nature of our quickness and speed, I purposely omitted the m-60 mm mortar.) Mortar and tow squads will carry C4 (PE). If possible, warriors should be familiar, with firing and identifying sounds from the AKM's, the USSR PPSH-41 SMG; SKS carbines; Czech Skorpion Machine Pistol; Tokorev pistol; and finally, all tow squads will carry 2 each M18A1 Claymores.

7. Additional Training

   All warriors must be able to identify friendly and especially *unfriendly* armored vehicles. NATO nomenclature for the USSR's T-55, T-62, T-64, T-72 and also the ASU-85, SAU-122, SP-152, ZSU23 & 4, BTR-50P, BTR-60P and also the 4 basic USSR anti-tank guided missile vehicles, the BRDM-2's. All must be able to spot and identify *unfriendly* aircraft such as Mig-17, Mig-27, SU-7, SU-20, Mi-8, (Hip-8) and Mi-24's (Hind-D).

8. Target Sites/Locations
   To be received from intelligence of friendly countries (i.e., Israel's MOSSAD or IDF, U.S. G2). Only myself and Battalion Commander will know in advance (need to know basis). Battalion warriors informed enroute.

9. Airborne Sites
   The threat of mine fields and the need of quick surprise dictates these. If possible, unmarked transports coming in at ground level, jump at 300 meters (T–10's); no spare. Evacuation by Hilos is desired but wishful thinking in the Middle East. Confiscation of unfriendlies' vehicles or leave by foot with unmarked aircover.

10. Method of Communication
    High frequency SSB radios. (80 kilometer ground wave, 2400 kilometer skywave.) Because of enemy RDF, radio messages should be sent by South Africans using AFRIKANA lingo. Israelis will also be equipped with radios to listen in for enemy (Arabic) chatter.

11. The Mission
    Jump at 300 meters, form up and move in fast, strike hard and finish rapidly. Combining the imperative principles of maneuver, mass, and surprise. All Phoenix units concentrating to quickly destroy the enemy. Only survivors should be those recognized as known terrorist leaders, and these should be brought out for questioning. Several of the captured will be needed to tie across front bumpers of confiscated vehicles to warn our withdrawal through mine fields. I have used this successfully three times in Africa. The last time only 2½ weeks ago, withdrawing from a raid on a terrorist camp in Mozambique. If time permits, all papers found to be brought out. No one will be left alive and all buildings will be leveled.

12. Phoenix Attackforce Equipment
    Each warrior will be dressed with olive green bottoms and cami-green tops because of the need for quick recognition. Each will wear a red or maroon beret with the same color armband (left arm). I have participated in terrorist raids and the need for color and dress is essential. Because of the need for speed and quickness I recommend the Israeli canvas boot or the U.S. jungle boot. Each warrior will carry:

a 360-degree lensatic compass
one K-bar
one canteen
one side arm (.45 or 9mm)
one primary weapon (Ghalil, *AK47* or Ml6al). I recommend
AK47.
six M–67 grenades
On the warrior's harness he will carry enough pouches for 8 magazines for his primary weapon, and pouches for 5 mag. for his
secondary weapon. Also carried will be nutriment for two days
and a combat first aid kit (with morphine). The above is for the
line-platoon personnel; the heavy-weapons platoon will have a
primary weapon (AK47) and will be carrying Laws and SAM's
M–79, M-60's and 203 grenade launchers. It will be their duty to
handle the Claymores and C4.

13. Casualties cannot be determined at this point until such time as a
target has been selected. Estimates will be given prior to the strike
and after information from intelligence sources has been digested.
(i.e., if the target strike is to be Balbac, Lebanon, a known terrorist camp, items to be taken into account are: method of drop and
distance of drop zone to the camp; will we have air cover before,
during withdrawal, and most important, our method of evacuation: Hilos, drive out, walk out? Because of safety, swiftness and
security of the withdrawal all friendly troops that are wounded
will be evacuated if it does not impede the safety of the Battalion.
However, this will have to be determined by Command on the
spot. No badly hurt warrior will be left there alive.

14. Salaries for Battalion Warriors

520	Line Soldiers (Warriors)	$20,000. per yr.	
18	Officers	25,000.	" "
2	Officers (Battalion Leader & Warrior Leader)	28.000.	" "

I recommend the following pay procedure that is practiced in
many parts of the globe . . . $1,000 bonus to sign warrior contract,
and a $1,000 completion bonus after each mission.

Estimated budget and cost breakdown for Phoenix Battalion

Bonus to sign
540 × $1,000 $ 540,000

Completion Bonus (3 missions per yr.)	
540 × $1,000 × 3	1,620,000
Salary for Warriors.	
520 × $20,000 line troops	10,400,000
18 × 25,000 officers	450,000
2 × 28,000 Battalion & Warrior Leaders	56,000
Uniforms (2 sets per man, includes boots and harness gear)	
540 × $200 × 2	216,000
Weapons (estimated high)	
1300 pieces at $600 ea.	780,000
Ammo (includes Claymores, rockets, grenades, practice rds., etc.)	220,000
Food and billeting (leasing of Negev base or Texas ranch, etc.)	3,888,000
Transportation cost (rough est. based) $1500 per man plus extra for Command trips for intelligence gathering and etc.	880,000
Misc. Expenses (medical, T–10's, emergency fund)	286,400
Approx. total for one year	$19,336,400
Estimated Budget for 6 months Bonus to sign	$ 540,000
Completion Bonus (2 missions only)	1,080,000
Salaries for Battalion	
520 × 10,000 Line troops	5,200,000
18 × 12,500 Officers	225,000
2 × 14,000 Leaders	28,000
Uniforms (remains the same)	216,000
Weapons " " "	780,000
Ammo	220,000
Food and billeting	1,944.000
Transportation (remains the same)	880,000
Misc. expense	143,200
6 Months total	$11,256,200

Cost for three more months
9-month cost add $4,310,100
to 6-month total

$15,566,300

16. Disclaimer for budget

Total cost for	ONE	year	$19,336,400.	(3 missions)
Total cost for	6	months	11,256,200	(2 missions)
Total cost for	9	months	15,566,300	(3 missions)

Budget may be altered drastically in the event Israel gives a 100%
"green light". (They may give us weapons and not charge for the
Negev base, etc.) If they give us Israeli troops already employed
by the IDF, then cost is drastically cut . . . as much as 35%.

Budget estimate is rough but close. Take into consideration my
experience in buying and bartering for weapons and ammo on the
black market in Southeast Asia 2½ years ago, and for the past 2
years in Africa. The preceding prices reflect current black-market
stickers.

17. Final Recommendations for PHOENIX Battalion
Israel is the key for us in the Middle East. They will play ball.
The question is how far do they want to go with us? How much
they give us has to be worked out. As you know, their readiness
and zeal is unsurpassed. Their security is one of the best, if not
the best. They want to strike but when they do they get raked
across the international coals from Beirut to the United Nations. A
friend of mine in Tel Aviv, and an aide to Minister (former Chief
of Staff for all Israeli Forces), tells me they are genuinely interested and have requested my return. (I refer to previously sent
telex).

From Mike Webb in South Africa, former British commando
and South African Special forces (also former group leader for the
famous Mike Hoare), we know that he has the contacts in England
with many of his British SAS friends just waiting for such a thing
as the *Phoenix Battalion*. Also, Webb has assured me of many
ex-South Africans waiting for final word to join the *Phoenix Battalion*. And then there is my former team, also in South Africa.

With a little more work, the *PHOENIX BATTALION* could
reach Division strength by Spring. At this time, however, I recommend Battalion level.

In summation, I need to once more fly to England with Webb (he'll have to have his way paid, round trip from South Africa) to meet our Brit group and work out all details. Then I will proceed to Tel Aviv and work out the final details with them. Finishing that, I will go directly to South Africa and finish what is needed there. On my arrival back in the States I will head to Dallas and work out the details with our American contact. I estimate this trip to take one month, costing between $11–12,000.

Mobilization could commence in late March or early April, and realistically our first preemptive strike/mission could take place the latter part of June, 85.

Before such a trip is undertaken I am recommending a weekend session in Fairfax, VA. Present at that meeting:
Capt. Hamilton
Cmdr. Fane
Sam N. Hall

> At your command,
> Sam N. Hall

Hamilton called me at Red Dog's place three days after I returned to the States. Since submitting my report I'd been wondering what Hamilton thought of it. Did I cover all the bases? Was there enough intelligence info in it? Was it professional enough? I knew the material I'd presented would be evaluated by the best and at least a couple of times. I was worried sick about whether Hamilton would approve the report.

On the phone I thought he sounded encouraging, saying that it would take him a few days to digest all the information I'd presented. However, when I tried to pin him down as to when he'd know for sure whether the plan would be implemented he said he couldn't say, that it would take a while.

He went on to tell me that I had been turned down by the CIA, which upset me greatly until he explained why.

Apparently it had been planned that way, that what I was doing was something I could not do for the CIA.

When I got off the roller-coaster Hamilton told me to contact three men who'd be taking over the planning of the Phoenix Battalion if it flew. I was never to mention their real names to anyone. When he said code names would be necessary, I suggested Tinker, Evers and Chance—names I used in setting up my POW rescue plan.

It turned out that Tinker was the Mr. Big of the operation, an American who had contacts in the highest places all over the world. Evers was British and the Phoenix fund-raiser. For openers, he was supposed to be approaching the owners of Greek and Italian cruise lines since they obviously had a vested interest in combating terrorism. Chance was an Hispanic, and word was he'd been a member of the 2506th, the private army based in Florida during the 60's—the one that had made the try at Castro at the Bay of Pigs. My personal guess was that all three were connected either with the National Security Council or the CIA.

Chance was the one who called me in the spring to say the Phoenix Battalion had been put on hold and gave me three reasons that didn't do anything to lighten the letdown. First, the plan looked like it would cost more than Evers could ever accumulate. Second, there was the fact that Uncle Sam was in some hot water over the Libyan situation. The third reason had to do with the way the Iran-Iraq war was going. About the time Chance finished explaining reason number three I tuned out and started cursing under my breath. It seemed too much of my life had been put on hold. But before I exploded Chance did toss me a crumb I couldn't refuse. He said he wanted me to go back to Central America until he received a definite yes or no on whether the Phoenix Battalion could be funded. I was to get myself aligned with Civilian Military Assistance (CMA), which was based in Decatur, Alabama, and headed by a man named Tom Posey.

In a few days I loaded up the car and headed for Alabama. Posey's Civilian Military Assistance outfit was serving at the time as one of the Contras' chief lifelines, Congress having cut off military aid. CMA sent boots and bandoliers and various kinds of support material to poorly equipped troops. I was anxious to meet

Posey, having already seen a great deal about him on television.

On the way to Decatur I decided to stop off outside Mobile to get a look at Frank Camper's famous warfare school. Camper, I'd heard, was said to be a cog in the CMA's wheels too. I'd seen pictures of his school on the TV news and I wanted to eyeball it in person. A day at his battlefield didn't overly impress me, but I did meet a couple of friendly British mercs who were passing through, trying to make connections with Camper and Posey to help them get to Costa Rica for some reason they wouldn't explain. But they caught my attention when they said they used to work out of South Africa. After a rag-chewing session with them about their combat adventures and the set-up in Central America, we decided to share a ride to Decatur. The British mercs had been there before, so I asked one of them what he knew about the head of CMA.

He claimed that Posey flew in supplies to the Contras from different places in unmarked planes and that the U.S. government was supplying the aircraft. Regardless, when we got to Decatur I realized I had to stick around *both* Posey and Camper if I wanted Chance's blessing in Honduras. Politics.

I must have done a pretty good job of massage, because within a few days Posey and Camper trusted me enough to put me to work. They wanted me to get some quick training so I could take over as chemical warfare officer for the FDN—the Hispanic branch of the Contra army camped on the southern coast of Honduras. The Indian branch was set up toward the east coast. There was a Creole unit in the Bluefields area too. The chemistry lessons sounded kind of dull at the time, but the two armchair generals spiced up the schooling with a tease; they wanted me to be part of a team they were putting together to steal a Russian helicopter from the Sandinistas. That mission really excited me because I'd heard about the capabilities of the Russian Mi–24. It could saturate a 200-yard long, fifty-yard wide patch of landscape with so many rounds so fast that probably none of the troops and not more than half-a-dozen fishworms in the fire zone could make it till morning. The Sandinistas used these so called Hinds to spray rounds and chemicals at the Contras—especially the Miskitos. If CMA could get their hands on a Hind we could study it and set up a defense against it.

The best place to get scoop about anything that flies was back in Dayton at Wright Patterson, where somebody at the airbase could fill in gaps in CMA's info about the Mi–24. And my old home-town was the world headquarters of a big chemical company just a stone's throw away in one of the suburbs. The next week I spent the morning pumping everyone at the base who would talk, and in the afternoons I took a quickie course from a friend at the chemical lab. I also talked to a civilian chopper expert who worked for Bell Helicopter in Dayton, and thought for a while he was going to end my military career. All my life my problem has been my mouth. This time I made the mistake of telling the chopper expert why I was so interested in the Mi–24. And I had the temerity to be critical of Posey and Camper! Next thing I knew two FBI-types spoiled my dinner at Denny's by indelicately presenting their badges in my face. They reminded me about a law called the Neu-trality Act and told me to knock off the Clint Eastwood routine. I told them I was just sent to get some information and that they of course wouldn't catch anybody with half a brain (ha!) plotting in the *States* to steal a helicopter from Nicaragua. Any planning like that would have to be done somewhere else. Sure. Like maybe a third world country. Of course. That *seemed* to appease them, they told me to be very careful and left.

The chewing out I got from the two FBI agents turned out to be mild compared to the one my brother the U.S. Congressman gave me. The agents told Tony what I was up to, and he got properly bent out of shape. It wasn't the first time he'd had occasion to land on me about my out-of-step life. That other time he'd come into my motel room before he was expected and found airline tickets and my passport and a couple of weapons. But now Tony was even more upset, and worried, afraid I was going to get arrested and thrown in jail or even killed—that my name would be plastered all over the newspapers and that I'd be scoffed at because of the old

drug problem and assorted other stupidities. He was naturally concerned about what it would do to mom and my three kids if I got
into trouble. I knew where he was coming from, but I still couldn't
tell him what I was really in to. I at least wasn't going to put the
plan for the Phoenix Battalion at risk, as well as my chance to help
people like the Miskito Indians.

Indeed, my opportunity to do just that came right after I got back
to Alabama with my new chemistry books and the chopper blue-
prints. The next week found me stationed in Honduras, right on the
border of Nicaragua. But a change in plans had me working on the
Atlantic Coast side, which was where CMA was helping the Misura Indians. The Misura were made up of the Rama and the Suma
tribes along with the Miskitos. My job was to help modernize the
Miskitos' fighting skills. It didn't take me long to get caught up in
their cause. Right away there were a couple of missions across the
border and I got a good gut-wrenching look at the Sandinista tactics. On both strikes we found mass Indian graves. Thousands of
skeletons. Men and women. Children with bullet holes through
their skulls. The most sickening things I'd seen since the graves of
those Canadian tourists in Africa, but on a bigger scale. These
graves said to me that the numbers I had been hearing weren't
exaggerated. One of the Americans along on the mission told me
the Sandinistas had already killed off fifty-four percent of the Mis-
uras—a high price for ordinary farmers and fishermen to pay for
being in the Sandinistas' line-of-sight.

In my first month in Honduras with the Miskitos I learned a
good deal about the Central American situation, including why the
Russians went into Nicaragua. Partly I believe they're testing us
there. If we won't deal with them in our own backyard they can
surely move into other parts of the world. But they want to do
more than test us. If they can hang on to Nicaragua they'll have
their first warm-water port in the Pacific, not to mention two more
in the Atlantic. The country also gives them a beachhead for a
route into the southern oil fields in Mexico and the northern ones in
Venezuela.

The only way to stop the Sandinistas from getting all the Russian materiel they need to stay in power is through a guerrilla war, and I believe the Contras could already have won that war or at least put the Sandinistas on the run if Congress had anted up with the Russians. Instead we gave the freedom fighters dribs and drabs and the set-up kept getting worse instead of better. The Russians were sending the Sandinistas more and more high-tech hardware and Congress got stingier and stingier with its Contra aid. Some *quid pro quo*.

Old Chairman Mao was right about one thing at least. He said it took fifteen sharp soldiers to take on one well-armed guerrilla. It was the "guerrilla factor" that helped make up some for our own relative inaction. Small teams of Contras could close down the ports in Nicaragua. They could also pepper the airstrips and take out the Soviet choppers from miles away. It was the only way for the Contras. After all, their total strength was just about 24,000 men, while the Sandinista regular army numbered 200,000 with another 200,000 in reserve.

All through March I taught the Indians commando tactics and fought next to them, seeing more death that first month than I ever want to see again. In the beginning, the CMA had about twelve men running things. The field leader of the Miskitos was Joe Adams—nickname, "Shooter." He got his nickname from being a pistol-marksmanship champ. He'd been Adolfo Calero's bodyguard for a while and I felt he was the best of the CMA group. The worst was the officer in charge of CMA forces—we called him "Colonel Flako." He managed to screw things up so bad that the CMA was being brought out of Honduras a few men at a time.

Early in April I got a handshake from a man who helped change my direction again. It happened just after a mission with the Miskitos. We'd just gotten back to camp and I was stretched out on the ground with a cup of beet juice when he introduced himself.

His name was Rob Owen. As I recall the conversation, Owen told me that he had gotten a message from his boss and that from that point forward I was to work with General John Singlaub through him. Singlaub was directing some of the Contra-aid operations from his home in Colorado, or so I was told.

When Owen asked me for my thoughts on the military situation in Honduras and Nicaragua I told him that the Contras were great soldiers but that they badly needed supplies if they were to get anywhere and pointed out that the Indians' situation was especially desperate. Owen said he didn't know how much he could find for them but he would look into it.

All through April the American advisors were pulled out one by one till I was the only American left with the Miskitos. My answer was to try to step up the raids across the border, and I was damned flattered when in early May the Indians named me their field leader and dubbed me Commandante Zulu. They'd decided on that handle because they knew about some of the work I'd done with the Free Lancers in Africa. Those Indians got to me. Lack of Congressional aid may have been turning the Contras into a rag-tag outfit, but the Miskitos were by far the worst off. The FDN Hispanics had a first claim on all the uniforms and supplies and medicine. If the Indians were good little boys they *might* get the leftovers—a couple dozen bandages and a few beans with some rice to wet with river water. Sometimes we'd go weeks without receiving food supplies. Those were the times when passing parrots were in big trouble, not to mention monkeys and iguanas.

The problem with the food supplies was aggravated by the fact that the Indians' families lived near the camp and the men were always hoarding what little grub they had to give to their wives and kids, who looked almost as bad as all those TV shots you saw of the Ethiopian famine. Even though I'd reached the point where seeing the worst combat wounds didn't much affect me I couldn't look squarely at those women and children. But all my calls to FDN headquarters were wasted. So while their loved ones suffered, my small army travelled on empty stomachs most of the time. Let me tell you, the Miskito fighters had balls on balls when they ran up against the Sandinistas, but they could hardly do their best in the shape they were in.

We also had to get along with a pitifully inadequate weapon supply. We only had a half dozen M–60 machine guns and no shoulder-mounted ground-to-air rocket-launchers to knock down enemy planes that might spray chemicals. (The Indians had been the victims of chemical warfare earlier in the war.) There were one or two mortars, but no anti-tank weapons, no gas masks, not enough rifles. We never saw a wheel, except on the dirt runway where charter flights landed once a month—if that—bringing in supplies. There was usually no medicine. Never any doctors or nurses. Not so much as a fresh battery for our field radio. Sometimes the Indians would go for days with slugs lodged in their bodies before they died.

And even when we got some supplies we had to use them fast, because everything in the jungle contracted instant rot. Even the ammo. Once, in the middle of an assault, we fired six rounds of 60 mm mortars and five turned out to be rusty duds. The cartridges grew a green slime right out of a Hollywood horror flick. Your boots lasted about three months before they crumbled away from ragged socks. And your boots were your best friends, because this was a war you walked to. The only break you ever got from the walking was the short trip in the dugout canoes crossing the Rio Co Co between Honduras and Nicaragua.

The more I complained about the puny supplies in messages to Tegucigalpa, the more the FDN brass turned a deaf and dumb ear. One night in early July I went back to headquarters to make my pitch in person. A Contra big shot who was close to Mario Calero, Adolfo's brother, was manning the desk that night. He gave me a song and dance that would've put the late great Fred Astaire to shame. It was clear he didn't give an iguana's ass about the Miskitos, even made a racist remark or two to prove the point, then tried to paper over his slurs with lame excuses about the monsoons and the jittery young Contra pilots who kept piling up DC–3s in the jungle. When I went back to my room at the hotel about midnight I felt really wiped out. It was clear now that intra-Contra politics were screwing the Indians just like Egyptian politics had screwed my Thai workers in Israel. I was on my way to the bar for a little hair of the Honduran dog when two Miskito leaders stopped me. They were the Indians stationed at headquarters to funnel messages back and forth from the field. It turned out one of our commando strike teams was in position to blow the Sissen bridge, which we'd been after for a couple of months. My two visitors had a diagram of the span. Our men in the field had radioed back with a question about where to put the charges.

I'd had extensive training in explosives with a Special Forces expert three months before. Still, when I looked at the diagram I knew I was in trouble. In the past the expert's lessons had helped me teach the Miskitos how to blow up every type of bridge except the kind pictured on the map. This baby was huge, and it was made out of thick steel cables. The area around it was mined and there were seventy Sandinistas nearby to protect it. The monsoons had turned the river into a cross between the Snake and the Mississippi that time of year, so it would be hard to place the charges. The worst problem, though, was that our 300 pounds of C–4 explosives had been buried in the ground four klicks from the site during an aborted mission six weeks earlier. There was no way to tell if the C–4 would be effective after all that time underground, and I'd need all 300 pounds to do the job. I marked the diagram as best I could, showing the men where to place the wires on the bridge, and crossed my fingers, as my Indian visitors took off on the run to send the word by our SC–130 radios.

Back at the camp the next day we got a message that half the charges hadn't worked, but the half that had caused the span to list about twenty degrees to one side. The bad news was that it wasn't leaning far enough to stop the traffic of military supply trucks. And the Sandinistas were combing the jungle for our men. The Indians would have to get out soon. Still, if they could play hide-and-seek with the Sandinistas one more day I might be able to get a few extra pounds of C–4 to them. And that just might be enough to bring the bridge down. They were willing to try, so I sent some helpers out with the explosives.

They didn't have time to make it to the bridge before I radioed them to come on back. I'd had a message from the front that made their mission a scrub. A recon team of the first party at the bridge reported that the span had fallen when two deuce-and-a-halfs tried to use it at the same time. You took your good fortunes as they happened, and didn't ask questions.

One day Rob Owen, who I understood carried my reports back to the States, was supposed to come down for a look-see and bring my mail with him. When his plane landed he explained that somewhere between Washington and Tegucigalpa he'd lost a stack of my letters but he had a present for me that more than made up for the missing mail. It was a flight jacket and in one pocket was a gorgeous hunting knife that could do everything from cutting concertina wire to shaving a peach. It was the other pocket, though, that held the real prize—two fifty-nine-cent tins of chocolate pudding. As soon as I saw them I took one and excused myself so I could get into the next room. Not even a "Cosby kid" could've made shorter work of that pudding. When I got back to Owens he was smiling over how fast I'd put away the pudding, but what did he expect after a month-and-a-half of rice and beans? If somebody had stolen the other tin I'd have used my new hunting knife on his family jewels.

A week later I led a team of Miskitos across the border to mine supply roads, a familiar mission. Eight Miskitos joined me on this trek, which took ten days going in and ten coming out. As usual our ammo was a joke. We each had three magazines—about ninety rounds per man. We did have seven grenades, though, that I'd brought in from Tegucigalpa. When the Indians saw them you'd have thought I was Alexander the Great. To make it for three weeks on the enemy's turf we'd probably have to supplement our fire-power with Sandinista hardware, and if we could surprise a unit or two we might even be able to recruit a few new Contras . . . some of the Sandinistas didn't want anything to do with the regime in Managua, and given the chance could be coaxed into fighting on our side.

The trip to the supply roads reminded me once again that this war was something out of the Middle Ages. Only worse. At least some of the troops had horses back then. We inched our way through thick jungles, attacking the undergrowth with machetes, waded waist-deep through stinking swamps, expecting to get ambushed any minute, wondering whether it was better to get killed on dry land or half submerged in muck. But the Miskitos kept me going. They were truly the greatest. I remember their beaded necklaces and the bags they always carried hidden on their bodies. The bags were made out of babies' placentas, and each contained a rock and a bird's nest. I never knew what they represented symbolically, but the Indians were certain no enemy round could touch them so long as the bags were hung on their bodies. Despite all the evidence to the contrary.

We finally got to the supply roads and set the mines without flushing any unfriendlies, but on the way home we bought trouble. We were just coming out of a swamp when our point man took a round in the chest. The rest of us backed into the swamp and headed for the dry land we'd left about fifty yards back. We couldn't tell how far away the enemy was when our point man got it or how bad off he was. We made it to firm ground, though, and set up a defense. Sure enough, six riflemen made their entrance across the swamp about five minutes later. They were crouched over with their fingers on the triggers of their bayonetted weapons, and when they got to our point man they kicked him to see if he was dead. About that time we opened up on them and they went down. After ten more minutes of no-show by any of their buddies we moved back across the swamp and discovered that our point man was still alive, but just barely. His chest was in pretty bad shape. I had just begun to check the Sandinista body-count when one of them lifted his rifle and sliced my side with his bayonet. He turned out to be the only one of the enemy we hadn't killed. We corrected the error.

In fact, my wound looked worse than it was. The bayonet went in just below the skin and ran up along my rib cage. The one who really needed help was our point man. We used a couple of the Sandinistas' uniforms to make a litter for him and moved out. Once back at the camp I did what I could for him with the medicine we had on hand, and a month later he was back in business. The Indians were *tough*.

Since early May I'd been planning a major strike into Nicaragua and updating Rob Owen on details. If we could get some help from headquarters with supplies, we might be able to hit some key Sandinista positions that made a handy cluster. When we had them in our hands we'd be able to shut off the arms and ammo coming to the enemy in the Atlantic Coast area, not to mention their food and medical supplies. Control of the Sandinista positions would make the turf from just above Bluefields all the way north to the Honduras border Miskito territory. We'd have the East and West as far as Bonanza-Rosita too. I called the operation the Rainbow Mission.

To make Rainbow work we had to blow up four bridges plus the wharf and airstrip at Puerto Cabezas. We'd also have to mine a lot of roads. The tricky part was that the damage had to be inflicted simultaneously, and by a force big enough to take over some bases. And that called for using every one of the 1800 Indians at the camp, plus weapons and ammo and support equipment. Most of all, we needed some good boats.

The Indians loved the plan when I laid it out for them. It was their biggest chance yet to score a major victory and they couldn't wait. Except they'd have to, because we might not be able to get the hardware we needed. When the plan was polished I brought Owen up to date and sent the idea with a courier to General Singlaub in Colorado.

As I waited for a response from General Singlaub the monsoons hit us and there was very little food to go around—rice and beans, parrots, white-faced monkeys and an occasional K-ration.

One rainy night as I sat in my thatched-roof houch crouched over a field radio and asking without success for supplies, I threw down my mike in a fit of pique and walked outside. What the hell was I doing here? No supplies, no food, no ammo, no medicine, no dry socks, no mail . . . I was operating in total darkness. At the bottom of a well.

I had had my ass shot at a number of times; I had been stuck like a pig by a bayonet; and I had been told that the Administration approved of what I was doing. Except who the hell would believe that one? If I was ever captured on one of my foot-sorties into Nicaragua I would be promptly disavowed. I was, to use the popular vernacular, plausibly deniable.

Standing there in the rain, it seemed to me that somebody had drawn up sides, and that the world was on the other side. Here I was, working under the auspices of "Mr. Chance," presumably answering to the National Security Council, and as I understood it taking orders from General Singlaub and . . . ah, forget it. I was being used again, had become an obscure instrument of a U.S. policy that refused to declare itself openly.

What I, of course, didn't know at the time was that things were about to change. Not only were the Saudis about to contribute several million to the Contra cause, but I was informed five weeks later in a secret briefing with "Chance" that there was an additional $38 million being given secretly.

In mid-June I was contacted by Rob Owen and told that General Singlaub wanted to see me. I *understood* Owen to say that the Rainbow mission had been tentatively approved but that the general had some questions. I flew from Tegucigalpa into New Orleans and then went to Denver, where I rented a car and drove up to Boulder. When I got into town I ran into Tom Posey and Colonel Robert Brown, publisher of *Soldier of Fortune*. I told them I was there to see Singlaub and they asked if they could come along. I didn't see any harm, but when we got to Singlaub's place the general told the two of them in the plainest English I'd heard in a while that they weren't sitting in on our meeting.

Once Posey and Brown left the room we got down to business. I told the general all we needed was the right hardware. He said it would be difficult to get Sam-7's.

He must have noticed my disappointment. He then told me that on my way back to Tegucigalpa I should make a stop at Aggacote, a secret supply base in Honduras and the headquarters of the Contra brain-trust. I took it that being told to stop there meant that my summer Christmas stocking would soon be filled with some helpful weapons and supplies.

Much later, as I understand it, General Singlaub and Rob Owen would give testimony at the Iran-Contra hearings that indicated the Rainbow mission had never even received tentative approval. Without intending to cast any doubt whatsoever on the honesty and integrity of either of these gentlemen, I do say that what was said to me by Rob Owen prior to my trip to Boulder, and by General Singlaub during my meeting with him, at least indicated to me that all that stood in the way of my carrying out the Rainbow mission was logistical support—support that I believe I was given to understand would be forthcoming. (In May of 1987 I arranged for an independent polygraph service, Locaters International, to question me on this point and I passed the polygraph with apparent vindication.)

Returning to my narrative, at Aggacote the next afternoon I was walking over to the main office for a three o'clock talk with some suppliers when a supply sergeant I'd struck up an acquaintance with stopped me and pointed out a man with short-cropped hair and wearing gym shoes, a T-shirt and khakis. The man had "Marine" written all over him and I guessed who he was.

"That's the man from Washington—Colonel Ollie North," the supply sergeant said, confirming my speculation. "They say he planned the Grenada invasion in his basement. He's with the National Security Council now."

Across the way, Colonel North stopped to talk to a wounded commander from the Bluefields area, reached into his leather case and gave the Creole commander something. When Colonel North walked away I went over to the commander. His son had fought with my unit a couple of times. When I got to where the Creole was sitting I saw that the colonel had given him a leather pistol holster.

"Do you know that man, Sam?" the commander asked.

"I'm not sure," I said.

"He knows you."

I didn't say anything further, but wondered to myself how Colonel North might know about *me*. Through Rob Owen, I guessed. Or maybe General Singlaub? Whatever, I was damn pleased.

At the three o'clock briefing I was told my wish-list might be soon filled. Soon turned out to be August. When I was called back to Aggacote I found out materiel had started coming in. I never saw so much military hardware in one spot. I even got three emergency frequencies so I could get air-dropped supplies. When I left the hut that August day a "package"—as I understood it from Singlaub—was waiting. A Contra soldier ran over to tell me. "Come and see, commandante." I tried to keep from slapping his back too hard when I saw the SAM-7 ground-to-air missiles and the M-60 machine guns. Before I could get the rest of my new stoppers loaded for the flight to the base I got another surprise. A message from Singlaub. According to my notes, when I placed a call to him he told me he had the boats I'd asked for, and more. They were classified Kevlars. The notes I took while listening to the general's description read:

"Bullet proof; self-sealing fuel tanks; cannot be detected by radar; 800-mile range; operates in depths of two feet: 2500 pounds of load capacity; anti-infrared tracking system: cruises at 65 mph; 180 degree turns at 40 mph in 4½ seconds; twin 50 caliber machine gun mounts in rear; 20 mm mounted in front."

I was sure when I got on board the supply-stocked plane that my Rainbow mission would be a success. It was set for early October.

I had, of course, no way of knowing that all hell had broken loose back at the jungle camp, that while I was away the Indian nation had been conducting its once-a-year meeting to elect their council of elders and administrators and their military leaders too, that not only were intramural tensions at an all-time high but there were other problems as well . . . heavy rains keeping the food supplies from being delivered, three companies of Miskito troops surrounded by 2400 Sandinistas near Puerto Cabezas inside Nicaragua. As soon as I learned what was going on I used my new emergency frequencies to call for some air-lift aid for the hemmed-in units, and a fresh Contra force of forty helped the trapped Miskitos break the Sandinista circle at its weakest point and pull off an escape-and-evade tactic. But it took a week to work. At the same time I called headquarters for more fire power, I asked for an emergency food drop as well. The troops at the base camp had only eaten three meals in the last week. The same for the refugees. Once I had rations on the way I then turned to the politics.

When the command staff huddled in my thatched houch we got down to the root of the problem, which turned out to be a self-proclaimed leader of the Indians named Stedman Faggot (his real name).

Faggot was an asset of the FDN—someone counted on to keep the Indians under control and prevent them from having too much of a say in the new government should the Contras ultimately be successful. Rumor had it that Faggot had grafted over $70,000—some of which was funds collected in the U.S. for the express purpose of aiding the refugees.

With the money Faggot had access to, he hired thirty men who could be used as enforcers. He was also paying as much as 200–300 limpiras (100–150 U.S. dollars) to Indians who would vote for him in the upcoming election. But word of the corruption was spreading and Faggot, apparently getting desperate, began making death threats to key Miskito leaders.

Before I could move to intervene Faggot made good on his threats, beating up one of the elders and killing five higher-ups and burying them in the dense jungle. I was captured as well and held at the hospital camp site, but I succeeded in escaping through an open hospital window and outran my pursuers back to the commando base. Once there, I called my aide into my houch and dictated a letter that could be carried back to Faggot's men. In the letter I told them to lay down their weapons, that enough death had taken place, that Indians should not fight Indians. I also told them that since I was, in effect, the representative of my government in the region and controlled supplies flowing into the area, I had the option of cutting off supplies to their families and friends back in the refugee camps.

The bluff worked. Preceded by a runner with a white flag who carried the letter to the rebels and told them I was on my way, I walked back to the hospital camp site unarmed and alone. When I arrived I found that half the rebels had left their weapons and fled. The others surrendered to me peacefully. As for Stedman Faggot, he and six others had ventured off the hospital grounds earlier in the day and been captured by the Honduras military.

It took a few weeks before the Miskito political situation showed signs of stabilizing, and at that point my thoughts turned, inevitably, to the Rainbow mission and the logistical problems we still confronted. I was in the midst of puzzling out some of these problems when General John Singlaub intervened.

I had been asked by Rob Owen to get in touch with the general. When I did by phone I received the worse possible news, telling me that the Rainbow mission would have to be put "on hold" until after the elections, that I was to go back to the States to be treated for a mild case of skin cancer I'd contracted and after the treatment was finished wait for word about coming back.

Skin cancer? *That* could wait. Of course I was concerned about it, but I felt it was more important to help the Indians get a leg up, and the Rainbow mission could do that, providing it went into effect quickly.

As the general ended the phone call I ran those two words "on hold," over and over again in my head. It seemed as if once a government took over a war, nobody wanted Sam Hall. It was fine and dandy for me to spill blood but only if it was on an "unofficial" basis. I guess by now I should have been used to it, but still, the order to go home left me feeling deep-bone depressed, and I don't think I was afflicted by self-pity—more like anger and frustration.

I had a tough time telling the Miskitos I was leaving. As I've made clear, I'd come to love them in the months we fought together. I shook hands with each one of them and told them if there was ever a way I could help in the future...but at that point it didn't seem likely that I'd ever get the chance and the words struck me as ringing hollow. I got the hell out of there.

Back in the States I just couldn't stop thinking about the Miskitos, wondering how they were doing in the fighting to get their land back and how the new leaders were working out and whether Stedman Faggot would make any more trouble. I just didn't feel any fight except the Miskitos' could interest me enough to make me go back to the war. I knew, though, that I had to get a job soon... my adventures had used up nearly all of my share of the family money. Finally in late December a friend offered me a job with Roberds' Furniture in Bradenton, Florida. Furniture never exactly turned me on, but Roberds' was doing ninety million in sales every year; and when my friend dared me to work my way to number one salesman, I shrugged and took him up on it, and for the next four months talked myself hoarse in a pitch that would have put a carny con-man to shame. By the middle of April I'd beat the dare and made my mark as Roberd's top salesman. Big deal. It didn't keep me from following the Contra war news in the Florida papers.

One rainy afternoon I was on the floor at work, winding down after a day of selling, when I spotted a wealthy-looking gray-haired couple in their sixties. They were wandering around the bedding department and our man in mattresses was busy with another customer. Hall to the rescue. Waiting on the two seniors turned out to be a big turning point in my wonderful selling career. "Could I help you?" I said. "We have a sale on Sealys today." The woman's reply was, "Thank you, no. We don't need any help. You may go."

Well, this was a hell of a comedown from the days when I was Commandanté Zulu with my own army. I felt like settling the score for poor old Willie Loman right then and there. *Death of a Customer.* One thing was sure, I wouldn't spend another day of my life selling furniture.

A week later I called a couple of contacts and joined a rescue mission in Africa, but that didn't work out and left me bone-beat and way way down. Once again, back in Florida the rest didn't do that much to pick me up. I was forty nine years old now and still tilting at windmills. There was no way I could keep soldiering for much longer and I had to get steady work. So in spite of all my promises to myself I went back to Roberds again. This time they sent me to their Tampa-St. Petersburg store, where I lasted scarcely a month. Fortunately the paper on a piece of property I'd sold fifteen years earlier matured and I was sent $25,000.

In late May I moved in with my best Dayton-days friend, Jim Bonbright, who had made millions in the beer-distributing business and built a huge house at Tierra Verde outside St. Petersburg. His wife had moved out and left him with 9000 square feet and a patio door that opened onto Tampa Bay. I settled in but couldn't stop reading the papers and their news that things weren't going so well for the Contras.

There were reports they would be kicked out of Honduras because they presumably were causing the government there too much upset. When the Contras made strikes into Nicaragua now, the Sandinistas were chasing them back over the border into Honduras, which meant the Honduran army was doing some fighting and the government was afraid they'd get too deeply drawn in. They were taking a few casualties too, and their people would soon find out what was going on. It also didn't much help that the Contras were calling the Honduran border areas where they were camped, "New Nicaragua." Not exactly diplomatic.

* * *

The reports during the summer and into the fall were increasingly grim and with them I was getting increasingly antsy for action and even more worried about the Miskitos. If things totally fell apart down there they'd be the first to feel the worst of it. I was more than ready when Chance called in November to set up a meeting with me in El Salvador to talk over the Contras' situation.

On the 13th of the month I flew to San Salvador and checked in at the Sheraton. After dinner Chance showed up on schedule in my room. He told me it was almost certain the Honduran government was going to make a move and that the Contras had only a few months more at the most in Honduras.

I asked about the refugees, reminded him that they were promised a sanctuary. He told me that the refugees would also be forced to leave, that El Salvador couldn't take them and neither could Costa Rica, which was neutral. Our Ambassador Tambs couldn't help. Chance said his people had tried Belize, Panama and Guatemala—without any luck.

All of which meant the refugees would have to go back to Nicaragua. I asked Chance what I could do to help and he told me that if I wanted to become involved he would call me soon, that there was some information I might be able to help him with.

I settled for that. There was no doubt in my mind that I wanted to become involved. I already *was* involved. After praying and fighting and eating and bleeding with the Contras, there was no way I could just forget them. If the 1800 Miskitos who were still in Honduras had to go back home and face the Sandinistas with their Russian arms and equipment, they'd be wiped out along with the rest of the Indians left in Nicaragua—and then the whole race would disappear.

It was the first of December when Chance called and said to meet him the next day at the Orlando Day's Inn. When he came to my room he gave me some expense money to cover the El Salvador trip and then got down to it.

He told me he wanted me to go to Nicaragua in ten days—not,

as it turned out, to fight with the Miskitos but to make a contact. In Managua.

That one flattened me for more than a few minutes, but I told Chance I was interested. He then described the mission to me and told me about my contact, code name "Roberto." With Roberto's and my help, Chance hoped to update some of his situation stats. A bit cryptic for me, but what the hell.

Back in St. Pete I waited for word from Chance and wondered about the assignment. It was one thing to lead freedom fighters against the Sandinistas in the jungle, but a spy mission? Not precisely my speed.

On December 7 the headlines splashed the news in the Miami paper. "Honduras to Expel Contra Forces." That night Chance called with his orders, told me to make a commercial reservation for the 11th, Thursday, with a return date of the 16th. I was supposed to meet him at the Tan-Sahsa ticket counter in Miami two hours before the flight and receive further instructions.

Thursday morning I wrote out a note for my friend Jim Bonbright asking him to take care of some odds and ends while I was away and letting him know that I couldn't tell him where I was off to but that I'd be back on the 16th. I put the note on the kitchen table and left the house before Jim woke up, then drove to the airport and flew to Orlando and on to Miami. When Chance showed up at the ticket counter, he gave me a scare.

There had been a change in plans, he said, and right away I started thinking that once again I'd been put "on hold." Chance suggested we get a cup of coffee at the snack bar where he laid out his problem.

His people had gotten word that the Sandinistas were increasing their armament and improving their defenses. The Managua newspaper was full of advertisements for volunteers and news of reserves being called to duty. There was a possibility that the Sandinistas had decided that the time was ripe to strike at the Contras, especially now that the Contras' position in Honduras had been weakened. So under the circumstances it seemed that more than just the stats from Roberto was needed. Chance now began filling me in on the situation at some of the major Nicaraguan air bases. According to him, the bases at Puerto Cabezas, Sandino, Montecino and Punta Huete had been rebuilt to accept Soviet fighters. His people also had word that work was being done on the runways to ready them for long-range Soviet reconnaissance planes and bombers.

Chance rang a bell with that last. I had gone to Puerto Cabezas on a mission with a Miskito team a year or so before and had found a very modern military base nearby bulging with some 6000 Sandinista troops. The airfield runway was 13,000 feet long and the tarmac was twenty-four inches thick, which meant the heaviest Russian bomber could land on it. Three years earlier the runway had been 5500 feet and thin enough to break up under the big bombers.

Chance interrupted the briefing to take out a map. He pointed out the military installation at Puerto Cabezas, calling my attention to drawings of the Kukalaya and Bombanita bridges, and told me that after I got the information from Roberto about enemy troop strength and number of planes, helicopters, tanks and frigates I was to look around the Puerto Cabezas area and see what kind of security was set up at the bridges. If the Sandinistas moved against the Miskitos left in the country, the Indians would need some time to escape to the Sukitpin mountains. Blowing up the bridges would help.

At that point Chance pointed to the area around Punta Huete air base, which was sixty kilometers north of Managua. Supposedly the Sandinistas were building an underground tunnel there for MIG fighters. I understood that Chance invited me to get a look at the base and see if the reports were true. Also I was to see if the Cubans at the base were assembling Mi-24s.

Chance's final request, as I got it, was that I look around the Sandino air base if there was enough time. There had also been reports of Mi-24s being assembled there, though spy satellites had not confirmed the rumors.

Chance then walked me to the loading gate, wished me luck and shook my hand. As he turned and walked away, the PA system broke the news that Tan-Sahsa was boarding passengers for the flight to Managua.

I was back in it.

On a mission in Nicaragua.
The Rio Coco river is in the
background.

Preparing for an assault on a Sandinista base near La Tronquera, Nicaragua.

Tom Posey, founder of
CMA (Civilian Military
Assistance), and I pose for
photo in Denver, Colorado
just before meeting with
General John Singlaub.

Reviewing troops at Commando Base T.E.A. in Honduras.

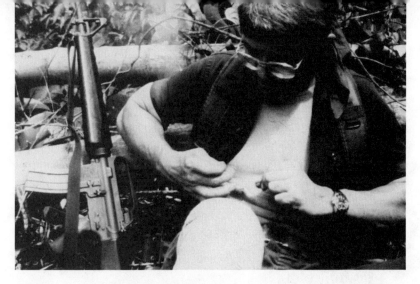

Stitching up a bayonet wound suffered during a firefight in Nicaragua.

During a lull in the fighting I had a 28-bed hospital built in my camp in Honduras. I financed it with some of my own money and with money sent to me from friends back home. Here we are working on the thatched roof.

Conducting a briefing just prior to entering Nicaragua for an attack against the Sandinistas.

Although the Miskitos had made use of bows and arrows early in the war against the Sandinistas, they never saw a collapsible, fiberglass Sniper bow. Here I'm teaching them to use it.

Each Sunday, if I was not inside Nicaragua, I brought to the outlying refugee camps clothing, medicine, toys and candy that had been donated by friends back home. I also held sick calls and offered what little medical help I could.

UNITED STATES COUNCIL FOR WORLD FREEDOM		1390
P. O. BOX 39027		91-170/1221
PHOENIX, AZ 85069		

August 23 19 85

$ 794.15

PAY TO THE ORDER OF * * * * Sam Hall * * * * *

* * * SEVEN HUNDRED NINETY FOUR AND 15/100* * * * DOLLARS

VOID AFTER 90 DAYS

19TH AVE. & THUNDERBIRD OFFICE (067)
1910 WEST THUNDERBIRD
PHOENIX, ARIZONA 85023

THE Arizona BANK

W A Johnson

MEMO

067 176975

⑊000 1390⑊ ⑊1221017 06⑊

I never accepted a salary during the time I was in Nicaragua. To cover expenses, though, I would occasionally receive cash from my contact, Rob Owen, or checks from the United States Council of World Freedom, an organization headed by General John Singlaub. One such check is shown here.

Collecting identification from dead Sandinistas inside Nicaragua.

After 14 days in enemy territory (Nicaragua), I'm on my way back to safety via a dug-out canoe on the Rio Coco River.

I nicknamed this little girl, "Doveness." Here she's holding her pet chicken. Two months after this photo was taken, her 13-year-old brother, "Tiger," graduated from my commando school.

Map I created showing targets to be hit as part of the "Rainbow Mission." The mission called for a simultaneous attack against two bridges and a military airstrip and would have required over a million dollars in logistical support.

Instructing staff in placement of explosive charges under the Sissen bridge. Five weeks later, the bridge was blown.

Here I inspect Tiger's weapon. Six weeks later the boy was wounded in fighting outside Puerto Cabezas.

Jimmie Bonbright and I talk with Pete Rose at the Cincinnati Reds' spring training camp in Tampa, Florida (1987). I am indebted to Rose, a longtime friend, for providing support and encouragement during the years I had a drug problem.

TEN

By the time I got on the plane the adrenaline was flowing, and it hadn't let up when we touched down at the Managua airport at six-thirty. I went straight to the InterContinental Hotel and downed a couple of drinks and dinner. At ten-thirty I went up to my room and got ready to fire up Chance's plans.

I put on a pair of Levis and dark top over my khakis and yellow t-shirt, stuffed a blue bandanna in one of my pockets. I also ran hot water into the tub so that I wouldn't broadcast my return through the hotel plumbing system hours later.

Outside the InterContinental I waited as planned on the cement bench by the taxi stand. I was supposed to sit there every night at the same time till contact was made and I heard the right code words. I scored at 11:01 the first night. An old blue Toyota pulled up and a window rolled down. A couple of Spanish eyes checked me over while two Latin lips formed the magic circle.

"Zulu."

"Roberto."

"Commandanté."

I eased into the passenger side and shook Roberto's hand. He smiled, revealing two gold teeth. He was a little man, about thirty years old.

"The set-up has changed, Roberto. Let's get out of here and I'll clue you in."

As we drove off I told him about the mission to Punta Huete. He didn't like it. Getting up close to the base would be tricky and besides it would crowd his time. I knew from Chance that Roberto needed to get some first-hand information about the area south of Vegas on the Honduran side of the border. The country below

295

Vegas might make a fast southern getaway route for the FDN toward the Nicaraguan gold mine country of Bonanza and Rosita. Those two places would give them a safe haven where they could set up a base camp that would replace the one in Honduras. But Vegas would be a long drive and a tough area to reconnoiter once Roberto got there. And he had to hand over his information sheets to me on Saturday the 13th. If we missed our meeting that day I'd allow Roberto at most two extra days to do his work and catch me before I had to leave on the 16th. Roberto would have to send his findings to a drop in Costa Rica if we didn't connect before I left. That would cost Chance weeks. With all the numbers we'd be dealing with in our reports, I didn't want to forget our date, so I wrote down December 13th on the Punta Huete-Sandino map and stuck it in my back pocket.

Roberto reluctantly agreed to help me with the Punta Huete probe, and we headed for the base. On the way he pulled into a darkened shopping center, I got out my pen-light and Roberto updated my stats on military hardware and troop strength. I quickly noted that the Nicaraguan Air Force had jumped from 16,000 to 18,000 men. Before I studied the rest of the numbers on the ride to Punta Huete I scotch-taped both sides of the paper so that the numbers wouldn't bleed from all the sweating I'd be doing in the Nicaraguan heat the next couple of days.

At 12:30 in the morning we pulled up to what looked like a farm with corn fields and a red water tower.

"This is the base, commandanté. Here is the water tower on your map."

"I'll see you in two hours, friend. Don't forget to flick your headlights each time you come to a curve in the road. And don't forget the bicycle either."

The bike was my ticket back to Managua from Sandino, where Roberto would take me after he picked me up again. Meanwhile he'd take a two-hour joy ride outside the area so as not to tip off the Sandinistas that something was up.

When the dark swallowed the Toyota I headed through the corn fields past some barracks and climbed over two six-foot cyclone fences. I knew they weren't wired for shock because there were vines climbing all over them. My map led me to the big mound where two rows of bricks spelled out the number "25," which stood for the 25th Nicaraguan Aviation Wing. From the ID mound I could look down on the base and check out the action. The mission had been a piece of cake so far. There were sentries working in pairs, but they didn't see me and penetration was easy.

Down below on the base there wasn't much happening except for a little welding. I took some mental notes on the aircraft and the buildings and then retraced my steps back over the fences and past the barracks to the water tower and waited in some weeds by the road. In fifteen minutes Roberto's flickering headlights signaled he was through cooling his wheels and a couple of curves later he pulled up beside me. The moon lit up an old bike that looked like a reject from the Managua Salvation Army store. It was roped to the trunk of the Toyota with the rusty handlebars sticking through the glassless back window.

I got in beside Roberto and we headed for Sandino, Roberto complaining the whole way about how he was losing time for his Vegas mission. When we got near the base he dropped me and the bike near some bushes by a small hacienda. By that time it was about three-thirty and still moonlit. I hid the bike behind the bushes near the hacienda sign and tied the blue bandanna around my head to hide my light hair from the full-moon glare. I picked my way then through the bushes and a stand of trees and crawled through more brush and high grass. I jumped a fence and found myself fifty or sixty feet from a Mi-24 and a Mi-26 parked on a helicopter pad. There was a lot of welding going on here and I was trying to figure out what was being bonded when all of a sudden I heard what sounded like a pistol shot. By the time I dove into some high grass it was clear the "shot" was just a welder's mistake, but it turned out I wasn't the only one the noise put on alert. Thirty or forty feet ahead a guard with a big German shepherd on a leash was checking the area. My heart was thumping, but the man and his dog went by

me without breaking stride. Either I was downwind of them or the
pooch had a bad cold. Once the canine patrol was out of sight I
retraced my steps and headed for the bike.

A quarter mile of pedaling later I realized I didn't have my bandanna, but it would be forty-five minutes before daybreak and
maybe I could make it if the bike's wheels stayed attached to the
frame. It was supposed to be a five-speed, but I'd only been able to
locate one. After about twenty more minutes I stopped at an alley-
way in a little village and took a cigarette break. When I came out
of the alley on my bike I met a flatbed truck headed in the right
direction and grabbed one of the metal supports that braced the
sides, then held onto the handlebars with my left hand for the ride
of my life. The truck driver couldn't see me because his rearview
mirror was tilted up. In ten minutes I was inside Managua and
parted company with the truck and stashed the bike and the Levis
behind a sign, then walked the last six blocks to the InterContinental.

At the hotel I peeled off my clothes and slipped into my pre-
filled bath. After an hour's soak I dressed and lined up my stage
props for the day's operations. I stuffed a small canvas bag with
my camera and film plus a pair of binoculars and my passport. I
also put on a pair of Banana Republic pants that had *seven* pockets,
filling them with maps and Roberto's up-date. No way was I going
to leave any of those items in my room. When I felt certain everything was covered I made like a tourist and went down to the
dining room for breakfast. Four eggs and six sausages later I was in
the lobby buying a map of Nicaragua, then found myself a chair
and drew a hand map of the main roads. When I asked the desk
clerk if he could find a driver to show me around the country he
said he didn't think he'd be able to scare one up so I decided to
grab a cab and rent it for the day.

When I'd hailed one I told him I wanted him to drive me around
the countryside near Punta Huete. "*Quanto?*"

"*Si, si*, fifty dollars. *Si*."

Actually I wanted the cabbie to drive close to the base so I could get some pictures. When the driver got us within two or three miles of Punta Huete, though, it turned out he didn't even know which road to take to the base. I tried to tell him I knew the way but he wasn't listening. Ever find a cab driver who did? We did a lot of backing up and turning around, and finally came to a spot just around the corner from where I had penetrated the base the night before.

The trouble started when we turned the corner. Two helicopter officers in uniform and an old peasant woman were standing by the road, and the driver stopped the car before I could say anything and actually asked the three of them for directions. Worse, the two pilots and the woman were piling into the cab for a ride to the base.

After we took off, the tall pilot in the front seat immediately started asking me questions that went like this . . .

"You *Norteamericano?*"

"Yes. I'm a reporter. Here's my ID. I'm doing a story on Nicaragua's farm products."

"How long here?"

"A couple of days."

Up ahead I could see the corn field and the water tower. Then we were 150 feet from a guard station about the size of a one-hole outhouse. Then seventy-five feet. God, the crazy cabbie was heading straight for the guard. When we stopped three feet from him the young guy, wearing civvies plus a baseball cap and a pair of high-top boots, walked out of the booth bored as you please and dropped the rope that blocked the way. The driver went on through and up the road near the mound where I had done my observing the night before.

At a fork in the middle of the corn fields the woman got out of the cab and I figured she must have been a support worker at the base, which still couldn't be seen from that spot. She started off up the right fork. After the two officers traded a few words with the driver they shook my hand and got out, then they too started up the right fork. I told them I'd like to see what was down that way and asked if could I go with them. They said no, so I asked if I could take the left fork. That was okay and the driver started down the road. A half mile later I spotted at least a million linear feet in all diameters of pipe and counted thirty spanking new fifteen-by-forty fuel tanks protected by sheds without walls. While the driver watched the road I stuck my right arm halfway down the outside back door of the cab and snapped as many pictures of the sheds as I could.

After another mile we came to a seedy looking little clump of ten or twelve houses, then turned around and started back—and spotted two Sandinista MPs back at the fork in the road. How at that moment I wished I'd told my driver ten minutes earlier, "The InterContinental, Jaime." The MPs shouted at the cab to halt, ordered me to get out and show them some ID. I fumbled in my bag and produced the passport. When they asked me to empty my shirt and pants I somehow managed to shift the maps and Roberto's stats from pocket to pocket. When their search was finished they had my hand-drawn road map, but not the sketches of the bases with Roberto's stats.

I had noticed earlier that down the road the pilots took was a tall farm house that looked deserted but had to be the base intelligence outpost. There were no windows or doors on the farmhouse, but there were two big radio antennas on the roof. The two MPs told me to stay by the car while they went to the farmhouse to radio the Secret Service headquarters in Managua. They knew I wasn't going anywhere, they had my passport and false correspondent's card plus my camera and binoculars. While I stood by the car waiting for the two MPs, two more showed up. Then there were four. Then six. Finally the first two came back and we all got in my rental car and headed for Managua.

As I sat in the back seat wedged between two Sandinista soldiers who turned every now and then to eye me with suspicion, all I could think of was the L-23 "suicide" capsule lying in my vitamin case back at the hotel. The capsule had been issued to me in the event that I was captured and tortured for information. I'd taken care to tape it under my right lapel the night before when I'd penetrated the two airbases but hadn't brought it along on this trip because I hadn't expected trouble. As my mind churned with thoughts of what might lay ahead, the consequences of that decision began to loom larger. Would I have the guts to swallow the capsule, were it still in my possession? I still am not sure.

It was noon when we got to the Sandinista Information Bureau and the MPs hustled me into a room where an information officer and an interpreter were waiting. Before the door closed behind me two interrogators joined the group.

For three hours they directed fairly polite questions at me.

"Why did you not apply for a correspondent's certificate this morning?"

"I started out too early. I just wanted to drive around."

"What publication do you work for?"

"Washington Centre."

The interrogators then handed me back to the MPs, who drove me up near the top of the highest hill just outside Managua. We stopped at a squat building that I figured from the talk between the MPs was the Secret Service headquarters. There I got four more hours of grilling that got considerably less polite by the minute. A two-man team would ask me the same questions for about two hours and then be replaced by another team. Altogether there were six teams, each team having at least one English speaker. I kept giving them answers they didn't seem to want. As I reconstruct the q. and a. it went like this:

"Have you had any military training?"

"Yes, the United States Air Force in 1961."

"We have your passport. Do you expect us to think you are not CIA? Four trips to South Africa. Two to Chad. Thailand. Israel four times and eight to El Salvador!"

"I write novels. I need to make sure the background is real."

"Truly, Señor Hall? How many novels have you written?"

"Three."

"And what are their names?"

"Oh, *The Eye of the Storm, The Lay of the Land* and *Debbie Does Dayton.*" (Smart ass to the last.)

"And who is your publisher?"

"The Popular Press."

The more the interrogators badgered me the more I tried to lighten things up to keep from panicking.

"Do you know any military officers in the States, Señor Hall?"

"A few."

"Their names, please."

"Well, Colonel John E. Appleseed and Major Buster Brown."

"We will check on them. Your plane arrived from Miami. Do you live there."

"No. I was just staying there a few days."

"Where were you staying?"

"The No Tell Motel." Not funny, their stony faces told me.

At seven-thirty they decided to feed me some dinner. But I couldn't eat much even though I hadn't seen a calorie since the InterContinental. By eight I was back on their hot seat. The interrogators still came in teams of two, still six different teams. But now they were joined by observers whose ranks were getting higher. Word must have been out about me by then, because fresh faces kept gawking at me from the hallway. About nine-thirty the powers decided I could go to the bathroom. As soon as I got in the john I took Roberto's update out of my pants pocket and inserted it up my ass. I couldn't figure out why, but the Sandinistas still hadn't searched me after the two MPs watched my sleight-of-hand back at the road fork. I knew I couldn't flush the map down the toilet because of the scotch tape so I put it the first place I thought of and hoped the gentlemen in the interrogation room wouldn't notice my slowed-down awkward gait. If they did I doubted I could convince them I had a sudden onset of hemorrhoids.

Back to the room and the questions:

"Did you come here to kill Eugene Hasenfus?"

"No."

"Did you go anywhere besides Punta Huete?"

"No."

"What are the names of your novels?"

"Debbie Does Dayton, The Eye of the Needle and The Lay of the Land."

"The Eye of the Needle?"

"Yes."

"You are a liar."

I wanted to say right you are and shove it.

When after another hour-and-a-half of questions an officer told me I was going to be taken to the maximum security prison I knew I had to get that map out of my backside. The prison guards would find it for sure in a body search but there was at least a *chance* they might let me keep my socks if they decided to hold me. I asked for a last trip to the john, the major okayed it and I quickly transferred the map to my left sock.

El Chipote prison was at the very top of the steepest hill that climbed out of Managua. My first stop was a small room where a couple of portly guards proceeded to operate on my belongings, ripping my bag to shreds, then breaking my camera and binoculars down into more pieces than the makers probably knew existed. They took my clothes and money and then gave me the body search I was expecting. When it was over they threw a canvas T-shirt and a pair of canvas pants at me. No shoes. My heart sank. Where were my socks? I got my answer soon enough. I was in an interrogating room being grilled by two captains when one of the body-search guards came down the hallway yelling. When he turned the corner into the interrogation room he was holding my sock in one hand and Roberto's map in the other. Which, of course, was when all hell broke loose. There was much shouting in Spanish and running up and down the hallways. The officer who had been in charge of the questioning when the guard ran in now had Roberto's update in hand and started going at me about the December 13th date I'd written on the slip of paper.

"Are you *espía*?"

"No. I'm a correspondent."

"What is going to happen on December 13th?"

"Nothing."

"Are you *espía*?"

"No."

The same questions kept coming from different interrogators all night. The room had whitewashed walls and was bare except for a back-breaking straight chair I sat in and a raised platform with seats and a small table. Above my head I could see a microphone in the air-conditioning duct. What I judged to be every couple of hours the officers would give me a break by putting me in a two-by-three room with an air-conditioner going full blast. I froze clear down to my bone marrow in that little hacienda. About three in the morning one of the colonels got the bright idea I'd planted a homing device at Punta Huete and motioned to one of the guards to make me talk. The burly sergeant walked over to my chair and hustled me to the cold room, then kicked me hard in the ankle. Back to the grill room. A thousand questions and repeated kicks to the same ankle later, it was now nine in the morning. Which was when I met Lieutenant Lopez. He was in the middle of his quiz session when he tossed in a comment from the raised platform. "You are going to die, Señor Hall." Those words I remember exactly. I just stared at him. "You are *espía*. You knew the risks. We will kill you."

There were now three officers and two guards in the room. When my answers didn't please one of the officers, who didn't speak English, he pulled out his pistol and held it against my temple. One of the guards grabbed a wastepaper basket and held it in back of my head, presumably to catch the resulting mess of blood and brains. I could feel the pistol begin to move over my forehead. Was the man's gun-hand unsteady from nerves or rage? Sure then it would soon all be over, I said a last prayer and asked God to forgive my life of sins. The officer, however, abruptly pulled his pistol away and the questions started all over again.

About noon I finally decided they'd indeed kill me if they believed nobody knew I was in Nicaragua. Accordingly I decided to fatten up my story and switch gears. Capt. Ahvarado was doing the questioning. He spoke the best English of all the officers, having gone to college, I learned later, in Washington. But he'd been trained in intelligence in Cuba and Russia. He offered me smokes and once even coffee or coke, obviously to relax me so I'd talk.

"Are you a spy?"

"No. I was only looking for information."

"Mr. Hall, you must come to your senses. Who do you spy for? The CIA?"

"No. I gather information for the Phoenix Battalion."

"What is the Phoenix Battalion?"

"A private organization that sells information to interested parties."

"To the United States government?"

"I don't know."

By now there was a small crowd of officers and guards in the room. Apparently they'd been so entertained listening to the Sam Hall show through the air-conditioning ducts that they wanted to be part of the studio audience.

Capt. Ahvarado was just warming up.

"Who is the leader of the Phoenix Battalion?"

"I don't know."

"Who are the interested parties you spoke about?"

"I don't know."

"What were you doing in Managua?"

"Meeting a contact."

"You have a contact in Managua?"

"I don't think he lives in Managua."

"What is his name?"

"Roberto."

"His surname?"

"I don't know."

"Describe him—one minute, Mr. Hall."

One of the other officers left the room and came back with one of those plastic cards like you see on TV police shows, the kind with the outline of a human face on it. He had an art pencil so he could draw in the details from my description. I knew I couldn't afford any more slip-ups like forgetting the title of one of my "novels," so I started describing a guard named Garcia who was either in the interrogation room or right outside all the time. He was a tall character with glasses thick as goggles. And sunken cheeks. Fingers long enough to pick pockets. A start toward a potbelly. About fifty years old.

"Roberto is a tall man."

"Go on, Mr. Hall."

"Well, he's got cheeks that are sunk in."

"And?"

"Long fingers. He looks like he'd make a good piano player. But he's a little bit out of shape, needs to drop a few pounds."

"You are showing intelligence to cooperate in this way, Mr. Hall. Now, what is going to happen on December 13th?" . . .

The interrogators just kept coming in those teams of two the rest of the day, and I was getting increasingly groggy. I hadn't slept at all since arriving in Managua. At times the officers seemed more interested in Roberto than me, so I just kept describing Garcia minus, of course, his thick glasses. A couple of times during each of the next two days an interrogator named Guiterrez would draw his pistol and put the barrel against my skull while a guard repeated the wastebasket at the back of my head. Each time it happened I said my silent prayers, sure those were going to be my last few moments on earth, and then I almost wished they had been when one of the guards would rush me through the door of the cold room and bang my head against the wall or kick the same spot on my left ankle. Say this for them, they knew how to avoid bruising a whole body in case some human rights type should happen by.

About seven at night I got the worst scare yet. Instead of the team of questioners I'd come to expect every few hours, Captain Ahvarado walked in the room.

"We are taking you to Punta Huete."

"Why?"

"You are a spy. Since you will not talk, we will take you to Punta Huete to kill you. It is appropriate that you die there."

He let that sink in, then a homely little man I'd never seen before came to the door of the whitewashed room and said in the King's English, "The van is ready for Punta Huete, captain." Ahvarado pushed me toward the door. *"You heard. The van is ready."* I didn't move. I was sure I was going to die. No point in cooperating now. I was groggier than ever. No sleep. I tried to think, told myself I had to keep caring if I wanted to live. But at that point I really was about ready to throw in the towel. Strange, but what kept me hanging in was my terrific thirst. If I only had a cold drink . . . I decided to play for time.

"Captain, could we make a deal? If you give me a cigarette and a drink of cold water, I'll give you some names."

"Of course."

Ahvarado called one of the guards. *"Un cigarillo y agua para Señor Hall, por favor. Y una pluma y papel."*

"Si, capitán."

When I got the "last meal" Ahvarado lit the cigarette for me and I took a gulp of the water. Then I started writing down names on the paper. "General Mike Motors. Colonel Harland Sanders. Major Doug Domo." I was taking as long as I could, then asked for another cigarette and more water. Ahvarado provided them. I kept writing names and drinking and smoking, all in slow motion. "Admiral Perry Moore. Commander U.S. Able." When I saw Ahvarado getting restless I wrote, "Send my body back to my son. David Hall. Dayton, Ohio." Then I read the last line out loud. As soon as I did two guards grabbed the water and cigarette, cuffed me and led me through an outer door to the big van. The tailgates opened and I was shoved in. There were three or four compartments in the van but no windows. A guard behind a screen told me to keep my chin on my chest at all times so I wouldn't see anything. I was still barefoot.

With no outer windows my compartment was black as night. If I lifted my chin off my chest the man behind the screen would yell out an order in Spanish. I was on my knees in the rear left corner of the compartment. If my hands hadn't been cuffed behind my back the position would have been appropriate, since I was praying as hard as I could.

Amid shouted Spanish commands from outside, the van finally started to roll. I counted the stops—for traffic lights, I guessed—to try to figure out where we were in Managua till there weren't any more stops and the van hit a steady pace. I moved my head up a fraction of an inch at a time till I could just get a glimpse of the guard, and when he turned his head away I raised mine to work the painful kinks out of my neck. That ploy worked three or four times, but then he swiveled his head before I was expecting it and caught me.

"Tú estás muerto, gringo." I believed him.

My heart jumped at every turn, down-throttle and stop the van made. Once we parked, the engine idling for what seemed like at least ten minutes, and I thought This is it. But the engine revved up and we were rolling again.

Some two hours after we left the prison we stopped again, and this time the engine cut off. For about half an hour nothing happened. The van just sat there. When I managed to get off my knees and into a sitting position the guard didn't leave the screen but he also didn't say anything. Then I could hear four or five vehicles pull up behind the van, their engines stopped, followed by Spanish commands and footsteps on all sides of the van. Something was going to happen now—but it didn't. The talking and walking let up. I sat and sat, figuring I was going to cash it in at any minute, and needing to piss worse than I could ever remember. But still nothing happened.

Finally there was a surge of activity from outside and I heard the bolt on the van door slip. The doors opened and I raised up my head, but the lights from three or four vehicles blinded me. Then I recognized Captain Ahvarado's voice from about twenty yards away.

"Keep your head down."

"*Por favor, capitán,* permissible to urinate?"

"One moment, Mr. Hall."

By now my eyes were adjusting to the light and I could see uniformed soldiers all around me. I was standing on concrete. The soldiers wore machine gun magazine vests, their rifles were at port arms. One of them took an order in Spanish and walked over to me to take off my handcuffs. After some minutes that seemed like a whole day Ahvarado broke the silence.

"Now, Mr. Hall."

"Right here?"

"Yes."

With my chin still on my chest I did my best and finally nature began to overcome humiliation. Before I'd finished a deep rich voice I didn't recognize suddenly broke in. "It is three-thirty in the morning and you are now pissing on Punta Huete." It may sound funny reading it here, but at the time it sounded like a death sentence. I was back at the base where I'd been arrested, they were sure to kill me here. I raised my eyes as far as I could get away with and saw a column of soldiers facing me in the firing-squad position.

A soldier grabbed me by the arm, spun me around and pushed my head against the van doors. He put a pistol to my head and said, 'Pray." Another voice asked, "Are you Catholic?" Ahvarado answered for me. "No. He is a Baptist." The soldier held the gun to my heart for several minutes, leaving me to wonder when he would pull the trigger. Now there was another order in Spanish, he took the pistol away and put the handcuffs back on me. I never thought I'd be so happy to feel a set of cuffs.

Ahvarado's voice was next. "Lie down on your stomach." The soldier pushed me down and ground my face into the concrete. My best view was undercarriages of the van and two other vehicles. Not a sound for the next twenty minutes. I filled the time trying to figure out just exactly where we were . . . it looked to be an airstrip tarmac on the military base but I obviously couldn't see much in my position and without my glasses.

Suddenly Ahvarado and the rich deep voice began talking, and then Ahvarado walked to one of the vehicles and got on the short-wave radio. After he signed off he came over and stood looking down at me. "Any minute now, Mr. Hall." But it was more like a half hour later when Ahvarado said, "You can get up now, Mr. Hall. We have sent your picture to Ronald Reagan."

It turned out they'd been waiting there all that time for the American spy satellite to make its every-ninety-minutes pass over the tarmac. When I picked myself up I stole a look to my left and spotted a row of what had to be jet-fighters.

Quickly somebody grabbed me and pushed me back through the van doors. Then absolutely nothing happened for several hours.

Suddenly there was again much talking and the van's cab-doors opened, then shut. The engine turned over and five or six other motors followed suit. We were rolling again, but less than an hour later we were stopped and I was pulled out of the van at the fork in the road where I'd been arrested. From there the Sandinistas tried to make me retrace my steps up to and after the point where they caught me. I was still convinced I was going to die, so again there was no percentage in helping them out. Besides, I still didn't have any shoes and damn well didn't feel like leading them through all that underbrush with its spiders and snakes.

When they were convinced I wasn't going to help they shoved me back in the van and we headed off to El Chipote.

Days later I did replay the Sandino mission for them. By then they'd convinced me that somebody had seen me come into the InterContinental around six-thirty the morning of my mission and they were at me to account for the hours in between. They obviously knew so much now that I figured there wouldn't be anything lost in telling them where I'd broken their security net. In fact, it could have the advantage of shaking them up. They already knew I was spying at Punta Huete.

The van now took us out to Sandino and they put me in a glassed-in jeep and drove me around till I recognized the hacienda and the sign where I'd hidden the bike. We got out and I led them through the bushes and trees and the tall grass where the dog with the bad nose had missed me. After about ten minutes searching the area, a non-com picked my bandanna out of the tall grass and waved it over his head. So now the Sandinistas had to know I was telling them the truth—at least about aspects of the mission.

As we headed back toward Sandino there was a lot of traffic on the road, cars being stopped by the military police and traffic jams everywhere. At one point we passed an open car carrying three American women who had the look and air of reporters. When one of them pointed at me and shouted something like "There he is," I wanted to jump out of the jeep and kiss her, figuring that now that they'd seen me the outside world would know too . . .

Once back at El Chipote guards hustled me out of the van and showed me to my new digs—a cellblock in a maximum security "hard time" prison. The cell that was going to be home for who knew how long was one of about twelve connected holes burrowed under the Nicaraguan hillside. Behind the heavy metal door with only an eleven-by-fourteen-inch square peep-slot for air and a food plate was a nine-by-seven bunker. The peep-slot was locked shut most of the time. The ceiling and floors and walls were all concrete. No windows. One dim light that looked to be early Thomas Edison was recessed in the wall above the door. Living here would be like being buried. My furniture was a slab of plywood sitting on some rods mortared into the wall. And the mattress: a six-foot long, two-foot wide, one-inch thick sack of little lumps that smelled badly and always felt wet. The "shower" was behind a little passageway cut into the concrete. (Janet Leigh was better off at the Bates motel.) There wasn't any soap. No toilet paper either. About four in the morning they turned on the water for an hour, which was when you could stand next to the pipe that was flush with the wall and enjoy the trickle while you swatted the cockroaches that came out with the water. The bugs were bigger than I'd seen anywhere, even in the Sinai. Besides the cucarachas there were outsized spiders and mosquitos. I tried to pass the time seeing how many bugs I could kill in twenty-four hours but I never knew what my record was because I couldn't accurately keep time. That first day I found a chunk of concrete on the floor and made four notches on the plywood to count the days since I'd landed in Managua, but when I toted up the scratches a couple of weeks later they didn't match up with the date one of the guards gave me.

As for the menu, rice and beans got top billing. Once a day a hunk of meat came along with them that was shoe-leather tough. The big treat, though, was an occasional piece of stale bread. It was more filling and you could use it to sop up the juices. There were no utensils so you ate with your fingers. An old tomato can half-full of beet juice or maybe a little water washed down everything.

The heat was fierce. Never any air stirring. When they locked me up they had given me prison issue: thick canvas shorts and a shirt that couldn't be ripped up to make a choke tool to use on a guard. Also a pair of thongs just thick enough to stun a spider. I stripped off the shirt right away and tried for the first sleep in days, but after a couple of hours I was so sweat-soaked that the sleep wouldn't come.

That first day I also met my new roomie. A few minutes after I got pushed through the cell door my eyes—still minus my glasses—barely made out through the dim light a fuzzy figure on the bunk across from the one that would turn out to be mine. The figure whispered, *"Buenos dias, amigo."* Later he would identify himself as a captured Contra captain. I never did get a real good look at his face in the bad light. He seemed to know enough about the guerilla war to be an insider. Anyway, we whispered and flashed sign language to each other during the three weeks he was in the cell, but for some reason he always seemed to be afraid of me. I gave him the shoe leather from my tray most every night because I couldn't choke it down, which still didn't win him over. Mostly he was whining, and constantly bugging me to trade bunks with him because my side of the room blocked out the little light and he wanted to sleep in the dark.

The guards were all sergeant-majors and higher. Interestingly, they didn't carry weapons. I guess they figured they didn't need them against the likes of us. One I got to know a bit rather quickly was Joaquin. The first night I was there he gave me two cigarettes through the peep-slot, but when I asked for the third one I bought trouble. His mate Julio, who was built like a tank, let him light it for me. But when I stuck my fingers through the slot Julio grabbed them along with the cigarette and hung onto my fingers while he burned the back of my hand. Getting scorched by cigarettes at El Chipote happened so often the first two weeks that I finally stopped asking for smokes.

If you didn't play up to the guards with just the right words you wouldn't get any perks—an extra half-can of beet juice, for example. The meanest guard was a Rama Indian who was a whiz at all kinds of abuse. The guards who were regularly stationed at the cell door would bring me over to the headquarters annex for regular grillings and stay in the room where the officers questioned me. If I got sent to the cold room it was Rama or one of his buddies who went with me. Joaquin would just lock me in, but the Indian could be counted on to add a few extras. I would be facing the wall in the cold closet. My chin would be on my chest like it was supposed to be. Rama would grab my hair and bang my head against the wall. Or he would kick my left ankle a few times. Back at the cell door he'd taunt me with "You get shot *manaña*" or "This your *casa muchos años*." Rama, about forty, seemed to have the younger guards in thrall. They looked up to him, tried to be as tough as he was.

The day after I was moved into my cell Rama and the officer of the day took me over to the annex for my regular grilling. Captain Ahvarado and a light-haired officer named Rodriguez had pulled the duty this time. Ahvarado started us off like this:

"Describe Roberto for me, Mr. Hall."

"Very tall. A little out of shape. Long fingers." (I'd done this before.)

"I will read you some names, Mr. Hall. Tell me if you know these names."

"OK."

"Posey"

"No."

"Singlaub"

"No."

"Secord"

"No."

"Owen"

"No."

"Poindexter"

"No."

"MacFarlane."

"No."

"North."

"No."

"You have few acquaintances, Mr. Hall."

"I don't get around much."

"Please no smart talk, Mr. Hall. This is serious business. Do you think you are in what you people call a banana republic? This is Nicaragua. We are at war, our two countries. You are a prisoner of war."

Ahvarado started talking about the Sandinista revolution then, said it had cleaned his country of all the Samoza thugs. He even handed me a pamphlet about Bebe Sandino, the father of the rebellion.

"Read this. It will show you what we have made of Nicaragua."

"Why do you take orders from the Russians?"

"We do not take orders from the Soviet Union. They give us guns. In a revolution you do not look behind to see who is handing you the gun. We make the decisions for ourselves."

No sooner had Ahvarado finished that last sentence than two guards crashed in from the hallway and grabbed him under the arms. He was out the door before Rodriguez or Rama or Julio could react. Rodriguez then called off the interrogation and my two keepers took me back to my cell. I never laid eyes on Ahvarado again.

Back in the cell I started working out in spite of the heat. I guess I wanted to show the Sandinistas that Americans were tougher than they might think, and the best way to do that, besides not breaking down under questioning and physical abuse, was to stay in shape. I forced myself to do 200 push-ups and then ran in place for ten minutes. The Contra captain couldn't figure out what the hell I was trying to do. I hadn't seen him move a muscle yet. He just kept saying "loco" over and over. When I got outside for the hour's exercise period I would push myself even harder.

After the last interrogation, about midnight, I knelt down next to my bunk and prayed for my mother and brothers and kids, and for good measure for people I hoped were praying for me. I couldn't tell how long El Chipote would be my address but I asked God to make it a short stay. I told Him I was sorry for all the sins I was guilty of and that I'd try to be the best Christian I knew how even if it turned out I was going to be a lifer. Just about every time I woke up during the night I closed my palms together and prayed. And I woke up quite a bit. Every hour or so a guard would bang on the steel door just to remind us he was there. The praying made me feel closer to God than ever before, and *that* was real comfort.

One morning I woke up after what I thought were a couple of hours sleep and felt differently than before. I was more tired than I'd ever been and I couldn't focus on anything. There was a weird fear grinding my gut and yet at the same time I felt detached and numb. A couple of hours later, when the feeling wore off, I was sure I'd been drugged, presumably to draw out new and startling secrets from me. Apparently nothing new had been forthcoming while I was under the influence because at that morning they kept right on asking the same old questions.

* * *

All during those early days in prison I kept wondering what, if anything, was being done back home to try to get me out of this godforsaken hole. As I would discover, much was going on via the State Department. I also would hear later that a friend contacted Ross Perot and asked him for assistance in getting my release. According to my friend, Mr. Perot wanted to wait forty days to see if the State Department would be effective. Of course, I couldn't know any of this at the time and was dying to find out anything I could.

The first ray of hope came on the morning of what must have been the 17th of December when Julio and Joaquin ushered Rodriguez into my cell. The officer had a message for me:

"You will have a visitor later today, Señor Hall. A senator from the Congress of the United States."

As soon as Rodriguez and the guards left I started running in place to keep my excitement from boiling over. If a senator was coming to see me it must mean some fairly important people were working on my case. I spent the morning interrogation half-listening to the Sandinistas' questions and half-guessing which senator it might be.

It turned out to be Senator Christopher Dodd from Connecticut, the new chairman of a Senate Foreign Relations Subcommittee on western hemisphere affairs. The senator had messages from my family and we talked for about a half hour, but he couldn't throw too much light on my case. He was in Nicaragua on a fact-finding visit and he'd be seeing the downed pilot and prisoner Eugene Hasenfus too. When we ended our mostly social talk I went back to the cell at least fairly hopeful that I wouldn't be killed.

The next day another meeting was set up—this one with Louis Moreno, the U.S. Vice-Consul in Nicaragua. "Sam, the Sandinista Secret Service is only giving us twelve minutes together. We have no time to talk, so sign this." He handed me a paper. It was headed "U.S. Privacy Act" and it said something about information that could be given to people I chose. I skimmed a couple of lines and signed it. Moreno was working as fast as he could. He pushed three long pages full of names under my nose and said, "These people are Nicaraguan attorneys. You'll have to choose one. The People's Tribunal is going to try you. That means you'll have to have a lawyer from down here." I asked what the charge was and he said attempting to carry out President Reagan's plot to overthrow the Sandinista government. I'd be tried as a spy. I told Moreno to recommend a lawyer for me and he said he would. Moreno ended the interview with the news flash that Eugene Hasenfus had just been released to Senator Dodd. Did his release mean I'd be getting out soon too? The more I thought about that the less I could make myself believe it. Hasenfus was a hired hand. I was an *"espia."*

But from what Moreno had said it sounded like I'd get the first part of the Hasenfus treatment anyway, which would mean a kangaroo court and a thirty-year sentence. Then unlike Eugene Hasenfus, I'd have to serve time, who knew how long? Hasenfus had spent only a couple of months in jail—the first few weeks at El Chipote, then relatively easy time lock-up in Sandino.

One thing that was easier to figure than the Sandinista court system was when somebody important was coming to see me. Just before Senator Dodd's visit, the guards passed me a bigger food ration. The same thing happened the actual night of Dodd's visit, and the next morning Moreno showed up. Now it was the evening of the diplomat's visit and my supper told me somebody even bigger than the senator or the consul was probably on his way. When the dish came through the peep-slot the boring rice-and-bean mix was topped by a *tomato* and a piece of meat. I ate the rice and beans first and then slurped down big chunks of tomato. The meat turned out to be tough as a turtle's tit but I chewed and chewed till every drop of the juice was gone, then deep-sixed the sucked-dry wad down what passed for a john. The Contra captain had told me that you never wanted to leave any food uneaten or you wouldn't get your next meal.

The last interrogation of the day ended at five in the morning.

I'd been kept up for about thirty-six hours now but had no idea why. Around five-thirty a loud clanging nearly split the cell door, and Rama and Julio's wake-up call led to another long interrogation. At about ten two guards hustled me out of the annex and into the prison van. A dozen officers left the building at the same time and got into two cars and a jeep.

After a short ride we turned in at the Sandinista Information Bureau halfway down the hill and I was taken into a room where a couple of colonels were waiting for me. One of them, his finger in my face, informed me, "You will be interviewed now. Do not say anything against the Nicaraguan people. Above all do not describe any details concerning your spying activities. Remember that you have been treated well. Do not tell anyone you have not slept. If you do not comply things will go badly for you."

He then nudged me through a door, and there in front of me was a man I'd seen many Sunday nights on TV. He reached out and shook my hand. "Good to meet you. I'm Mike Wallace. Larry and Felicia say to hang in there. Your mother sends her love." Mike Wallace told me the Sandinista Secret Service said we didn't have much time so he should clip on his microphone to my shirt and we should get started. I barely had time to catch my breath before Wallace was saying, "Are you a spy?" I was shocked and starved for sleep and couldn't think straight. Wallace's questions came too fast. I kept wishing for Diane Sawyer.

The interview took ninety minutes. I tried to tell the man everything I thought I could get away with but it really didn't work out well. Wallace kept saying he was trying to help, and maybe he was, but his attitude got to me. For example, he said, "Ortega thinks you may be crazy. Are you crazy?" Now how do you answer a question like that? I told him the story about the spy satellite at Punta Huete but he didn't seem to respond to it. It occurred to me that maybe he thought he was helping me by trying to make me seem crazy. I was reaching, I know. At one point when the cameraman was changing the tape I leaned over to Wallace and said, "I don't like the way this is going. My kids are watching this. I don't want to look like an ass." When I looked around another camera behind me was grinding away. I was afraid then I'd sound like *I* thought I was crazy myself. As it turned out, Wallace used that part of the tape.

At another point when the camera *wasn't* rolling Wallace asked me for some backup on the Phoenix Battalion. I asked him for a pen and paper and wrote down the names "Commander Douglas Fane and Navy Captain William Hamilton." "Check my story with these two, Mike," I said, "but whatever you do don't use their names on TV." I'd only mentioned the names to let 60 Minutes know I had some government tie, reinforce credibility. I would learn that Wallace had used Fane and Hamilton's names in the segment broadcast and their pictures were included. I'm not saying he didn't have a right, although I had said in effect their reference was off the record.

Wallace also kept trying to tie me with Steve Carr, a reputed ex-junkie who overdosed—with somebody's help perhaps—the day before he was supposed to face a grand jury in Miami. Carr was a friend of the two British mercs I'd met in Alabama. The three of them, plus a Frenchman, had been charged with an alleged 1985 plot hatched in a Miami Howard Johnson's, and there was official suspicion that the idea was to incinerate the Costa Rican Embassy, kill the American ambassador, then blame it on the Sandinistas. Presumably the desired result would be that the American public and Congress would blow their stacks and support an avalanche of aid to the Contras. Wallace's questioning about Carr had me off-balance. All three of my government contacts knew my whereabouts at the time of the alleged plot in Miami and would confirm I had no involvement in it. But I couldn't tell Wallace Tinker's, Evers' and Chance's real names.

It was no surprise that the Sandinistas were none too happy about the possibility of my being involved in the Howard Johnson's plot to blow up half of Costa Rica and blame it on them, or that I'd told Wallace on tape that I hadn't slept in quite a while. Their pique translated for me into a night in the two-foot by three-foot cold closet.

It was a couple of days later that I heard what the outside world was saying about me. A snappy looking major named Perez, who was Ahvarado's replacement on one of the interrogation teams, gave me the news through an interpreter.

"Your acquaintances have not been saying good things about you, Señor Hall. We have some press clippings here. You told us you did not know Tom Posey."

"What's he been saying?"

"He says you are unstable. He calls you 'Sambo.' And that you expect your brother in Congress to come to your aid. That you are jealous of your brother's achievements. He says he expelled you from his organization because you were crazy."

"Does he?" (Not much of a response, never mind my anger.)

"Mr. Frank Camper calls you a crazy also."

"He does?" (Sam Hall, word-man.)

"Colonel Robert Brown says you are sponsored by no one. And that you sent photographs to *Soldier of Fortune* magazine that were dishonest."

"Is that so?"

"Who is Lawrence Hussman?"

"One of the writers of my book."

"He says you saved the lives of some children in Africa. Did you?"

"Yes."

"Tell me about that . . ."

Back in my cell I was even more angry than during the interrogation. Call me naive, call me sentimental, vainglorious. But crazy? A liar? Come on. Nobody fitting that description could, if I may say so, have even survived the missions I'd been on, led and planned. I'm sorry, but I'd always felt Posey was rather jealous because I'd gotten to stay in Honduras after the CMA was pushed out. As for Camper and Brown, I can only say their achievements did not seem to qualify them to pass judgment.

On the twenty-third day of December the Sandinistas took me out of El Chipote once again. It seemed they wanted to parade their captured spy in front of the world press. A large conference was set up in a building off the main plaza in Managua near the InterContinental Hotel. The press corps, it seemed, did want to know about my mission, though there was one reporter from my hometown paper who asked if it was true that I'd come down to Nicaragua to be captured and thereby sell my book. I wish that reporter could have spent a night with me in the cold room.

Toward the end of the conference a reporter asked me about the papers I was carrying when I was arrested. And that's when I decided to give it back to the Sandinistas. I answered the reporter with a question. "Didn't they tell you about the first night?" I'd been warned by the interrogators at El Chipote not to talk about my "spying" at Punta Huete and Sandino. Now the press was at least seriously listening.

"What happened the first night?"

"I penetrated two bases." That sentence was no sooner out of my mouth than two guards behind me took over. Welcome back to the cold room.

Christmas at El Chipote was a bleak holiday that I got through by praying and exercising. The interrogators left me alone Christmas Eve and the next day as well. The break from the questions was a godsend, but I couldn't stop thinking about my family. My mother wasn't young. Could she handle all this? It seemed as though I had spent my life hurting the people that loved me the most.

About six o'clock on the night of the 25th my only present arrived, and it genuinely moved me. There was a loud clang at the cell door and Rama's voice could be heard through the peep-slot. "Señor Hall. Merry Christmas. Come." When I got to the slot there was a smile on Rama's face and his fingers poked a lighted cigarette through the slot. Filter first!

During the next month I was shunted back and forth between the cell and the interrogation room, but I never gave the Sandinistas what they wanted:

"Who are Tinker, Evers and Chance, Señor Hall?"

"I don't know."

"Who do you work for?"

"The Phoenix Battalion."

"Do you know Eugene Hasenfus?"

"No."

"Why would a serious spy talk about his activities?"

"I was retired, I felt free to talk about them."

"Describe Roberto."

I added a few more details about Garcia and of the goggle-like glasses. Roberto was still well camouflaged. "Tall fellow. Small red scar on his forehead."

The colonel added the scar to the face on the plastic card. If they kept at it they might figure it out yet—and shoot old Garcia at sunrise for treason.

"Were you involved in the plot to kill your ambassador to Costa Rica?"

"No."

"Were you sent to kill Eugene Hasenfus?"

"No."

At one session they asked me about the plot to steal the Mi–24 helicopter. They knew exactly what was said and by whom during the meeting at Jerry's restaurant in Decatur where the heist was planned. When they told me they'd gotten the details from French intelligence I knew the only way Paris could know anything was through the Frenchman involved with Steve Carr and the two British mercs.

* * *

The long stretches in the cell dragged deeper into January. I tried my best to keep up and even increase the exercise pace—two hundred push-ups a day climbed to 225 and then 285, with much running in place and an hour's workout outside every day the Sandinistas weren't too annoyed with me to allow it. The exercise helped keep my mind sharp and tuned, and the spirits from sagging too deeply. When you're locked up you can give up hope if you aren't careful. I used to think about knocking the steel door off its rickety hinges with a karate kick or escaping from the outdoor exercise pen. I wondered if I could spring the other prisoners in the block, if there were any. Defending myself or pulling off an escape were too good bonus reasons for staying in the best physical shape possible—the primary reason, of course, being survival.

My strongest emotional tie was to my bunk mattress. It was my prize possession in those weeks at El Chipote. My *only* possession. A citizen who's never seen the inside of a jail can't appreciate what a mattress means to a prisoner, especially a prisoner in the kind of mess I was in. I spent so much time lying on it and sitting against it and coming back to it after the grillings or the cold room that I came to love it, well, almost like a woman. Every inch of "Maggie" was kneaded and patted and coaxed into place. 72-1-24. Lumps in all the right places, you might say. It takes more than exercise to keep one's head straight in solitary. Fantasy had its place too.

Early in January I was taken to a meeting room and introduced to a Nicaraguan psychologist and psychiatrist. For three hours on two different days they hit me with a set of tests and asked me endless questions. I made the gratuitous mistake of telling them about the drugs and the suicide attempt in my past, which, of course, gave the Sandinistas and others more fuel for the claim that I was "unbalanced." The set tests, to their disappointment, proved to be no problem just as was the case with similar tests I requested in the Miami Veterans Administration hospital after I was released;

I was given the results of those Miami tests and told I'd "passed with flying colors."

On the 9th of the month some officers took me to a building down the hill toward Managua to meet four congressmen. An interpreter and a Sandinista secret service officer stayed in the room during the meeting. One of the congressmen shook my hand and introduced himself.

"Hello, Sam. I'm Representative David Coats of Indiana. This is Alex McMillan from North Carolina, Guy Molinari from New York and Frank Wolfe from Virginia."

After we talked a while about my situation I switched to some really important news, like how's the Super Bowl shaping up and what was going on in basketball, especially with Indiana and North Carolina. They said the Hoosiers were doing fine, ditto the Tar Heels. I told them how much this talk meant to me, starved as I was for any news from the States. I asked how Reagan's operation had gone and heard the good news that he was okay, no cancer.

They also had some messages from my family. Congressman Wolfe was a friend of Tony's and he passed on a message from him. I asked him if he could get me a Bible, told him the Sandinistas still hadn't given me one. He said he had one in his hotel room and he'd see that it was sent to me. (I finally got it about five days later, and it helped me shape my prayers in a way impossible before.) Maybe the best that came out of the meeting was a pamphlet Congressman Coats gave me—*Thought Conditioners*, by Norman Vincent Peale. I would read it over and over again, and each time I did I felt better. It was also the first possession the Sandinistas allowed me besides the obvious propaganda piece about their founder Bebe Sandino.

When I finally got the Bible the passage that affected me most was Mark 11:25: "And when ye stand praying, forgive, if ye have thought against any: that your Father also which is in heaven may forgive you your trespasses." I knew I needed to forgive my enemies if I wanted God's favor, and prayed for hours trying to exorcise my hates. I had always wanted to kill the guards, and the officers. Maybe I could learn from St. Mark... "Dear God, I forgive the Sandinistas. I forgive the Contra captain. I forgive the terrorist kidnappers in Lebanon." And on and on. It was a prayer, and a fact. All one could do was try, but clearly I was and am no saint. I honestly felt though, that God was happy that I was at least trying. I could sense his pleasure. I would lay on "Maggie" or kneel next to her and pray like never before. I told myself there were many praying for me, so I tried to return the favor. I also asked God to give his richest blessings to the ones who weren't praying for me. I felt I was really prepared to face years in El Chipote, because the more I prayed, the more God lifted my burden. I now had the conviction he was with me, all the way. From that time on I felt like I could serve my sentence standing on my head.

Approximately a week after the congressmen's visit the interrogators and the guards started to lighten up on me. The grilling sessions slacked off and they even got friendlier. My food dish was graced by more edible meat once a day now. I wasn't sure what it all meant, but I still prepared myself for a long stay. It wouldn't, after all, be smart to build false hopes about getting out any time soon. Earlier on, some of the guards would say such things as, "You fly home Tan-Sahsa *nieve* days," then the next day it would be, "You leave *ocho* days." There wouldn't be any evidence they were telling the truth but I'd take the bait and even say, thank you, sweet Jesus. But, of course, they were just taunting me. I tried not to forget that when my hopes were in danger of rising.

One morning I heard a ruckus outside my cell and went to the peep-slot to check it out. About six of the guards were standing around watching two others playing some kind of game that I finally figured out was soccer. First two bodies would flash by the peep-slot toward the right, then they'd run past toward the left. Every once in a while there'd be a special shout indicating some-

one had scored. About twenty minutes into the game there was a
tie-up in mid-field and I got a look at the ball—it was a dead rat
the size of a groundhog. The guards played another ten minutes or
so before an officer broke up the match. By my shout-count the left
side won 5–4. That night the rat came through my peep-slot along
with the rice and beans. Those guards had some sense of humor.

The first week in February I had what would be my last interrogation—from eleven o'clock to one-thirty in the morning, courtesy
of Rodriguez and a new officer named Sanchez. It wasn't lost on
me that the questions were quite friendly now:

"Would you like some beet juice, Señor Hall? Or would you
prefer a peanut drink?"

"Peanut."

"Are you sure you will no longer pursue your career as a spy."

"I'm not a spy."

"Would you describe Roberto for us, once more, *por favor*,
Señor Hall?"

I *knew* something had to be in the air when one of the guards
brought in a cup of coffee for me. It was the best one I'd tasted
since that last breakfast at the InterContinental.

About a half hour before the end Rodriguez switched from questions to the one answer I'd been afraid to hope for.

"You have a surprise coming in the morning, Señor Hall."

I kept quiet, holding my breath.

"We understand your son's birthday is February fourth."

Now I knew I was going home when Rodriguez said that. I still
tried, though, to play it cool but I'm sure Rodriguez and Sanchez
saw my eyes were getting wet. They were the first tears I'd managed during all my time in Nicaragua. Only when I was back in my
cell did I let my feelings wash over me, and the anger against my
interrogators and the guards nearly was swept away as well. I also
allowed myself some pride in not cracking under questioning. I'd
kept intact Roberto's identity and the identities of my stateside
contacts. If things went as I now dared to expect, I'd be able to put

my foot on American soil in a few days and see David and Samantha and Kelly. And my mother. And all my friends.

No way to sleep after that news. Once the rush of feelings ebbed I tried to figure out why the Sandinistas were finally letting me go. I had no way of knowing what kind of pressure the State Department or other agencies might be putting on the Sandinistas in my behalf, but there were some known and plausible reasons for my release . . . I'd done a good job of convincing the interrogators that the Nicaragua mission was my last—that in fact I'd come out of retirement to take it on . . . probably the five visiting House members had some effect, not to mention Senator Dodd. One thing I was sure of—my brother Tony had done everything he could.

It also occurred to me that the likely ramifications of bringing me to trial could have motivated them. I had been expecting to go before the People's Tribunal ever since the U.S. consul handed me the list of lawyers that first week. I was always asking the interrogators when I'd be tried, but they never answered me. Now I thought I understood why. They couldn't have a trial without a formal charge, and once they formally charged me with spying they'd have to get down to *details*, and then it would be revealed that I'd penetrated two top-secret Sandinista bases and had almost made it into one a second time by *taxi*. The Sandinistas were red-faced about that.

Actually they would have to have a way to save face, whether it was red or not. They'd need some excuse for letting me go without ever making a formal charge. Not only that, they'd need to taint me in case I talked about the physical abuse in El Chipote. If they could get enough poison into the well, maybe nobody would believe me. I thought about it a while and decided that just one key fit the door—they'd take up the refrain that was apparently being sung by some other nay-sayers and add their own melody. "Sam Hall is off-center," they'd say. "We're turning him loose."

When about five that afternoon I was taken to a different room in the annex, Gary Froelich walked in. Froelich was the lawyer my family had hired to work from their end for my release.

He told me we would be leaving together the next morning!

"We'll be flying to Costa Rica then Miami. But don't say anything about spying, Sam. *Nada*. The word is out that there are some radicals down here who want you killed. Security is tight."

I said okay, whatever he and the embassy people thought.

"Something is supposed to be happening in Miami. Maybe a trade of some kind."

That night word came from the officers that I was to be ready the next morning to meet Gary Froelich for the flight out of Managua. My clothes and glasses were returned to me in the cell. At about five A.M. I was ready to go but I wasn't led into the prison van until six, which summoned up visions of missing the plane and spending thirty years at El Chipote after all. One of the guards, though, told me they wanted everybody boarded and the plane ready for takeoff by the time I got there.

Half an hour later the van pulled up at the airport and when they let me out I saw it was about a city block to the plane. There were 150 to 200 reporters lining the tarmac between me and the boarding ramp. When I turned around I could see another swarm running toward the van from the terminal building. A U.S. embassy man whispered that it would be better not to say anything. Then we started for the plane, and all hell broke loose . . . reporters walking backward firing questions, photographers flashing cameras in my face. When we came to a line of bushes a clutch of budding Sam Donaldsons and their buddies fell over backward into a fairly comical pile, accompanied by appropriate expletives.

The embassy man was trying to keep me moving through the crowd, and did a good job of it in spite of the reporters.

On board, the seat next to Gary Froelich was waiting for me, and as soon as I sat down I told him I was worried about flying into Costa Rica. I couldn't say that to him the day before because our talk was being taped. I knew I had been linked by flat-out lies to the plot to blow up the Costa Rican Embassy, so I didn't really know what to expect in Costa Rica. Conceivably assassination or arrest.

Gary, though, said there wouldn't be any problem. When we landed in Costa Rica we exited the back of the plane by a long ramp. Secret servicemen were all over the tarmac. The wind was blowing and their pistols were peeking out with every flap-flap of their coats. Within minutes I was on the Miami-bound plane.

Looking down at America was an even bigger thrill than I'd anticipated. It did not diminish when the wheels touched down. At the top of the ramp I was met by a knot of officials, one of whom said, "Good to have you back." And then another, and another. A customs agent stamped my passport and a federal marshal told me that my brothers were waiting for me in the van over on the tarmac. "Welcome back, Sam, and good luck," he said.

After some unabashed tears and hugs from my brothers I talked to them about what had happened, then checked myself into the Miami Veterans Administration hospital. I was anxious to see my kids and mom and all my friends, but I knew resetting my biological clock would take more than a few twists of the knobs. I was right. The doctors warned me that my system was desert-dry from all the working out in the El Chipote heat and put me through a series of tests that freed hostages customarily took when returned. There were x-rays and blood work and urinalysis. EEGs and EKGs. Also dental work—El Chipote did not supply its guests with toothbrushes.

The hospital staff was absolutely terrific. They said I had to take it easy and eat as balanced a diet as I could to make up for the Sandinistas' bean cuisine. A female doctor named Trujillo gave me a series of psychological tests, more Rohrschachs then you'd think possible. She said I was in fine mental shape, especially considering what I'd been through, and in a couple of weeks I had a clean bill of health from the Veterans Administration and was ready to *enjoy* my freedom.

To that end I headed for my best friend Jimmie Bonbright's place on Tampa Bay to find the big house lit up like the national Christmas tree when I pulled into the driveway. I was still poking at the doorbell when my buddy handed me a gin-and-tonic, and that night he and I got roaring drunk in good ole St. Petersburg, Florida.

Two days later, still feeling the effects of the celebration, I went through my debriefing with Chance. First I gave him the stats so far as I could remember them from Roberto's update. If nothing else, it helped authenticate the report he had already received. I then gave him my mental notes from Puenta Huete and Sandino, as well as everything I had learned in prison that might help. He thanked me and said he could use all I told him, that it was still valuable.

And then he asked me if I was available for any more missions.

"I've retired, sir," I told him.

He told me he'd heard that before.

"You mean you don't want to go back to Nicaragua for us?"

"The only part of Nicaragua I want to see again is Managua—as the guest of the new Contra president."

Chanced nodded, wished me luck.

Not long after, my writer-collaborators called to say that they had run across a quotation from Shakespeare that seemed to fit my case. It was in Act V, Scene II of *Othello*, they said.

I headed for the library and located a fat complete volume of Shakespeare's plays. Then at Jimmie Bonbright's I leafed through the pages till I found *Othello*. It wasn't until near the end of the scene that I found the quote:

I have done the state some service and they know it. No more of that!

God, I hope so. I'm fifty years old at this writing. Time to forget the crusades, let the dust settle. I don't regret for a moment the past five years. There are things I'd have gladly changed in the first forty-five, but since then God knows I've tried to do my best. I've been ready to give up my life for what I believed in—my friends, the Israelis; the POWs in Cambodia; the Miskitos in Nicaragua; and those African kids. One man can't do a lot when there are so many causes that call. But the little I have accomplished has, I dare hope, given my life a sense of worth it never had before.

I think my dad would be proud.

INDEX